# How to get i
# advertising

NC    BE
TA    AY

**Second    ion**

**A guide to careers in
advertising, media and
marketing communications**

Andrea Neidle

**THOMSON**

Australia  •  Canada  •  Mexico  •  Si

GC 107364    GRIMSBY COLLEGE

**THOMSON**

**How to Get Into Advertising**

**Copyright © Andrea Neidle 2002**

The Thomson logo is a registered trademark used herein under licence.

For more information, contact Thomson Learning, High Holborn House, 50-51 Bedford Row, London WC1R 4LR or visit us on the World Wide Web at: http://www.thomsonlearning.co.uk

All rights reserved by Thomson Learning 2006. The text of this publication, or any part thereof, may not be reproduced or transmitted in any form or by any means, electronic or mechanical, including photocopying, recording, storage in an information retrieval system, or otherwise, without prior permission of the publisher.

While the publisher has taken all reasonable care in the preparation of this book the publisher makes no representation, express or implied, with regard to the accuracy of the information contained in this book and cannot accept any legal responsibility or liability for any errors or omissions from the book or the consequences thereof.

Products and services that are referred to in this book may be either trademarks and/or registered trademarks of their respective owners. The publisher and author/s make no claim to these trademarks.

*British Library Cataloguing-in-Publication Data*
A catalogue record for this book is available from the British Library

**ISBN-13: 978-0-82645-767-7**
**ISBN-10: 0-82645-767-3**

**First edition published 2000 by Continuum**
**Second edition published 2002 by Continuum**
**Reprinted 2004 and 2006 by Thomson Learning**

Designed and typeset by Ben Cracknell Studios
Printed in the UK by TJ International, Padstow, Cornwall

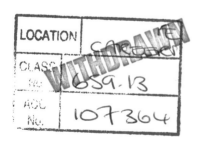

LOCATION
CLASS 659.13
ACC No. 107364
WITHDRAWN

# Contents

# Acknowledgements

I am grateful to everyone who has contributed to this book, in particular the following: Paul Alexis, Gini Arment, Brad Abrahams, A. Baginsky, Michael Bartman, C. Blackburn, Tony Bodinetz, A. Botting, Harriet Bruce, Olga Budimir, Rachel Burrows, Andrew Canter, D. Chambers, Andrew Croft, L. Cronin, Vic Davies, Gareth Dimelow, Richard Eber, Salim Fadhley, Corinne Fahn, Anna Forsyth, Cheryl Garber, Ted Goater, Linda Goodman, Paddy Hall, A. Hellerman, N. Holker, John Holmes, Andrew Hyde, Lara Richardson-Hill, Dave Katz, Scott Knox, Bob Lampon, Jamie Maker, Charlotte Middleton, Wendy Milne, Alan Morgan, Gareth Morgan, J. Muggeridge, Jan Newbold, Carolyn Park, Emma Payne, J.E. Peerless, Karl Perry, S. Peterson, Archie Pitcher, Simon Prindiville, Maureen Purbrook, L. Richardson-Hill, Jason Ross, Adam Scholes, E. Sergeant, Ajay Shah, Charlie Snow, Elizabeth Steadman, Duncan Stokes, Hugh Todd, Louise Wall, Carol Wilkins, Kate Woolf and Carolyn Youdell. If you don't see your name here, you'll find it in the notes and references at the end of this book. Thank you all.

In memory of my parents – Freda and Ralph Finn.

# Foreword

This book vividly conveys how talented individuals can prepare themselves for a career in advertising, media and marketing communications.

*How to Get into Advertising* dispenses conventional and unconventional wisdom for entering the profession. It includes common-sense tips as well as maverick approaches. Helpful hints for job preparation – such as knowing oneself, doing one's homework and networking – along with recommended reading are included in each chapter. The importance of internships and placements are also emphasized as useful ways of obtaining preparatory experience. An entire chapter focuses on writing the résumé/CV and letter of application.

I strongly recommend *How to Get into Advertising* for young people aspiring to careers in the dynamic marketing communications profession. Its fundamental recommendations are applicable worldwide.

Professor John H. Holmes, PhD
Former Director of Professional Development
International Advertising Association, USA

*To my husband Stephen*
*and children Dan, Ben and Hannah,*
*who have always been a great source of*
*encouragement, support and inspiration,*
*and to all my advertising students,*
*past and present,without whom*
*this book would never*
*have been written*

# 1 Getting started

## Where do you start?

If you want to work in advertising, where do you start? What jobs are available? Where are they advertised? And how do you hear about them in the first place? Every year the average advertising agency receives approximately *three thousand* applications for every available graduate training position. But there are many other job vacancies that the industry would like to fill. Jobs in media, planning, creative services, direct marketing, sales promotion and new media, for example. Jobs that you didn't know existed. And even if you did, you wouldn't get to hear about them because they are not usually advertised.

It's quite ironic that the advertising industry is not particularly good at advertising itself – you probably didn't even know that these types of jobs were available. That's because most people tend to think of advertising as just consisting of two jobs – account handling and copywriting. In the same way that most people have only heard of one advertising agency – Saatchi & Saatchi. Yet there are over 600 advertising agencies in London alone. And there are countless jobs out there waiting to be filled and employers eager to meet applicants with the right aptitude and skills to fill them.

## The tip of the iceberg

In an average day you'll probably see 33 TV commercials, 25 posters, 33 newspaper ads, four sponsorships, two pieces of direct ('junk') mail and hear three radio commercials. What you may not realize is that the ads that you see are only the tip of the iceberg of the work that goes into making them.

## A team effort

Virtually all the advertising you see is produced by people working in advertising agencies. Whether it's a TV commercial, a radio ad, a magazine or newspaper ad, a huge billboard or an ad you see when strap-hanging on the tube. Each ad you see (and it's said that you are exposed to about 2000 ad messages in a day) is the result of the work of many different people – a huge team effort of people in a variety of roles, working behind the scenes.

## Everyone loves ads

Everyone thinks they know everything there is to know about ads. Everyone has an opinion on the ads they see. And everyone who has ever seen an advertisement thinks that they can do better. They think that they know all there is to know about advertising – that it's 'easy', a 'soft' job that anyone can do. They think, 'yes, it's fun and it's glamorous but it's not really *work*'. As a result, advertising is probably one of the most misunderstood careers, as well as being one of the most sought after.

## Getting your foot in the door

Many years ago I wrote an article that was published in *Ad Weekly*, the forerunner to the advertising journal *Campaign*. It was called, 'Getting my foot in the door' and it described my frustration at trying to find that elusive first job in advertising. This is the book that I wished someone had written then. As an agency friend recently said to me, 'I wish something like this had been around twenty years ago.'

## How this book will help you get started

Throughout this book you'll find people's first-hand accounts of their own experiences. For example, a day in the life of an account handler, a creative team or someone working in sales promotion. Students have answered questions about what they found good about their courses and tell you honestly about their interview experiences. Experienced recruiters – including the personnel assistant at top agency Saatchi & Saatchi – tell you what they are looking for in an applicant and how you can get your CV on top of the pile.

## How to get into advertising

This book does not set out to be prescriptive – all it can do is give you some idea of the *scope* of jobs available and the different ways of approaching them. It's designed to help you find out what of kind of jobs exist, who does them and how to go about getting them.

Chapter 2 tells you how to get started in your job-hunting. Chapter 3 gives you some basic information about the advertising business. Chapters 4 to 10 outline the different kinds of work available and introduce you to some of the people who are working in the industry today with first-hand accounts of their experiences. They recall how they got their jobs and give you tips on how to get yours.

There's also information on what you can expect to earn and what you have to do to earn it. At the end of these chapters there is advice on what books to read and where to go for more information. This new edition features updated book lists with many new recommended books, publications and websites.

## New media information

Since I first wrote this book there has been a huge growth in new media ad agencies. So this edition includes a new chapter on 'new media': what it is, what it involves and how to get into interactive advertising. You'll find lists not only of the top twenty interactive ad agencies but also details of some of the best interactive websites.

## US agencies and graduate programmes

Most chapters also include lists of ad agencies to help you in your job-hunting – not only in the UK, but worldwide. This new edition has a special focus on the American market, with information about top ad agencies (including what you can earn in them) and courses.

Chapter 11, 'Selling Yourself', tells you about application forms, CVs/résumés and interviews, and advises you how, when and where to apply for jobs. Chapter 12 explains about graduate training, while Chapter 13 helps you find out about advertising courses. Which colleges have the best reputations for advertising training? Should you study advertising in order to work in advertising? And at what level? In Chapter 14 students reveal what has worked for them. Chapter 15 helps you with work experience. And to show you what can be achieved with persistence and determination, Chapter 16 contains some first-hand accounts of how people (including myself) secured the jobs they wanted.

In Chapter 17 you'll find an *extended* directory of useful information to aid you in your job-hunting, including a list of the agencies offering graduate training, their web addresses and other helpful information. There are useful addresses, phone numbers, company websites, listings of different types of ad agencies (e.g. new media/interactive agencies) and other invaluable information to help you in your understanding of the advertising market.

The world of advertising is such a dynamic one that there are bound to have been some changes in the industry before you read this. To the best of my knowledge all the information in the book was correct at the time of going to press.

## What advertising is not

> If you're looking for a regular routine job with a nine to five mentality, don't head for advertising.
>
> *Bob Lampon, Director, Making Waves*

If you're someone who likes to work on their own, craves stability and security, enjoys a nine-to-five job, never wants to work late and hates taking risks . . . close this book now. An advertising career is not for you.

## Exploding myths

If you think advertising is glamorous – that it's all about long lunches, lots of booze, beautiful people, clubbing, holidays in exotic locations, mixing with celebs and supermodels and earning a lot of money very quickly by doing very little – think again. True, some of it can be glamorous, but mostly it involves long hours of hard work – as you'll discover in later chapters.

But, having said that, if you're adventurous and energetic, like mixing with all kinds of people, are able to cope with more than one job at a time, are good at thinking on your feet, thrive on stress and – above all else – have ideas . . . then advertising might just be the career for you.

## The business of advertising

Let's talk about what advertising is. First and foremost, it's a business. And it's big business. According to the Institute of Practitioners in Advertising (IPA) the UK advertising sector is worth around £13 billion (IPA, 2001). But it's a business with a difference. The IPA, which is the industry's professional body, describes advertising as 'a fascinating fusion of business and art. The planner, the negotiator, the writer, the artist, the production expert and the management co-ordinator combine to form a team which delivers pertinent and hopefully first-rate advertising solutions to help clients achieve their business goals' (IPA, 1998).

## The most fun with your clothes on

Above all else, advertising is fun. It's an advertising adage that it's the most fun you can have with your clothes on. That's because it's a job like no other. Every day is different. Every job you are asked to do is different – presenting different problems for you to solve. It's a dynamic and varied industry with a diversity of advertisers, ad agencies and people. You need to be a team player, someone who is able to work alongside and get on with people at all levels. Contrary to what you might have read in the press, the industry has no time for prima donnas.

## You will want to get up on Monday mornings

You're expected to work long hours and never clock watch. In my experience, the job is never boring, so you won't be watching the clock anyway. Times passes quickly – there's never enough of it. Most of the time you're working under enormous pressure to deadlines. You have to please people who have very high standards about what is acceptable and what is not, not least of all the great British public when your ads (because they are *your* ads, even if you did not write or produce them) appear on posters or on TV.

## Juggling for a living

Invariably, you are working on more than one job at a time. So you need to be able to juggle your work and prioritize. You have to work quickly and think quickly. It helps if you're creative – if you have ideas. Most people in advertising do, even if they're working in so-called non-creative jobs.

## Passion and persistence

You need to care about the work you do because that's the way great ads are made. You need to feel passionate about things – particularly about advertising. You're expected to have strong feelings and opinions. Passion, persistence and diplomacy are prerequisites of the successful ad person. You must be able to defend your work and to know when it's not necessary to do so.

## 'Get up again'

You need to be what I call a 'get up again' person. Someone who will fight his or her corner and when faced with rejection doesn't give up but gives it another go. This applies to job-hunting and job-keeping. In other words, you need to be fairly tough to survive in advertising.

## 'Butterfly brain'

Advertising people (and obviously I'm biased here) are interesting people. They often have unconventional backgrounds and unconventional views on life. They know about a lot of different things because it's their business to do so. It's quite useful to have a 'butterfly mind' so your brain can flit from one thought to the next and back again. You'll develop a superficial knowledge of a lot of deep things. And a deep knowledge of a lot of superficial things.

## Read, read, read

You should be reading as many different newspapers and magazines as you can, not just those that particularly interest your own age group.

## Get paid to watch TV

At last you'll have an excuse to watch a great deal of television, because part of knowing what's going on includes being aware of who's doing what to whom in the news and in all of the soaps. You can channel hop and say you're working.

## Streetwise

A good advertising person needs to be aware of the latest trends in popular culture – what's in and what's out. You'll need to be in tune with what was described years ago as 'the man on the Clapham omnibus', because it's important that you know what's going on at all levels of society.

You'll need to know what's at number one and what plays, shows and films are playing to the biggest audiences. You must be aware not only of the latest fashions but also streetwise enough to be able to predict the next trends. You need to know what kids are talking about in the school playground, and what's the latest gossip in the coffee bar and in the pub. It's important to be able to talk to people and be interested in what makes them tick. That's what successful advertising is all about.

## It's not who you are, but how good you are

Advertising prides itself on being a meritocracy. There's a saying that you're only as good as your last job – the last ad you wrote, the last TV commercial you directed, the last campaign you planned. People are promoted, not according to their age or experience, but according to how good they are at doing their job. It's as simple as that, which is why you may find yourself working alongside someone many years younger than you, or that someone who has only just joined the agency is earning more money than you are (even though you've been there for years).

Most ad agencies pride themselves on their youthful image. However, if you're a little bit older there may still be a place for you somewhere – you may just have to work that much harder at finding it. A few years ago Saatchi & Saatchi employed a 53-year-old copywriter, but then, their motto is 'Nothing is impossible'.

To sum up. In order to be successful, you need to be hard working, long working, business-like, energetic, passionate, committed, dedicated, diplomatic, relatively young, resilient, an intelligent, tenacious, tough and persistent juggler who is full of ideas and has an interest in everything and everyone.

Still want to work in advertising?

# 2 Getting in

Advertising people have to be like sponges – you have to absorb everything that's going on around you.

*Linda Goodman, Copywriter, Lowe Direct*

Daily life? Are you kidding? There is no such thing as a typical day . . . ever.

*Gini Arment (2001), Rhea & Kaiser*
*Marketing Communications, Illinois, USA*

This chapter gives you some tips on how to find that elusive first break. Where to look, who to ask, where to go. First of all, some general points to help you get started.

## Be focused

Know what you want to do, where you want to go. Have a plan for the future – a goal. And be single-minded about getting there. Don't be put off at the first obstacle, the first rejection. Keep coming back for more. If you are rejected for a job, ask for a work placement and always ask for feedback. If you are determined and not put off by the first rejection, you will get there in the end. Those who want to work in advertising, do. Those who give up easily are generally not suited to the business anyway.

## Be aware of ads

Read books around the subject and study the advertising press. Listen to ads on the radio. Watch ads at the cinema and on TV. Be aware of the ads you see when you're outdoors or travelling on the tube or in your car. Be knowledgeable about ads, good and bad. Make sure that you have an opinion about what you like and what you don't. Have a favourite ad and be ready to talk about it, if necessary, at interview.

## Find out about advertising careers

Know about the jobs available to you. Don't apply for graduate training if you want to be a copywriter or art director – agencies do *not* offer graduate recruitment schemes for creative positions. Don't talk about copywriting if you want to be an account handler. For careers information write to the IPA and the Advertising Association (see the addresses in the Directory at the end of this book).

## Job opportunities

*ALF* (*Account List File* – the advertising bible) has over two thousand entries for advertising – that's well over two thousand job opportunities in ad agencies, consultancies, direct marketing, media, new 'interactive' media, outdoor advertising, public relations, recruitment, sales promotion, sponsorship and web design. And we haven't even begun to list all the jobs available on the client side in product development, brand management and other areas of marketing.

## 'Just do it'

Once you've decided what you want to do, choose the agencies where you'd ideally like to work and research them thoroughly. Here's a list of thirty leading agencies just for a start (addresses for many ad agencies can be found in the Directory at the end of this book). Check out their websites – find out as much as you can about them before you apply for work experience or a job.

### Top 30 ad agencies*

| | | | |
|---|---|---|---|
| 1. | Abbott Mead Vickers BBDO | 16. | WCRS |
| 2. | McCann-Erickson Advertising | 17. | Leo Burnett |
| 3. | Lowe | 18. | HHCL & Partners |
| 4. | Ogilvy & Mather | 19. | Bartle Bogle Hegarty |
| 5. | Publicis | 20. | Banks Hoggins O'Shea/FCB |
| 6. | J. Walter Thompson London | 21. | Mortimer Whitaker O'Sullivan |
| 7. | Saatchi & Saatchi | 22. | cdp-travissully |
| 8. | Bates UK | 23. | Partners BDDH |
| 9. | M&C Saatchi | 24. | Delaney Lund Knox Warren |
| 10. | Rainey Kelly Campbell Roalfe/ Y&R | 25. | St Luke's Communications |
| | | 26. | Leith Agency |
| 11. | BMP DDB | 27. | WWAV Rapp Collins |
| 12. | TBWA/London | 28. | Mother |
| 13. | Euro RSCG Wnek Gosper | 29. | ARM Direct Group |
| 14. | D'Arcy | 30. | Roose & Partners |
| 15. | Grey Worldwide | | |

*Agencies ranked according to billings/revenues by AC Nielsen MMS

Campaign Report *(February, 2002), data supplied by AC Nielsen MMS*

## Do your homework

Begin by reading *Campaign* (or any other advertising journals you can get hold of) and familiarize yourself with the advertising scene. Discover all you can about the agency you want to work for and build a file. Use the internet to help you. (A list of agency websites can be found in the Directory in Chapter 17). Look up the agency in *ALF* or *Campaign* to see what 'accounts' (clients/business) it has and who works on what. Find out who is the director of the 'account' you'd like to work on. That way, you can actually write to a *named* person rather than sending a general letter that will never reach its target.

Keep a cuttings file about agencies and their brands. Be aware of current trends in advertising. Follow the media columns in the *Guardian* (Monday and Saturday), the *Independent* (Thursday), the *Evening Standard* (Wednesday), *The Times* (Friday) and the advertising trade press. Try to get hold of a show reel of the agency's current TV commercials so that you are familiar with the work they do. Be aware of their most recent work, their most famous work and any of their work that has won awards.

You can try phoning the agency or company and asking them to send you information. In my experience, very few agencies respond to requests from students, but it's worth trying. Some agencies, such as M&C Saatchi, have a press officer you can talk to. Most major agencies publish their 'credentials' (information about the agency for clients), and if you're lucky, they might send you a video or a brochure.

Sometimes you may actually be able to get through to someone who works at the particular agency you're interested in – or at least, leave a message on their voice mail. If you manage this, forget your homework and ask if you can come in for a chat. This could lead to work experience and then you're halfway there. Work experience is considered to be one of the best ways of getting into advertising – you can find out more about it in Chapter 15.

## Answer an ad

Recruitment ads for agency staff are few and far between. Most jobs in advertising are not advertised. Agencies either use their own recruitment programmes (see graduate training in Chapter 12) or use recruitment consultancies – 'head-hunters' to help them find people. Often jobs are found through the grapevine – by word of mouth.

If you do find an ad (and you're more likely to see one in the media supplements of national newspapers than in the advertising press), it will probably ask for experience. It's that old chestnut about how can you possibly get experience without having had any experience in the first place? If you've had work experience in an agency, that might help.

Most advertised jobs are more likely to be offering work in a specialist area, such as health care, sales promotion or direct marketing. If you have Mac experience you might be able find work in an agency specializing in web design. Even if you don't have the technical know-how, many new media agencies are looking for people who can 'think outside the box' and have an understanding of what's achievable with the new technology.

## Think beyond London

Many of the ads you see will be offering work outside London and this is fine as long as you realize that it might be harder getting back into a London agency afterwards, if that is your goal. That doesn't mean to say that only London has the good agencies – there are plenty of excellent agencies outside the capital.

If you're able to 'think beyond London' you will probably find a first job more quickly. Many of the agencies north of Watford are subsidiary companies of agencies in London – for example, J. Walter Thompson. The journal *Adline* is a good source for finding jobs in out-of-London agencies. Every January, subscribers to *Adline* receive a free copy of their yearbook. Here you'll find published what they consider to be the best agencies in advertising and media buying outside London. Some of these agencies are listed in the Directory at the end of this book.

### Top twenty UK regional agencies*

| | |
|---|---|
| 1. Leith Agency | 12. Advertising Principles |
| 2. Faulds Advertising | 13. The Bridge |
| 3. BDH TBWA | 14. Poulter Partners |
| 4. Cheetham Bell JWT | 15. UK Advertising & Marketing Services |
| 5. Publicity Bureau | |
| 6. Attinger Jack Advertising | 16. Blair Fowles Advertising |
| 7. Bray Leino | 17. Nexus/H UK |
| 8. Robson Brown | 18. Yellow M |
| 9. Union Advertising Agency | 19. Typestyle Advertising |
| 10. BCMB Pilkington | 20. Cravens Advertising |
| 11. Coltas | |

*Ranked by billings/revenues. Data supplied by AC Nielsen MMS.

Campaign Report *(February, 2002)*

## Think beyond Britain

To start you off, here's a list of the world's top twenty advertising organizations:

### Top twenty advertising organizations worldwide

| | |
|---|---|
| 1. WPP Group (London) | 11. Hakuhodo (Tokyo) |
| 2. Omnicom Group (New York) | 12. Asatsu-DK (Tokyo) |
| 3. Interpublic Group of Companies (New York) | 13. Carlson Marketing Group (Minneapolis) |
| 4. Dentsu (Tokyo) | 14. TMP Worldwide (New York) |
| 5. Havas Advertising (France) | 15. Digitas (Boston) |
| 6. Publicis Group (Paris) | 16. Aspen Marketing Group (Los Angeles) |
| 7. Bcom3 Group (Chicago) | |
| 8. Grey Global Group (New York) | 17. Tokyu Agency (Tokyo) |
| 9. True North Communications (Chicago) | 18. Ha-Lo Industries (Niles, Illinois) |
| 10. Cordiant Communications Group (London) | 19. Daiko Advertising (Tokyo) |
| | 20. Incepta Group (London) |

Advertising Age *(2000)*

## Write to agencies

You've chosen and researched your top twenty agencies. Now you need to write to them. For most jobs it's best to do a straight CV and accompanying letter rather than attempting to be creative, which often misfires (see Chapters 11 and 12). Be specific about what you want. Don't say that you'll do *anything*. Instead, let them know what your goals are. Even if you're asking for work experience, you should make it clear what area you wish to work in. If you don't know, research the job market first before you apply.

If you want to work as copywriter or art director no amount of letter writing will get you a job. You will need to have a portfolio of work, and the way to go about this is explained in Chapter 6.

## Graduate training

Most of the established ad agencies offer graduate training programmes for those who want to go into account handling, planning or media. Entry is by application form obtainable from the advertising agency you wish to join. It is advisable to apply to as many agencies as possible. Full details of the graduate training process, applications and interviews can be found in Chapter 12.

The IPA publishes a Graduate Factfile that lists all the IPA agencies who offer graduate training programmes. All you have to do is visit the IPA website: www.ipa.co.uk. If you're not yet online (and you should be) you can phone the IPA and ask them to send you a copy of the Factfile by mail.

## Business sense

Today, more than ever before, the industry recognizes the value of qualifications, and many employers favour applicants who have some understanding of a business environment.

## Do a course

If you're not fortunate enough to find a job straightaway, you might like to consider taking a course. Many people choose to take an advertising or marketing course because they believe it gives them the edge over other applicants. They argue that it shows their commitment because they have invested their time and money. Some courses, like the ones at Watford, have an excellent reputation and their students are usually successful at finding jobs in advertising.

## Hit the ground running

Agencies want people who can 'hit the ground running'. Not all agencies have the time or resources to train their own recruits and are pleased to have people who can work without supervision from day one.

Chapter 13 lists some of the many courses now available, including specialist courses for those wishing to study advertising or marketing in depth.

## Visit a recruitment consultancy

Many graduates don't realize that they can find work through an advertising recruitment consultancy. It costs you nothing. It is the employer who pays the agency, not the job-seeker. You will find many recruitment agencies advertising themselves inside the back pages of *Campaign* and other trade journals. Again, you need to do your homework, because most recruiters have their own specialist areas, such as media or creative. Make sure you know who does what before you waste their time – and yours. You'll find more information on recruitment consultancies in later chapters and in the Directory.

## Be open-minded

Be flexible about where you want to work and what you want to do – in your own mind – but be focused and single-minded at interview. Don't have set ideas about only working for the top ten or twenty ad agencies. Think about working outside London or even abroad. Agencies have networks everywhere and it is fairly easy to move from one to another.

Think about working in sales promotion, direct response or new media. These are huge areas of growth, offering tremendous job potential and rewarding careers. If you narrow down your options too much, you may find it difficult to get the job you want – although you might be admired for your single-minded determination.

Sometimes it's worth taking *any* agency job – even if it isn't the one you've set your heart on – just to get your foot in the door. You can always move on in the future. And in the meantime, you're getting valuable experience for your CV.

## Network

Ask around among your friends and family for contacts. Take the plunge and phone up complete strangers. If they can't help you, they might know someone who can. Mingle with people in the advertising business – try the pubs and wine bars around Charlotte Street and in Soho.

Let everyone know you're looking for a job. Don't be embarrassed about family connections – use them. You'll discover that many of the people currently working in ad agencies got started in their careers because they were connected in some way with someone in the industry. Every time you meet someone, use that lead to help you meet someone else. That's what is meant by networking and it's done all the time in business.

The trick is to know when to stop. Don't get to the point where you are annoying people. Be friendly and assertive but not pushy. Most people are only too pleased to help and are often flattered to be asked. Remember to thank people afterwards even if the contact doesn't lead to a job.

## Apply online

Surf the web – many companies now recruit via their websites. You can post your CV online. Try emailing someone and asking for work experience. You could even create your own website to market your skills.

## Luck

In the end a lot of jobs come down to being in the right place at the right time – or simply luck. Someone I know got her job because she was overheard chatting to a friend on the train about the difficulty she was having finding a job in advertising. A stranger leaned across and said, 'I couldn't help overhearing your conversation. I run an ad agency – you can come and work for me.'

## Recommended reading

Read the Media sections of the following newspapers:
The *Guardian* (Monday and Saturday)
The *Evening Standard* (Wednesday)
The *Independent* (Thursday)
*The Times* (Friday)

Also the trade press:
*Marketing* (Wednesday)
*Marketing Week* (Wednesday)
*Revolution* (Wednesday)
*Campaign* (Thursday)
*MediaWeek* (Friday)
*Adline* (monthly)
*Creative Review* (monthly)
Ad agency websites (see the Directory)

# 3 The business of advertising

## The advertising business

The people who own the brands, products or services are known as 'clients'. 'An agency' is the name given to the company that makes the advertising. Within agencies there are various specialist areas. On a very basic level these are as follows:

- Account handlers – liaise with the clients (Chapter 4).
- Account planners – analyse the problem (Chapter 5).
- Creatives – who come up with the ideas (Chapter 6).
- Media – decide where the ads will appear (Chapters 7–9).
- Production/creative services – get the ideas made and make sure that the ads appear (Chapter 10).

## Job ladder USA

As the world becomes smaller in terms of advertising and public relations agencies, with agencies branching worldwide, the answer to job titles is not so much what country you are in, but more so what agency you work for. Typically, the job ladder in the USA would be as follows:

intern > assistant account executive > account executive > senior account executive > account supervisor > senior account supervisor/managing supervisor > vice president.
*Brad Abrahams (2001), Rhea & Kaiser Marketing Communications, Illinois, USA*

## Job ladder UK

Every agency has its own way of doing things. However, a typical medium- to large-sized ad agency in the UK might have the following career progression for those working in client services/account management:

graduate trainee > junior account executive > account manager/account supervisor > account director > group account director > board director

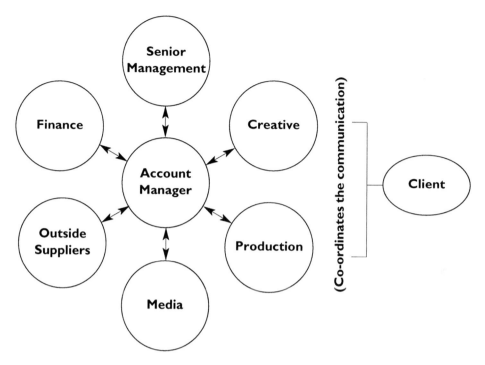

Figure 3.1 shows the major interfaces of an agency account manager in a typical advertising agency.

## What's it like working in a typical advertising agency?

There is no such thing as a *typical* ad agency – there are many different types of agencies. Just as different agencies handle different brands, there are many specialist agencies that handle specific areas of advertising.

## Job opportunities

There are ad agencies offering all kinds of specialist services – agencies that specialize in recruitment, sales promotion, the internet, direct marketing, financial services, healthcare, business-to-business and many others. You'll have a lot more scope in finding employment once you realize that you can look beyond conventional ad agencies for work in advertising – there are more jobs out there than you ever imagined.

## Recruitment advertising

The demand for highly skilled employees and executives has meant that recruitment advertising has become big business. Recruitment agencies are responsible for writing, designing and placing job ads. (You can see some examples of these in Chapter 6.)

## Business-to-business advertising

Business-to-business agencies specialize in business and industrial advertising. They mainly advertise within the business press and also through the business pages of the national press – advertisements for conferences, office equipment, computer software and so on.

### Top ten UK business-to-business agencies*

| | |
|---|---|
| 1. McCann-Erickson Business Communications** | 7. Anderson Baillie Marketing** |
| 2. Banner Corporation*** | 8. Wyatt International** |
| 3. Ogilvy Primary Contact | 9. IAS Marketing & Communication** |
| 4. Tidalwave Technology | 10. = A V Browne Advertising |
| 5. Hunterskil Howard** | = HPS Group |
| 6. AGA | = William Murray |

*Agencies ranked by declared income; ** Members of the Association of Business to Business Agencies; ***Full-service income only

Campaign Report *(February, 2002)*

## Corporate advertising

This is the name given to advertising designed to promote a company's image and, at the same time, give a 'feel-good feeling' about the company to its employees.

## Trade advertising

What use is a massive advertising campaign if you can't find the goods in the shops? You can have the greatest ad campaign in the world, but if it doesn't have trade advertising behind it, it's likely to be a flop. Specialist agencies – responsible for trade and point-of-sale advertising – advertise to retailers, wholesalers and stockists.

Advertising to the trade is used to promote brand distribution and increase awareness of advertising campaigns. Incentives are developed to encourage retailers to stock brands on their shelves. Ads directed to the trade appear in the specialist trade press – for example, *The Grocer*, *Travel Trade Gazette* and *Checkout*, the supermarket trade publication.

The advertising industry, of course, has its own trade press (*Campaign* or *Adweek*, for example), as does almost every profession and specialized market. Interestingly, there are more trade and business publications in existence than there are consumer magazines.

## Healthcare advertising

Healthcare agencies handle medical and pharmaceutical accounts. These may be specialist independent agencies or part of an existing agency network such as

Saatchi & Saatchi Healthcare. Most agencies will have access to professionals who advise and help them with their work, so you don't need to be a medical expert to work in a healthcare agency. A growing number of medical professionals are now working full time for such agencies. Euro RSCG's healthcare division, for example, now employs five pharmacists and a doctor on its account planning team (Carter, 1999).

### Top ten UK healthcare agencies*

| | |
|---|---|
| 1. McCann Healthcare UK | 6. Saatchi & Saatchi Healthcare |
| 2. Bray Leino | 7. PTK Healthcare |
| 3. Paling Walters Targis | 8. Brader Perryman |
| 4. VB Communications | 9. Matthew Poppy |
| 5. Bates Healthcare | 10. Herman Beasley |

*ranked by declared billings/revenues

Campaign *(1999)*

### Top ten US healthcare ad agencies

| | |
|---|---|
| 1. CommonHealth | 6. Torre Lazur McCann Healthcare Worldwide |
| 2. Nelson Communications Worldwide | 7. Lyons Lavey Nickel Swift |
| 3. Lowe Healthcare Worldwide | 8. Klemtner Advertising |
| 4. Bates Healthworld | 9. Cline Davis & Mann |
| 5. Grey Healthcare Group | 10. Sudler & Hennessey |

Advertising Age *(2000)*

## What do ad agencies look like?

Each agency prides itself on being distinct. They all look very different from one another – each has very much its own style. There are traditional department-centred agencies that, if you were to walk round them – aside from the ads on the walls – look like any business. Then there are the new open-plan, no-desk agencies where everyone has a lap top, mobile phone but no personal space.

In one such agency, St Luke's, staff are free to work anywhere they like in the four-storey building. The agency has a 'brand' room for each of its clients where staff can go to soak up the atmosphere. For example, a brand aimed at the youth market might have a client room set out as a typical teenage bedroom – complete with posters on the walls and trainers on the floor. A room like this might be used for client meetings or to brainstorm ideas for a new campaign. The agency also has a number of 'mood' rooms to foster creativity, such as a womb room and a cave (Stuart, 1998).

## The working environment

It's no exaggeration to say that working conditions at most agencies are extremely good.

> Most industries pay at least lip service to the idea of meritocracy, but few can really deliver in quite such spectacular fashion. And few offer the same mixture of enviable working conditions and attractive salary that the successful adman can command. Those little extras that make office life worth living . . . corporate croissants in the morning . . . a session down the subsidised gym at lunchtime . . . a gentle five-a-side kick around . . . Afterwards they can repair to the company's bar to embrocate the stresses of the working day, at suitably subsidised prices.
>
> *Richard Cook (1998)*

## Below the line or above the line?

In the past, agencies separated traditional advertising media (TV, cinema, press, posters, radio, magazines) from other media. Leaflets, mailers, inserts, direct mail, point-of-sale and sales promotions such as supermarket offers of 'two for the price of one' were known as 'below-the-line' advertising. All the sexy media that everyone wanted to work on was called 'above the line'. Now everyone is going 'through the line' and the buzz word is '*integrated*' advertising. In other words, there should be no separation – simply one cohesive, integrated campaign that works across all the media.

## Integrated full-service agencies

In order to offer a fully integrated advertising campaign, some agencies either offer their clients everything under one roof (full-service) or are made up of a number of different but related companies all providing specialist services, but still remaining under the umbrella of one agency's name. For example, the advertising agency Bates Dorland offers the specialist areas of interactive advertising, healthcare and sales promotion to its clients. In this way, an agency can offer a coordinated, personal approach to its clients while remaining efficient and flexible.

## Dis-integration

On the other hand, M&C Saatchi offers their clients the opposite of integration. Their philosophy is one of dis-integration. They have what they call the 'M&C Village', a reciprocal relationship with *independent* specialist companies who work in partnership with the agency. In this way, M&C Saatchi can recommend their clients to specialists – that are companies in their own right – who know exactly what they're doing and can act for M&C Saatchi clients on the agency's recommendation. For example, in the areas of sales promotion, new media, graphic design, sponsorship, media buying and product placement.

## The ideas business

The industry is going through a massive change – we're moving away from advertising to *communicating*. Even the household name Saatchi & Saatchi no longer want to be known as an *advertising* agency – they now call themselves 'Saatchi & Saatchi *Ideas*'.

In today's advertising-literate society, agencies are now having to 'think outside the box' and apply greater creativity and lateral thinking in order to reach their customers.

Consumers have less time to soak up advertising messages than they did 25 years ago . . . To get the message home it's now necessary to communicate with people at every possible stage of their daily lives, whether this be on rail tickets, boxes of matches or through a website . . . when ad agency Michaelides & Bednash helped launch Apple Tango, the brand took over the page three girl in the *Daily Star*, replacing her with a can of Tango in a bra and knickers.

Ad agency Circus sent actors dressed in period costume on to the Central Line to promote the Museum of London. According to Tim O'Kennedy, a founding partner at Circus, 'clients are waking up to brands as things people experience in a number of ways. They are experienced rather than observed.' Graham Bednash, founding partner at M&B says, 'Everything communicates and anything is a medium.'

*F. Newland (1999)*

### Top ten agency brands worldwide

| | | | |
|---|---|---|---|
| 1. | McCann-Erickson Worldwide (New York) | 5. | J. Walter Thompson Co. (New York) |
| 2. | Euro RSCG Worldwide (New York) | 6. | Grey Worldwide (New York) |
| 3. | Ogilvy & Mather Worldwide (New York)) | 7. | Y&R Advertising (New York) |
| 4. | BBDO Worldwide (New York) | 8. | Publicis Worldwide (Paris) |
| | | 9. | DDB Worldwide Communications (New York) |
| | | 10. | FCB Worldwide (New York |

*Advertising Age (2001)*

## What can I earn?

A recent IPA survey (April 2001) of UK agency salaries shows that the average starting salary for most agency positions is between £15,000 and £17,500. However, you should be aware that these are for the larger and medium-sized London agencies. For agencies outside London and smaller agencies, starting salaries might not be so high.

## How do salaries compare in the USA?

*Advertising Age* recently published the salaries for *senior* agency employees. Bearing in mind that these are *average* salaries, right across the USA, and for both men and women, the results are as follows:

- account executive: $48,792
- lead account planner: $67,838
- management supervisor: $101,543
- media director: $77,896
- copywriter: $59,148
- art director: $57,240
- associate creative director: $97,732
- creative director: $115,668

## The gender balance in British agencies

According to the IPA (2001), the advertising workforce is now made up of 51 per cent of men and 49% women. Interestingly, there are now far *more* women working in client services (account management) than men. The 49 per cent does not include those women in a secretarial role, so it would seem that things are looking up. However, most creative departments are still male dominated; most creative teams are male and most creative directors are men.

## Where can I find information on ad agencies and their clients?

The best place to start looking is online. The IPA have a very useful website, as does the American Association of Advertising Agencies. Many of the ad agency sites contain helpful information – see the Directory at the end of this book for addresses that will help you in your search.

ALF publishes an up-to-date list of advertisers and all the ad agencies every month, but you may only be able get hold of a copy in an ad agency. At over £200 for a single copy, it's not something you could ever hope to buy over the counter in your local bookshop or newsagents. However, if you can get hold of a copy, it would prove invaluable, because it lists everything you need to know about finding a job in advertising – for example, the addresses of all the different types of ad agencies, lists of personnel, which agencies hold what accounts and what brands are with which agencies.

An easier solution might be to read *Campaign*, which regularly publishes an up-to-date list of the top accounts and agencies.

Ad agency addresses, websites, recruitment consultants, advertising journals and professional associations can all be found in the Directory at the end of this book.

## Recommended routes

- See Chapters 4–16 and the Directory in Chapter 17.
- The Institute of Practitioners in Advertising (www.ipa.co.uk).
- The American Association of Advertising Agencies (www.AAAAdvertisingjobs.com).

## Recommended reading

*Campaign*
174 Hammersmith Road
London W6 7JP
Subscriptions: 020 8841 3970
www.campaignlive.com

*Adline* (for information on regional ad agencies)
Adline Publishing Ltd
Adline House
361–363 Moseley Road
Birmingham B12 9DE
0121 446 4466

*ALF* (*Account List File*)
Emap Media
33–39 Bowling Green Lane
London EC1R 0DA
020 7505 8459

# 4 Account management

If you're not fertile and imaginative and full of wonder and curiosity, I urge you to stay away from advertising.

*(Leo Burnett, 1995)*

## Typical ad agency progression

| UK | USA |
|---|---|
| graduate trainee | intern |
| junior account executive | assistant account executive |
| account executive | account executive |
| account manager | senior account executive |
| account director | account supervisor |
| group account director | senior account supervisor |
| board director | vice president |

## Account management

First, account management is not about finance or accounting (though you need to have some level of numeracy to do the job). 'Accounts' is simply the ad jargon for the client's business. As an 'account handler' you are said to be 'handling' an account – in other words, looking after the client's business on that account.

## Accounts

The accounts an agency handles are listed under different headings known as 'categories', and agencies like to have a good cross-section of advertisers in each one. These might include the following: some FMCGs (fast-moving consumer goods) – the everyday items you might purchase in a weekly supermarket shopping expedition, such as coffee, bread and tea; retail – advertising a store such as Woolworths or a supermarket; automotive – a car account such as Ford; travel and leisure, such as an airline or holiday company; financial, such as a bank or building society; corporate, such as BT or General Electric; one or more charities, such as the RSPCA or Cancer Research Campaign; and maybe a political party or pressure group, such as Greenpeace or Amnesty International.

## The account team

Most account handlers work on a number of different accounts at any one time and may be part of a team of people all working on that account. Accounts move around all the time, from one agency to another. If you need to know who has what account, *Campaign*, the advertising journal and gossip sheet, is a good way of keeping up to date on who is handling what business and what accounts are in the process of moving elsewhere. There are also many other trade journals, listed in the Directory and at the end of each chapter, that will help you find out who handles what and where.

## The role of the account handler

It is often said that the account handler is the client's representative at the agency and the agency's representative to the client. Figure 3.1 (p. 15) shows how the account manager acts as an interface between the client and the agency. The account manager's role is to define what advertising the client needs and then coordinate all the agency's resources to deliver it to the client's satisfaction.

You'll need to acquire a firm grasp of all the aspects of the advertising process from start to finish and have a good understanding of all your clients' business so that you can interpret their needs for the benefit of everyone involved. You're the team's linchpin – the person who holds everything together. And the one who has the ability to make things happen.

It is the account handler who is often responsible for getting the client's business in the first place, and then for keeping it. It is you who will receive instructions from clients about their business and you will be responsible for all the documents relating to the campaign. This initial briefing is the start of an important relationship between you, the client, your colleagues and the agency. It is the beginning of a whole chain of meetings and events that will culminate in the creation of what you hope will be an effective and successful (and maybe even award-winning) advertising campaign for the client.

Once the agency has agreed a campaign, it is usually the account executive who presents the ideas to the client for approval. You are the person who has the ultimate responsibility for all the work on the account. It is you who are accountable whenever there is work to be assigned or delivered. It is you who gets the praise when things go well and the blame when things go wrong.

## Jack of all trades

Some account handlers have described their role as being a jack of all trades: in order to do your job properly you really need to have a good knowledge of everyone else's job as well as your own. You need to be all things to all people: a spokesperson and team leader, a negotiator, salesperson and diplomat.

## Junior account management

Most account handlers begin as graduate trainees or at a very junior level, mucking in and learning on the job. If you're seeking to start as a graduate trainee, full details of the graduate training process are given in Chapter 12.

As a junior or trainee, you will probably not be given responsibility for your own account immediately. This will come once you have proved yourself. In the first few weeks or months you will probably be expected to do all the mundane jobs, such as collating reports, running errands, researching information, doing photocopying, maybe even sharpening pencils in the boardroom. You will probably sit in on meetings but may not be expected to speak. On the other hand, however, many agencies nowadays believe in giving you responsibility at the start and expect you to make a contribution (including a spoken one) from day one.

## Hunger, passion and broad shoulders

Here's how one junior account executive (Leagas Shafron Davis, 1996) describes his job:

> "It's fair to say that when you start in the business as an account executive you'll do your fair share of leg work. The key is to try and do it enthusiastically, diligently and above all, with a smile. It will help the others around you put the necessary trust in you to start running an account if the document you put together for the account director is delivered on time, free of spelling mistakes and in the order he or she asked for.
>
> When you get involved working on an account you'll quickly notice a few truths. Your clients may be difficult, but you've got to be their friend and earn their trust. You'll have a ton of paperwork, a load of deadlines and an ad to sell. In essence, the account handler's job is a thankless task. But, those of us who do it love it. You do get involved and you will run accounts. Colleagues learn to respect your point of view and as a result you can influence the whole substance and look of a campaign."

He goes on to say that to do well as an account handler you need the following attributes: hunger, passion, creativity and broad shoulders. 'If you want it enough and believe in yourself, you'll get in.'

## Making it all happen

A number of account executives were asked to sum up their work. Here's what they said:

- Jack of all trades and master of some.
- I make the advertising on my accounts appear on time and with the right quality.
- To provide the best-quality advice for the clients about their advertising

needs and then to ensure the quality of creative work and media planning delivers.

- Manage the accounts and account handlers – interface with the marketing director at the client end.
- To interpret my clients' needs accurately and effectively and to ensure they receive professional attention at all times.
- To maintain a strong communication link within the agency between creative, media, production, planning, etc.
- To ensure the advertising work for our clients is correct to the brief, right for the market and uses the most cost-effective media.
- In charge of making it all happen on behalf of my clients.
- Knowing the clients' needs almost before they do themselves.

## One account handler's day

An account executive at one of the top UK agencies describes what the work involves:

"There isn't a typical day in this job. However, I normally start the day by looking at my emails and correspondence. I then look at the list of things to do that I planned the night before. But before I start working on the most urgent one, I receive a call from a client who wants something done yesterday. And there goes my diary out of the window!

### Eight jobs at once

It's usually frantic. You try and do eight jobs at the same time, try to please all the clients who think you have nothing else to do but their project. And try to please your boss who keeps asking you if you have already done it. So by the end of the day I need to take a couple of headache pills and a strong black coffee. Then I go home and collapse . . . and a new day starts again. This is the life of an account handler.

However . . . if you are the lucky account handler who has a small and reasonable client, your job will involve meeting clients to discuss marketing briefs. Then, back in the agency, you meet with your planner and creative director and discuss the approach you are going to take. You or your planner writes the creative brief, which gets approved by your client. You brief the creative team and then coordinate the whole process: approval of creative concepts, production, printing, etc. Of course, all of the above involves a great deal of administrative tasks, problem and client crisis solving.

### Keep smiling

You need to have all these skills to successfully do the job of an account handler: good communication, negotiation and persuasion skills. You must be a good team player, be able to play the politics, put up with the bureaucracy, cope with the pressure and be able to smile the fourteen hours of your average working day! You must be sharp and be able to come up with ideas/solutions on the spot. Account handlers are constantly challenged by clients and you must have the right answer there and then. You need to have creative flair and to be able to think strategically, particularly if you work very closely with the planners or when you have to do the planning job yourself. **"**

## What makes a good account handler?

The job of account handling requires diplomacy and patience. You need to be enthusiastic too, because though the job has its rewards, much of your time can be spent simply keeping on top of the paperwork. So you need to be fairly well organized and methodical. You need to keep a cool head (when all those about you are losing theirs) and stay in control.

It's important to be a good team player – to be able to get on with, relate to and communicate with people at all levels. You also need to be numerate enough to be able to number crunch and budget. And a good manager – of time and people. Tough. Resilient. Confident. Articulate. Creative. Motivated and motivating.

Most account executives enjoy their work and find it rewarding. One summed it up well when he said that his job meant that he had to 'inspire, control and sell'. There's nothing quite like the buzz you get when work you have been responsible for appears for the first time and gets people talking.

### A day in the life of an account executive at Saatchi & Saatchi

**"**I manage the development of advertising from the client-briefing process through creative development to the finished commercial and subsequent research, amendments, etc.

Normally I would spend about 20 per cent of my day on the telephone, either to clients, suppliers or internal process managers, making sure the process runs smoothly. We spend time almost every day with various creative teams, developing ideas and providing feedback.

A couple of times a week I will have external client meetings and may be in a studio or at a shoot (filming an ad) as a result of all these discussions with clients/agency people.

#### Skills needed to be an account executive

Number one has to be a calm but completely unshakeable self-confidence. Being a 'middleman' much of the time between creative teams and clients means you've got to have complete confidence in your convictions.

Number two has to be a positive, enthusiastic outlook. An ability to communicate well and understand other points of view is essential, as is an ability to be highly organized and motivated. **"**

### Graduate trainee six years on

Carolyn Youdell, Regional Management Supervisor, OgilvyOne (1999):

"I got my first job in advertising through graduate recruitment – I joined the company's graduate training scheme six years ago. I am now the Regional Management Supervisor for American Express in Europe.

On average I get in at 9.30 a.m. and leave at 8 p.m. Some days I will speak to about ten people across the company in different disciplines. Briefing creatives, briefing production, calling research companies, talking to O&M staff about Amex etc. I will be juggling client calls and tactical demands all day. The next day I might be locked in my office writing an outline proposal or a strategy for a pan-European communications campaign.

Management of staff and client management issues come up a lot. Pan-European is a nightmare because of the different 'cultures' and attitudes. The UK is much more advanced in thinking as well, so to roll out a consistent approach across all the markets requires a lot of pre-planning."

### Account handling skills
These are the skills Carolyn feels she needs to do her job:

"Flexibility, attention to detail, political, persuasive, listening skills, literacy, inquisitiveness, juggling balls, patience, relationship-building skills, interpersonal skills, team player, crisis manager, cool head, memory, creativity, confidence, dedication, ambition, numeracy."

---

## An advertisement for a job in account handling

We are looking for either a graduate or someone who has gained experience within a marketing department. In both cases the candidate would be looking for their first position in an advertising agency. Although additional training will be given, the successful candidate will need to have the following qualities:

- self-starter
- natural, confident presenter
- good team worker
- excellent organizational skills
- prepared to tackle a mixed bag of tasks in order to gain agency experience
- sense of urgency
- ability to see a project through
- ability to remain calm under pressure
- familiarity with the following software packages: Microsoft Office, Powerpoint and Excel
- knowledge of new media such as websites, multimedia, etc. would be useful.

## Summary of the main roles of the account handler

- You are the client's first point of contact with the ad agency.
- You need to know their product inside out.
- You must know and understand the needs of the market.
- You work with the client on the advertising strategy.
- You help brief the creative team.
- You sell ideas to the client.
- You manage the ad process from concept to print/broadcast.
- You must be on brief and on budget.
- You manage team meetings.
- You present the agency's work to the client and feedback from the client to the agency.

### Two way communication

"An old Chinese saying goes, 'We have two ears and one mouth so we should spend twice as much time listening as talking.' (Unfortunately, this is hardly ever true!) I feel the most important skill required in account management is two-way communication. An account manager has to listen, understand and read between the lines of any client conversation and brief.

The most effective account people I have worked with have been pragmatic, flexible and team players.

It is hard work and can come in fits and starts, so you cannot be work shy. Above all, you need to retain your sense of humour.

The fact that every day is different should be your motivation. It should be fun, for however hard or difficult a client may be there is always a team around you that understands – to share the good and the bad times."

*Bob Lampon, Director, Making Waves*

## The secretarial route into account handling

Even today, it's possible to start in advertising by working as a secretary. Here, Cheryl Garber, who began as a secretary and now works as an account assistant at the ad agency BBH, describes her job:

"My day involves monitoring competitive brands (including ordering tapes), arranging many meetings – making sure they happen and that everyone attends – sending information to clients and others and keeping an eye on the general administrative side of the account (files all in place, things are filed, TV library is in order, etc).

The skills needed for my job are knowledge of the advertising industry, organizational skills and patience. The secretarial route is an excellent way into advertising and can definitely lead to many other things."

## Brand management

For every job in advertising, there is an equivalent key player on the company side responsible for coordinating a brand's marketing, performance and promotion. The key jobs include the following: product managers, brand managers, market research analysts, market research managers, research executives and marketing managers. As a research executive, for example, you'd be managing research projects for a company, with responsibility for research into new product development, products and packaging. As a brand manager, you're ultimately responsible for the successful sales performance of your brand.

There are plenty of jobs going in marketing – advertisers need people who are passionate about their brands. Many of today's brand managers started out in ad agencies and vice versa. Being able to move from the agency to the client side (and back again) gives you plenty of scope for job opportunities.

## How to know which companies to contact

Andrew Hyde of British Telecom suggests that 'just as with agencies, go for the dynamic company'. Networking helped him to 'get solid industry contacts and experience quickly'. Five years ago he was a student on a postgraduate course. After working for a few years in advertising agencies, he's now the Head of Strategy for BT Communication Products.

The advertisers listed in the Directory at the end of this book are just a small sample of the companies where you can apply for jobs. Surf the web, read *Campaign* and the media pages of the national press for jobs in marketing. *ALF* has an A–Z of national advertisers and a brand index. Chapter 13 outlines courses in brand management such as those run by Procter & Gamble.

### 'First marketing manager in forty years'

Here, Gareth Morgan tells you about his job as Marketing Manager for London Taxis International, manufacturer of the famous black cab – a company with a £70 million turnover, based in Coventry.

‶I head the company's marketing function and I'm their first marketing manager in over forty years. In 1998 the company launched their first new taxi – TX1 – the result of a £20 million investment and one of the first Millennium Products chosen by leading designers.

The scope of my role encompasses the marketing of our taxi, finance, parts and licensing/merchandise. I'm responsible for marketing strategy and planning, product development, market research and all the company's marketing communications.

### *A real understanding of business*

After over fifteen years in agencies, I'm currently working on the client side for the first time. I believe all agency and client staff should spend three months on secondment in each other's business. This would promote greater knowledge, understanding and respect.

The main benefit of working for a company rather than an agency is that you operate at the centre of marketing. You get experience of all the marketing processes. The breadth can be daunting but it gives you a holistic perspective. You also interact with other company departments and gain a real understanding of business dynamics.

In my experience, most companies have more mature training and information technology functions. They are more likely to support your personal development.

### My typical week

Each week is full of meetings. It is a constant battle for time between attending meetings and taking the action that results from them. There are also constant interruptions – phone, email, faxes and colleagues (I work in a large open-plan office). I therefore have to try and be very disciplined with my time.

### The skills needed to work as a marketing manager

- Diplomacy – the art of educating without patronizing.
- Discipline – to stay focused on your mission and objectives.
- Time management
- Organization – self and others.
- Sense of humour – as one of my old bosses used to describe advertising, 'It's only tomorrow's fish 'n' chip wrappers – it's not serious really.'

### My tips for getting into marketing/advertising

When I was starting out I wish someone had explained to me not just advertising agencies and how they function, but also placed them in the context of marketing in general. The best explanation is still to read *Ogilvy on Advertising* by David Ogilvy (1995).

First, understand yourself, your strengths, areas of interest and most importantly, what you really enjoy. Visualize the life you want and the part your work plays. I recommend *What Color Is Your Parachute?* by Richard Nelson Bolles (1998).

### The only way to find out is to do it

Check your thoughts against a job in advertising or marketing. Does it fit? The only way to find out is to do it, but you can also visit agencies and client marketing departments (to see both sides of the coin).

Information sources are now greater and more accessible. There's still good old Yellow Pages, but also the internet and recruitment specialists. You must identify who the decision-maker is for the job you seek. Receptionists are usually friendly if you're courteous and explain your motives. Most people respond to a request for help. Approach the right person and ask for fifteen minutes of their time to discuss your ambitions. Be persistent, but don't be a pain – a tricky balance. **"**

## Both sides of the fence

Here, Bob Lampon talks about his move from Marketing Director KFC (New Zealand) to Group Account Director BSB Auckland (New Zealand):

"Having spent a long time on the client side in my career, my move into advertising was not as traumatic as I envisaged. I had obviously worked with various agencies over the years and was generally regarded as a 'good' client.

I realized exactly what this meant when I began to work with some not so good clients – although there is normally at least one you really enjoy working with. My experience on 'both sides of the fence' has been invaluable and I would recommend to anyone a spell on the client side if at all possible.

I feel the basic difference is that in marketing on the client side you are very close to your product, brand or service and tend to be a little subjective. In advertising you must retain the flexibility and objectivity to work on very diverse industries.

To give you an idea, in one day I have had meetings with a major international airline, a computer manufacturer and a major film distributor – hectic but invigorating. It should never be dull!"

## Recommended routes

- Other agency departments, e.g. planning, media, creative services (see Chapters 5, 7–9).
- Graduate training (Chapter 12).
- Vocational courses (Chapter 13).
- Secretarial.
- Work experience (Chapter 15).
- Working on the client side of the business (Chapter 12).
- Working in related areas (direct marketing, sales promotion) – see Chapter 9.
- Working outside London (see Directory).
- Recruitment agencies (see Directory).

The Advertising Association Information Centre: 020 7828 4831
(www.adassoc.org.uk)

The American Association of Advertising Agencies
(www.AAAAdvertisingjobs.com).

Institute of Practitioners in Advertising (IPA) publications and information about Graduate training (Factfile)
44 Belgrave Square
London SW1X 8QS
020 7235 7020
www.ipa.co.uk

## Recommended reading

Anholt, S. (2000) *Another One Bites the Grass: Making Sense of International Advertising.* John Wiley & Sons.

Brierley, S. (1995) *The Advertising Handbook.* Routledge.

Broadbent, T. (2000) *Advertising Works 11.* World Advertising Research Center.

Bullmore, J. (1999) *Behind the Scenes in Advertising.* Admap Publications.

Farbey, A. (1998) *How to Produce Successful Advertising.* Kogan Page.

Hart, N. (1995) *The Practice of Advertising.* Butterworth Heinemann.

Jefkins, F. and Yadin, D. (1999) *Advertising*, 4th edn. Pitman.

Kapferer, J.-N. (1994) *Strategic Brand Management.* Simon & Schuster.

Parente, D. (2000) *Advertising Campaign Strategy.* The Dryden Press (Harcourt College Publishers).

White, R. (1993) *Advertising – What It Is and How to Do It.* McGraw-Hill.

White, R. (1999) *Advertising.* McGraw-Hill.

Any book by David Ogilvy.

*Adline* (for agencies outside London)
Adline Publishing Ltd
Adline House
361–363 Moseley Road
Birmingham B12 9DE
0121 446 4466

*Campaign*
174 Hammersmith Road
London W6 7JP
*Campaign* subscriptions: 020 8841 3970

*Admap*
*Advertising Age* (www.adage.com)
*ALF* (Emap Media)
*Creative Review*

*International Journal of Advertising* (quarterly review of marketing communications)
WARC Publications
Farm Road
Henley-on-Thames
Oxfordshire RG9 1EJ
Ijoa@ntc.co.uk

US office:
1625 L Street NW Suite 1220
Washington DC 20036
USA

See Directory (Chapter 17) for other useful addresses and websites.

# 5 Account planning

Go into planning where you get paid to use your brain and think.

*An account handler*

## What is planning?

The planner's role is intended to bring analytical discipline to the development and assessment of advertising campaigns, although, of course, account planners are not the only people in an ad agency concerned with planning.

Account planning is relatively new to advertising. It was invented in 1968 by Stanley Pollitt, one of the founder members of the advertising agency BMP. At the outset the idea of planning was greeted with scepticism by the advertising industry, particularly its creatives. Charles Saatchi said at the time, 'There's too much intellectual chat. Words like "marketing strategy" are used to hinder advertising, not help it' (Fraser, 1990).

Of course, not all agencies have planners. Where they don't exist, the account handler might be expected to take on the dual role of account management and planning. Or, as happens in some ad agencies, simply ignore planning altogether. However, more and more advertising agencies are recognizing the importance of the planning function in every stage of the development of an effective advertising campaign.

## What does the planner do?

Come up with good thoughts, sell them to the team and the client. Manage that thought over time and see if it proves to be effective.

*Board account planner*

The main role of account planners or strategic planners, as they are sometimes known, is to represent the consumer to the agency and the client. From the outset the planner is involved in developing the strategy and defining the brief that the creative team will work from. He or she is responsible for deciding what the advertising should be saying and to whom, in order to achieve the desired effect. It's the planner's job to ensure that the advertising an agency produces is relevant and to represent the consumer in the process. He or she uses research to check back with the consumer that the advertising the agency is producing is being perceived in the right way.

> Coming up with ideas is not an easy thing to do.
>
> *Agency planner*

A good planner helps the creative team understand the consumer so that they can come up with an effective advertising campaign. You need to have a sensitivity for the creative process and to be able to build a relationship with the creatives working on the account. You need to be able to get your ideas across and be so enthusiastic about them that you will be able to inspire the creative team into producing their very best work.

> A planner is a bit like a detective – search, probe and interrogate.
>
> *Agency planner*

The planner will also manage all the related research from start to finish and look at all the consumer issues. It's not enough, however, to want to know what the consumer thinks about the product; planners should want to find out for themselves. You need to be enthusiastic about the product and about its advertising at all times. Finally, the planner has to evaluate the effectiveness of the campaign and make recommendations for how future campaigns can be developed and improved.

## What kind of people become planners?

Many graduates who go into planning have a background in sociology or psychology, and these seem to be the backgrounds favoured by ad agencies. It's also thought that you'll make a better planner if you have had a broad experience of life – some planners may have done something entirely different before coming into planning. Agencies often choose people to work as planners who have done other things first and a number of planners have moved across from other areas of advertising or even other careers. An example is a planner who worked for many years as a solicitor before making a successful career in advertising. Whereas many account handlers begin as graduates straight from university, planners are often older and with more experience of work.

Planning is also part of the agency graduate recruitment process, as you will see in Chapter 12. What tends to happen is that you may go for an interview as an account handler and, if you appear to have the right skills and attributes, be selected for the planning role instead. Or, you may begin as a graduate trainee in account handling and, if you demonstrate that you are more suited to it, be advised to follow the planning route.

## What makes a good planner?

The planner is a very important member of the agency team and needs to be able to get on with and communicate well with people at all levels. You need to be equally at home in a McDonald's or at Ascot. Good planners should be adaptable to all kinds of situations and all types of people. You need to be straightforward and down-to-earth so that you can talk to people and be understood.

## What qualities/skills should a planner have?

Listening, patience, calm, interest in human beings, enthusiasm. Everyone needs to think in a creative way within an agency, whether you're an account handler, a planner or a creative.

*Board account planner*

Although planners come from all different kinds of backgrounds, the most successful tend to be:

- objective
- analytical
- systematic
- organized
- comfortable with data
- creative
- able to understand and develop research findings
- curious – interested in people and what makes them tick
- articulate
- a team player
- enthusiastic about advertising.

### '20 per cent doing, 80 per cent thinking'

Carol Wilkins, who worked as a strategic planner at Saatchi & Saatchi, describes her work:

"Account people will generally spend about 80 per cent of their time doing and 20 per cent of their time thinking. This is reversed for planners who, in theory, spend 80 per cent of their time thinking and 20 per cent doing. I say 'in theory' because the world and his wife will try and disturb you all day, and generally you will be so busy that having time to think will seem like a fond memory.

### *Watching consumers*

It is the job of the planner to identify the insight/consumer latent need that they can hook into their client's brand/advertising. On average I attend at least one consumer group discussion per week. I have just come back from a trip to Paris, Hamburg and Madrid which involved sitting in a viewing facility listening to consumers talking for six hours in each country.

### Commissioning research

I think most descriptions of planning harp on far too much about research. When you start you don't have to know anything about research. It's the job of researchers to know about research. Planners work with a pool of researchers that the agency trusts. The planner needs to know what information they need and how the information will be used. They will write this up in a brief which will go out to researchers for proposals. It is the responsibility of the planner to select the most appropriate research methodology from the proposals and advice given by researchers.

### Writing strategy

This is probably the most important role of the planner and takes up about 40 per cent of my time. It involves ploughing through heaps of data and distilling it all into a brand strategy. This will broadly follow the, 'where are we now, where do we want to be, how are we going to get there?' process.

### Presenting to clients

I will generally give one or two presentations to clients per week. The planner usually presents with the account director. He or she will look after the client's needs and deal with all the issues relating to the agency/client relationship as well as being the central logistics person dealing with questions relating to production, fees, etc. The planner will be responsible for presenting the brand strategy, market segmentation, creative brief, and gaining client buy-in to all of these.

### Writing creative briefs

I will generally write at least one creative brief per week. This will be a distillation of all the research and strategic thinking into one clear thought. It is the job of the planner to brief the creative director – this is critical to the process and should be brought to life in some way. It is imperative that the creative director buys into the strategic thinking and proposition and feels that he or she has something from which they can deliver great ads.

### Lunch

This is a great job for gastronomes. I normally do at least two bonding-with-client lunches a week.

### Travelling

I work on international business, which means that I travel a lot. I have been to more countries in the last six months than I have in the rest of my life. I will generally visit a foreign destination at least once a week.

### How I got into advertising

One week after leaving the Watford Postgraduate Advertising course, in 1997, I joined Saatchi & Saatchi on a placement attached to a planner. After one month I was offered the job of a strategic planner. The skills I acquired at Watford were critical in my ability to turn this opportunity into a job offer. **"**

Carol's advice on how to turn a placement into a job offer can be found in Chapter 15. Carol is now Co-director of Wonderworks, the ideas consultancy.

### 'No such thing as a typical day'

A strategic planner in a top London ad agency describes her work:

**"**As a planner, we are involved at all levels in the ad process, so there is really no such thing as a typical day. The work required is dependent on the type of brand/client. For FMCG ('fast-moving consumer goods') brands, there is a great deal of new product development involving brainstorming, while for a retail account, the work veers towards marketing/justification of sales results and so on.

For all accounts, it is my responsibility to understand the market place, competitive factors, future trends, etc. I have to devise the optimum strategy to market the brand, to pinpoint the appropriate target group and understand their beliefs and motivations to purchase using quantitative and qualitative research. It's my job to suggest appropriate media for this target group and to write creative briefs for individual executions.

Of course, evaluation is a key factor in the process – ultimately we need to justify our advertising budgets and strategic decisions to our clients using tracking studies and econometrics. **"**

### 'A job for lateral-thinking probers'

A strategic planner describes the skills needed to do her job:

**"**Planners are unusual creatures – with a strange blend of analytical and creative skills. It is ultimately a job for lateral-thinking 'probers' – individuals who like to pinpoint an area (like the perfect slice of white bread) and turn all previous thinking on its head. It is a job for curious people who like to get under the surface of brands and behaviour.

Numeracy is important for evaluation, and organizational skills are essential. In terms of qualifications, a good degree/postgraduate qualification is essential in any subject, though obviously psychology, marketing and advertising qualifications are an advantage. It can be quite tricky to get in straight from college – most planners have a client-side or market research background (two years' experience).

### Advice for future planners
- Show you're fascinated by people.
- Read any book or play.
- Feed your head.

### Interview tips

- Don't spiel out the textbook stuff.
- Give your view.
- Make them laugh. **"**

*Board account planner*

## What can you earn?

In London, average starting salaries tend to be in the £15,000–£17,000 range if you're working for a medium-size to large agency. However, you may be looking at lower starting pay if you're working outside London or in a smaller agency (IPA Salary Survey, April 2001).

## Recommended routes

- Graduate training (Chapter 12).
- A postgraduate course (Chapters 13 and 14).
- Work experience (Chapter 15).
- Work on the client side or in marketing/market research (Chapters 4 and 9).
- The university of life.

## Recommended reading

BMP DDB *Advertising Works* (all editions). IPA.
Cooper, Alan (1997) *How to Plan Advertising*, 2nd edn. Cassell.
Solomon, M. (1996) *Consumer Behavior*. Prentice Hall.
Steel, J. (1998) *Truth, Lies and Advertising*. John Wiley & Sons.

*Campaign* and other advertising journals (see Directory).

# 6 The creative team – copywriting and art direction

People who write the best ads are mad about ads . . . Copywriting is a learnable skill. Anybody who has some talent can teach themselves the art.

*Peter Souter (1999), Executive Creative Director, AMV BBDO*

Ask most people what a copywriter does and you'll get some strange answers. Someone once said to me, 'Don't you get tired copying all that writing?' Another misconception is that it is something to do with law, as in copyright. Yet another misconception is that copywriters spend a lot of time writing. In fact, most of their time is spent coming up with ideas – 'concepts'.

Don't become a copywriter if you enjoy writing: be a journalist or novelist. Count the words in any ad or TV commercial – usually, the fewer the words, the better the ad.

*Tom Rayfield (1998)*

Even if people know that a copywriter works in advertising, most don't realize that it's the creative team – the copywriter and art director – who dream up the whole creative idea. Not just the slogan but *everything* you see or read.

## Who does what?

A copywriter may have to write anything – from the words on the back of a cereal packet to a TV commercial. The art director works closely with the copywriter as a team. They brainstorm and bounce ideas off one another to generate the concepts that form the ads. The art director 'directs' how the ads should look. He or she will need to have a good understanding of layout and design, though not necessarily have great drawing skills. It's enough to be able convey the idea on paper with a quick sketch. These are called 'roughs', 'scamps' or 'concepts'. Agencies usually employ other people (either in-house – a studio of visualizers and Mac operators within the creative department – or freelance artists from outside the ad agency) who have the illustrative, design and Mac skills to produce the 'finished' artwork.

A copywriter may also have an idea of how the ad should look – that's not just the job of the art director. Equally, an art director may come up with the headline or the words in the ad.

## The creative team

The copywriter and art director combine in such a way that virtually all the work they do is a joint effort – they are truly a creative team. It's important to realize this if you want to work as a creative in an ad agency. Most agencies will only hire creative *teams* not individuals. So, if you're looking for a job as an art director or a copywriter, you need a creative partner. You also need to be able to show examples of the work you can do when you go for interview. This is called a 'portfolio' or 'book' and is an essential requirement if you want to get work in the creative department of an ad agency.

## What do you need to be a good creative team?

Curiosity about life in all of its aspects, I think, is still the secret of great creative people.

*Leo Burnett (1995)*

The most important requirement is to have ideas and be able to express them. You need ideas that keep on coming – never be satisfied with the first idea you come up with, however good it seems, but go on dreaming up concepts until eventually you come up with the big idea that everyone likes. Even then, the idea will need to be developed, changed and modified, and you may have to work on it over and over again until it no longer feels like your idea at all. So, you need to be resilient and to be able to bounce back again and again with fresh ideas.

You need to be highly creative, not only in your thinking but in the way you use media. Today's advertising has become so much more integrated and interactive. Anyone wanting to work as a creative team will need to know how the media has changed and be aware of how it may be used in the future.

You need to be a juggler – to be able to work on many different things at the same time. You could be simultaneously working on a colour supplement ad for a car, a trade advertisement for pet food, a local ad for an insurance company and a cinema commercial for a bar of chocolate.

Some copywriters and art directors specialize in certain areas. For example, in healthcare working on pharmaceutical accounts, in recruitment advertising, trade advertising or for a business-to-business agency.

There are two main steps to becoming a copywriter or an art director. First, you need to find a creative partner. And, second, you will need to build a portfolio/book of work so that someone in a creative department will want to see you.

## Step 1: how to find a creative partner

It is extremely difficult to find a job as a copywriter or art director on your own. If you don't have one, how can you go about finding a creative partner?

### College courses

Copywriters searching for art directors often approach art schools or advertising courses, either formally through a lecturer or informally by introducing themselves to students.

### Advertise

Creatives in search of a partner can advertise that fact on college notice boards. It's also a good idea to mention to everyone that you come into contact with that you are looking for a partner.

### Head-hunters

Advertising recruitment consultants, such as Kendall Tarrant, specialize in finding work for copywriters and art directors. If they think you have the talent, they might be able to help you find a creative partner.

### Book days

Kendall Tarrant hold a 'book club' on the first working Monday of every month at the Saatchi & Saatchi pub, 'The Pregnant Man'. If you have a portfolio but are without a partner, you can go along to a book day, display your wares and, with luck, find someone who wants to work with you.

### Get partnered

Occasionally, agencies will be looking for someone to partner an existing copywriter or art director. If you have an exceptionally good portfolio, it's possible that you might just find a partner in this way.

## Step 2: how to start a portfolio

> I don't care where my people come from but they must have a book . . . AMV's website contains a section about how to put together a book, which we point people to when they contact us.
>
> *Peter Souter (1999)*

Whichever route you choose, you will still need to develop a portfolio/book of your work that you can show at interview. A portfolio/book is a showcase of your work. It is usually a leather or leather-effect carrying case (obtainable from art shops) with an integral ring binder that holds A3-size clear plastic sleeves. Work should be done on A3 white layout pad paper with a black felt-tip pen such as a Pentel N50.

The people who see your book will be looking for ideas not fantastic drawing skills. You should not use coloured pens, pencils, paints or any additional materials to enhance your work. Just black felt-tip and paper. Do *not* use computer software – just basic drawing skills. If you really can't draw, you can photocopy or use scrap art.

The most important thing is to get your ideas across. Keep them simple and clear. You will need to spend as much time as possible working on your book with your partner, and it's important that, as a team, you are constantly updating and improving your work.

## What should go in your portfolio

You will need about eight to twelve campaigns for different brands/services. A campaign is represented by three or four different executions all along the same theme which all meet the same brief. At least three or four of the campaigns in your book should be for press, posters and TV. It's also a good idea to include some innovative uses of media. Most 'student books' contain charity ads, so you might not want to include them in your book. Put your best campaigns at the beginning and at the end of the book. Your portfolio should achieve a balance – don't have lots of campaigns for similar products and similar target audiences. You need to demonstrate that you can do work for a variety of brands and media.

## Focus on your goal

If you want to work in a specialist area such as direct marketing, you need to show that you understand the medium. Your book should contain examples of mailing shots and demonstrate that you can write long copy. If your skills lend themselves to writing for TV and you want to work in one of the major ad agencies, your book's emphasis should be on storyboards. If your interest is in one of the specialist areas such as computing or healthcare, your book should focus on work in these areas. Obviously then, you need to take your book to the appropriate companies. There's no point in going to a small, local ad agency with a book full of TV work, or to Saatchi & Saatchi with small-space, local ads. Think about what you are good at and make sure your book contains the work you enjoy doing.

## Getting an appointment

More difficult than putting your 'book' together is getting an appointment to see a creative director. The more inventive you make your approach, the better. Whatever else you send include a one-page CV, a colour picture of yourself and your mobile phone number.

*Tom Rayfield (1998)*

Gimmicks aside, the normal approach would be to phone the creative director's PA (find out who this is from the agency switchboard) or the creative secretary. Ask if they could arrange for someone to see your book. It's not usually a good idea to let anyone see your work until you really feel you have a portfolio that you're proud of.

## Who sees your book?

You are very rarely present when your book gets seen, so your work must speak for itself. Remember that it should contain only ads, no descriptions or explanations. If the ideas need explanation, they're not working. The usual practice is for your book to be left at the ad agency, where a creative team will flick through it. If you are there in person, you may be surprised to find that the creatives concerned barely look at your work. They are experienced enough to know at a glance whether it is any good or not.

Don't expect feedback, but if you are given some, do take it on board and use it to improve your book. Creativity is subjective and a portfolio will often receive conflicting criticism. Don't react to every comment you receive, but if everyone who sees your book has only negative things to say, it's possible that you may need to rethink some of your work.

If you get helpful feedback from a creative team, act on it. If they are willing to see you again, do return to show them any changes you have made – let them see that you have listened and responded to their advice. Sometimes they will take a real interest in you and how you're getting on. Cultivate them – they could be useful allies in helping you to find work in the future.

## Make sure your portfolio is well presented

> The way a book looks is important. If someone is slapdash in how they present their work, they may be like that in the job.
>
> *Linda Goodman, copywriter, Lowe Direct*

## Practice, practice, practice

There are many good books on copywriting and art direction, but the only way to become a good writer/art director is by observation and practice. Spend time looking at ads in the D&AD (Design and Art Direction) annuals. These contain the best ads ever produced. They will give you the feel for what a good ad should look like and what makes a good idea.

# Ten ways to get started as a creative team

Once you have a partner and a book of work, there are a number of different routes to becoming a creative team, and these are just some of them:

## 1. A D&AD workshop

D&AD run evening workshops for aspiring copywriters and art directors in London, Edinburgh, Leeds and Manchester. The workshops are held four times a year – in winter, spring, summer and autumn. Applicants are selected on their creative ability. You are sent a creative brief in the post to work on and return by a deadline. If your application is successful, you are invited to attend a series of workshops where you work to a deadline on briefs set by advertising agencies.

You then take your work to the agency and receive feedback from a creative team. At the end of the session you are given a brief for the following week, and so on for six weeks.

Each session is held at a different advertising agency, so you get the opportunity to see inside an agency and meet their creative teams. The 'crit' (as advertising feedback is called) is as good or bad as the team giving it. Sometimes it can be disappointing, to say the least, to be told your work is poor without being told why. At other times, you may find that teams put a lot of effort into the feedback they give and that you will benefit greatly from their experience and expertise.

> D&AD places a high priority on education. We invest £1.3 million each year on running a range of innovative programmes that seek to identify talented graduates, support colleges and develop and train young creatives.
>
> *D&AD website (2001)*

### Who does D&AD?

You will find that all kinds of people attend these workshops. Some of them may already be working in advertising but want to make the move to a creative position. Others could be working in another area entirely. Chefs, secretaries, housewives, accountants and plumbers have been on workshops in the past. There may also be students who are hoping to get into advertising. Some may already be doing a creative or marketing communications course, others may have left university and be looking for work.

### What are the benefits?

A fee is charged for the workshops. They are worth doing because not only do they help you to build up a portfolio of work but you may also find a creative partner in the process. What's more, you can learn a great deal from seeing other people's work – good and bad. And, if you get a good crit, it can help you improve your own work so that your book becomes more marketable. Another benefit, of course, is that you will be making plenty of contacts that could be useful to you in the future. If you are really talented, your work might be spotted by a creative team and it could lead to some work experience or even a job. More information about the D&AD workshops is given at the end of this chapter and in Chapter 13 on vocational courses.

### Advertising advice from D&AD workshop tutors

- Don't think you know it all just because you did well at college.
- Don't do it for the money, there isn't any. It's no longer the 1980s.
- Be prepared to change your book drastically, and that could be everything.
- Don't over finish work. It's the idea that counts, not the art direction or access to a Mac.
- If you do TV . . . keep it simple, as few frames as possible with a minimum of written explanation, otherwise people just won't read it.

- If you have to explain an idea in a crit, it doesn't work.
- Be prepared to work hard on your book for anything from a year to three or four years. If you're not 100 per cent committed . . . don't bother!
- Visit lots of teams and agencies. Get to know as many people as possible.
- Remember it's only one team's opinion, not the agency's or the industry's for that matter.
- Never burn your bridges. You never know where someone might turn up.
- Be willing to learn.
- Have fun. Remember, some people have to work for a living.

*D&AD (2000)*

## 2. Work experience

There are no set rules. What counts is timing, luck, personality and skill. But work experience is essential. I would not take on anyone who had not worked with us first.

*Trevor Beattie (1998), Creative Director, TBWA Simons Palmer*

The usual way of finding work as a creative team is through work experience. But you need to have a really strong book to get the work experience in the first place. If you think yours is good enough, phone the ad agencies of your choice and ask to speak to the person who handles work experience for creative teams.

You may, if you are lucky, get paid expenses, but you are usually expected to work for nothing. Many teams continue indefinitely on work experience hoping to be offered a plum job. Some teams have even won awards for their agencies while on work experience and have still been asked to leave at the end of the allotted time. Some people feel that agencies take advantage of creative teams by paying them next to nothing (or nothing at all), using their work and getting it all for free. However, if you want to work as a copywriter or art director in the industry, work experience is probably the best known way of getting started, and you may have to be prepared to work for nothing in order to get it.

There is some good news. Since the introduction of the government's 'minimum wage scheme', an agency has to pay you if you work for them on a 'placement' for more than two weeks. In terms of money, it's not a great deal, but it will help put an end to agencies taking advantage of their placement teams. See Chapter 15 for more information on work experience/placements.

Agencies are looking for the best raw material to hire.

*Peter Souter (1999)*

There are stories of people, who are now well known in advertising, who started their careers with work experience. There's even one about an art director who refused to leave the agency at the end of his stint. He just kept coming back till, finally, his perseverance paid off and he was offered a job. There's also the story of the 53–year-old copywriter who got a job at Saatchi & Saatchi. He had been accepted for work experience but couldn't afford anywhere to stay, so he was sleeping rough. His secret was only revealed when he was discovered shaving in the men's room. Saatchi & Saatchi not only fixed up somewhere for him to stay but – because his work was so good – offered him a job.

### 3. Go on a course

Choose a copywriting or art direction course, such as the ones at Watford or Falmouth, where you are put into creative teams and work on live briefs for real agencies. See Chapter 13.

### 4. Networking

Use any contacts you have. If you know someone who knows someone in a creative department, ask them to help you find work experience or give you the names of people you can see.

### 5. Change jobs

Start work in another area, such as planning, and move across once you're in. It's worth a try – some agencies are more flexible than others. But they're only going to move you if they think you've got talent.

### 6. Be an account handling creative

Start at a very small agency where you have to do everything and get experience on the job. You may even be able to do this without a portfolio of work. Some sales promotion agencies, for example, allow the whole team to brainstorm and encourage their 'suits' to come up with creative ideas. The main drawback is that the kind of work you produce might not be good enough to get you a job as a creative in a mainstream ad agency.

### 7. Go below the line/interactive

Work 'below the line' in a trade, sales promotion or a direct marketing ad agency. See the Directory and/or chapters 8 and 9 for information on integrated, interactive and new media agencies.

### 8. Leave the country

Work outside London or even abroad. The main disadvantage is that you may have difficulty finding work in London afterwards – so much depends on the quality of the work in your book. It's important to remember that the world of advertising does go beyond London and that there are very many good ad agencies north of Watford.

### 9. Specialize

Choose to work in a specialist area such as healthcare, sales promotion, recruitment advertising or work for an interactive ad agency. According to Richard Lord (1999), writing in *Adline*, 'there's a crippling shortage of good professional copywriters and journalists working on the internet'.

To achieve success as a creative team you need talent, originality, determination, perseverance and . . .

### 10. Luck

Being in the right place at the right time.

## What happens if you don't work in a creative team?

With reference to numbers 9 and 10, here's what happened to Gareth Dimelow, a copywriter working at Peter Kane Advertising, a below-the-line ad agency. At the ripe old age of 23, Gareth had already experienced three copywriting jobs since leaving college.

### No such thing as a regular day

"The day starts off quite leisurely. I'm lucky, I get to start at 9.30 or 9.45, depending on the tube. The thing is, in this industry everything gets off to quite a slow start; it's the evenings where they take it out of you.

It's a very chatty studio with surprisingly few office politics in evidence. People talk, argue about which radio station we'll listen to (usually Melody FM or XFM, chalk and cheese I know!) and then buy breakfast.

Then the briefs arrive. Sometimes I'm given a scrap of paper with barely legible handwriting, other times, it's a fully printed five-page opus. Either way, I discuss with the designers any preliminary ideas, ask all the questions I need answering by the account handlers, then start thinking. As a point-of-sale copywriter, word association and puns play a big part in my work. This can be quite gruelling, and it plays havoc with your grasp of proper written English. I read a lot of magazines for inspiration and insight, but never plagiarize. That's something you're constantly aware of. There are, after all, only so many original ideas in the world. The creativity comes through in execution rather than in origination.

Lunch breaks are long and leisurely. The pubs and bars play a significant part, especially on birthdays, leaving parties and Fridays.

Meetings and mid-project internal reviews take place in the afternoon and tempers flare. This is where the real office divisions begin to emerge. All departments tend to be quite self-serving, so a thick skin is a prerequisite.

Work stops at 3.30 for an ice-cream. I usually have to get them, because I just want one more than anyone else. We then just carry on. We all enjoy our work (in varying degrees) and so 5.30 is not the time when pens are thrown down. Depending on the workload, some people may stay till midnight, others may be gone by a quarter to six. It just depends.

### Essential skills for copywriting

Basic literacy is quite important as a copywriter, although some of the people I've met in the industry have caused me to question this rule on occasion. Creativity is not about thinking differently. In fact, quite the opposite. It's more important to be familiar with those things which are popular and conventional.

### Make your own opportunities

Generally speaking, it is vital that you are prepared to take no for an answer and keep working, whether that's in finding a job or presenting something to the account people. But don't give up trying. Be prepared to make your own opportunities. It is worth the effort.

And finally, forget everything you were ever taught about the English language. Sentences do begin with 'and', clichés are our best friend and punctuation sucks. **"**

## 'Not a lifetime career'

There are about 1000 full-time copywriters employed in UK advertising agencies, plus a lot of experienced freelances. Most copywriters do it for a few years and then go off to write books, become journalists or write for television. Others drift into agency management, while some start their own agencies. There are very few old copywriters – 'old' means over 35. So, we are not talking about a lifetime career.

*Tom Rayfield (1998)*

## 'Unless you really want to do it, don't bother'

If you'd rather die than do anything else, then you've got the determination to succeed. Richard Eber is the New York-based Chief Creative Officer of MRM Partners Worldwide, a company that combines McCann Relationship Marketing with Zentropy Partners. Here's what he had to say when asked what advice he would give to someone trying to get into advertising:

Find a way to impress people with how talented you are. It's not an easy or cushy business, so unless you really want to do it, don't bother. Put together a strong body of work that shows how you think.

*Richard Eber (2001)*

## Working in recruitment advertising

The design and placement of effective recruitment advertising is the livelihood of a multi-million pound industry.

*Guardian (1995)*

You may not have realized that most of the ads you see advertising jobs have been specially devised by agencies specializing in recruitment. Writing recruitment ads is a particular skill – totally different from selling supermarket brands.

> A good ad has to be persuasive – you can't bore people into wanting to work for you – and it has to be competitive. Creativity is about using original thought not gimmicks.
>
> *Simon Russell, Creative Director of recruitment agency Bernard Hodes, Guardian (1995)*

> Eye-catching appeal is a number one priority. Then there's negotiating an ad's position – you get a very different level of response depending on where it appears on the page and in relation to other ads.
>
> *Blackburn (1995)*

> One of the most difficult tasks is communicating a corporate stance in a way that means something to individuals.
>
> *Holker (1995)*

One of the attractions of recruitment advertising is that you know how successful (or not) your ad has been by the number of responses you receive. This feedback enables the agency to know which advertising medium is best for which ad and what writing style attracts the most replies.

Here's a Barkers Human Resources ad that appeared in the recruitment pages of the *Guardian* Media section. It's not only an excellent ad in its own right but it also gives you a good idea of the skills required for working in recruitment advertising – at the same time demonstrating that recruitment advertising can be creative and fun.

---

**A recruitment ad for a recruitment copywriter**

*Write me off this page*

So you think you could, do you? Well pardon me while I fall off my chair with laughter. It takes years to learn how to do this. Just you try writing an ad that could persuade someone as bright, witty and literate as you to do a job like mine.

Recruitment advertising copywriter. Not nearly as glamorous as writing ads for cat food, and much harder. Very little money. Training that consists of having all the horrible jobs to do and then being told to take half the words out. Colleagues who, quite frankly, you couldn't take home to meet your Mum.

Oh yes.

And people who will change everything you write.

But if you are a graduate, hugely talented, reasonably presentable and you've worked long enough to know what you don't want to do, send me your c.v., plus one side of A4 demonstrating your intellect, humour, grasp of English, and ability to make me do what you've just done. Read to the very end.

Deny Coughlan, Barkers, 30 Farringdon Street, London, EC4A 4EA.

*Deny Coughlan (1998)*

Here are two more recruitment ads aimed at graduates:

### Want to be better at advertising? Try falling in love.

No, don't go all doe-eyed just yet. Because what we're actually suggesting is that you fall in love with advertising. (If that makes you want to laugh, or stick your fingers down your throat, then turn the page now.) You see, here at Barrington Johnson Lorains we believe that people who really love what they're doing produce by far and away the best ads. Which is why we encourage those who strive to do better work. Who refuse to give up until an ad is as clear and as relevant and as compelling as it can be. If, during your time at college, you find yourself falling head over heels for this cantankerous mistress called advertising, then call us when you're done. We can't guarantee there'll be a vacancy. But we never turn down the opportunity for a spot of pillow talk.

*Recruitment ad, Barrington Johnson Lorains, Manchester*

### Want to create award-winning soaps, comedies and thrillers?

Then perhaps advertising is for you.

After all, a firm grasp of showmanship has always played a big part in the art of selling.

If you think you have the ability to capture the public's imagination, we'd like to speak to you.

Because not only do we have to rivet an audience's attention on television, radio and at the cinema, but also on posters and press.

It's a profession which demands an endless supply of creative ideas from us writers and art directors – and planners and account handlers.

Which is exactly why we're always looking to discover new talent to work at McCann-Erickson Manchester.

'Manchester?' You say, 'But I need to start my career in London.'

Possibly.

There *are* more agencies in London and no doubt, some pretty damn good ones too.

Like Abbott Mead Vickers BBDO.

Whose chairman and creative director, David Abbott, says, 'If you're any good, all the material things in life will come your way anyhow.'

We agree.

Almost certainly, talent, drive and luck are more important than the city in which you start your career.

OK, now what?

Well, success still depends on you writing an engaging story based on personal experiences (a CV and letter).

Send them to Brian Child, McCann-Erickson, Bonis Hall, Prestbury, Macclesfield, Cheshire SK10 4EF.

Who knows? This could be the break you've been waiting for.

*Child (1996)*

## Working in direct marketing

Direct marketing is trying hard to throw off its 'junk mail' image. Much of what is produced today is exciting and innovative.

If you enjoy writing copy, direct marketing might be more fulfilling for you than working on one-liners and concepts in a traditional ad agency. Working as a creative in direct marketing means coming up with ideas that have a real empathy with the target market. The ideas have to be good because it's vital that you maintain the brand's existing image – one tacky mailshot can do untold damage to a brand. You also find out very quickly whether your ideas have worked or not by the response the ad receives.

The Direct Marketing Awards highlight the year's best work:

Direct marketing is a refuge for the copywriter's craft, offering a unique challenge: the direct mail letter. One well-argued, well-constructed letter can move mountains of response.

*Terry Hunt (1999), Chairman of the judging panel, Direct Awards*

### 'Go to the edge'

Linda Goodman, a copywriter, works in a creative team with art director, Paddy Hall, at Lowe Direct, coming up with ideas for Lloyds TSB, Orange and other major brands.

"An idea should not be dictated by an advertising medium. Sometimes you can take risks. We answer the brief and sometimes we go that one step further. You've got to be brave and go for it. Go to the edge. **"**

*Linda Goodman*

## Harness the internet

**"**It's essential for anyone coming into the industry today to have a grounding in and to be able to understand and harness the direct side of the internet – it's an enormous growth area for direct marketing. It's fulfilling to do things in a different way – if you want to make yourself marketable, learn about the internet and new media. It's very interesting and it's creative. You need to have an understanding of what's achievable. The more internet sites you see, the more ideas you'll get about how it can be used. **"**

*Paddy Hall*

## Writing copy for the web

**"**When you're writing copy for websites, there's no time for an introduction or a build-up. The heart of your topic has to be right there at the start. You have to get to the point immediately, because you only have *one* screen in which to capture attention. Then, if the reader wants to know more, he or she can dig deeper. If they're really interested, they can then dig deeper still. That's the amazing thing about the internet. You can write an infinite amount on any subject, so long as it's signposted well enough for people to find their way around. It's the opposite of writing a press ad. **"**

*Maureen Pubrook (2001), web copywriter*

## Eight rules for writing copy

1. Know your target.
2. Do your research.
3. Answer the brief.
4. Be relevant.
5. Be objective.
6. Keep it simple.
7. Know your medium.
8. Be ambitious.

*Dominic Gettins (2000)*

## What makes a good creative team?

**"**Being a successful creative team is like a marriage. You're going to be spending more time with your creative partner than you do with your husband or wife. Sometimes, if you're really lucky, you can work with the same person for years and years. There needs to be a chemistry – you develop a kind of shorthand with your partner. The test of a good team is the way you work together. If you produce good ads, if you win awards and if the client is happy. **”**

*Linda Goodman*

## What's it's like to work as a creative team?

Hugh Todd (copywriter) and Adam Scholes (art director) are one of the top senior creative teams. They met on the Watford copywriting and art direction course and have worked together ever since. Recently they moved from BBH (Bartle Bogle Hegarty) to Saatchi & Saatchi. Here, they talk about their work:

### Hugh Todd, copywriter

**“**My job involves coming up with ideas for ads – TV (mostly), posters, print, radio, ambient media, etc. – and executing those ideas with directors, photographers, illustrators, radio producers, etc.

Ideally time is split between coming up with new ideas on a new brief – TV scripts, say, for a large beer brand – perhaps ten scripts in a week, while also actually making a radio campaign for chewing gum which would take the best part of two days in a studio. I may also be helping with a pitch, sitting and brainstorming on a new product/client. The best fun is spending the whole week on a shoot in Miami in a large hotel making your own ad with a director and crew all mucking in together. To sum up, 'the most fun you can have with your clothes on'.

I got my first job by going round with my portfolio of work. You have to be completely focused on what you want. Copywriter or art director? Above or below the line? Good agency/bad agency? My advice is to pick ten agencies whose work you like. Find the creative teams who do that work. Hound them or their PAs for a crit of your book. Go back again and again to the same people. You'll get a job if you're good enough – two years max.

#### Skills needed to be a copywriter

Lots of ideas. A thick skin when those ideas get blown out by clients/creative directors/research/the BACC (TV script clearance committee). Resilience. An ability to have fun – enjoying pressure. An ability to drink a lot and dance well when things are going well and not so well. Get someone to believe in your ideas – the ability to sell to your creative director. The ability to do ten things at once – radio/TV/posters/press/mailers/speeches/drink/have a home life/play pool/sleep. **”**

### Adam Scholes, art director

**“**My job involves generating ideas for TV commercials, radio, press, posters and other media. The fun part is writing the ads. I find I write the best ideas in the morning for some reason.

A lot of time is spent dealing with problems from the clients – this is a grind. Arguing/debating your point with account handlers is crucial and often tiring. Unfortunately, keeping your idea 'intact' has become 50 per cent of the job now.

Of course, the shoots are a good laugh.

Our first job was after doing a work placement at Grey. Hugh and I got our jobs at BBH on the back of our campaign for Harley-Davidson motorbikes. This was our own client that we approached ourselves, sold the campaign, persuaded a production company (Stark Films) to shoot for free. We got a Gold Arrow at the British TV Awards and a job at BBH.

### Skills needed to be an art director

Imagination, energy, good with people.

I feel you can't dictate to someone how to get into advertising. You can lead a horse to water, but it doesn't mean it's a fish. Basically, if you want it enough you'll get a job. It's important to feel inspired – we went to see Trevor Beattie at HHCL and Tom and Walt at AMV. **"**

## A day in the life of a creative director

Tony Bodinetz, former Creative Group Head at DMB&B (now D'Arcy):

**"**As a writer, group head and board director, my job was necessarily extremely varied, involving writing ads with my partner, approving ideas from our 'teams', attending meetings, going to film shoots, radio recordings, photographic sessions, etc., briefing sessions, board meetings, interviews.

I would try to arrive early (8 a.m.) to spend some time working on some TV scripts and some body copy for a press ad, before the phone started ringing. Then I might have to dash to a recording studio for a music session on a new commercial. After lunch, there might be a pre-production meeting, with clients attending on an impending film shoot, after which I'd try to pick up the bits and pieces . . . teams waiting to show me some ideas, ads to proofread and an interview with a potential new team to end the day.

### Skills needed to be a successful copywriter/art director
- Empathy (never patronize 'housewives' or 'teenagers').
- Good health (you have to be resilient).
- Energy (impossible to exaggerate importance).
- A sense of humour (about the job as well as for use in ads).
- Thick skin (people can be very rude about your ideas).

### How to approach ad agencies
1. Find a partner (not necessarily for life).
2. Get a portfolio together (six campaigns, each of three ads, mostly in 48-sheet format, and not all for charities, Friends of the Earth or sex aids).

3. Write a simple, honest 'I'm sure you don't have a job right now, but we're really committed and half an hour of your time would really help us' letter to the top 40 creative directors, followed by early morning phone calls.

### Two things I wish I'd been told at the start

1. You may have to find something good to say about products (cigarettes, political parties, children's games, etc.) you'd rather not say something good about.
2. Keeping your integrity when everyone around you is losing theirs isn't easy. "

## A day in the life of a freelance art director

Jan Newbold:

"I have been a freelancer for the majority of my working life. As a 'full-time' freelance art director, my day could vary depending on whether there were pressing deadlines to meet. If this was the case, as it invariably was, myself and a copywriter would settle down after briefing to create around three ideas per each required ad.

Roughs would be drawn up and presented to the account director/handler and/or the creative director for their approval and discussion. The approved ad or campaign would be improved/finished up for final presentation to the client. On occasion, we, the creative team, would attend the presentation to client and assist in selling the idea. I personally preferred to opt out of these presentations as I couldn't spare the time as I had the next urgent deadline to keep.

During the course of a day's work, there were proofs to inspect for colour correction, mechanicals (artwork) to examine for correct layout, spelling errors, etc. and amendments, if necessary, to all of these.

These tasks, of course, were sandwiched between all the creative work that had to be undertaken for that day.

I often found that briefing meetings would go on too long and much preferred account handlers to give us a brief (of a familiar account) to read without them at first, to be expanded upon later when we'd mulled it over and had our questions prepared.

Time management was of the essence and it was our responsibility to decide which account was most pressing, even though many an account handler would implore us to work on theirs first!

Some days would be taken up on a shoot, sitting around waiting for the photographer to get his lighting right before shooting. I often used this opportunity to come up with ideas for the campaign in hand, if it was urgent.

Other days would be spent looking through photographers' and illustrators' portfolios for suitable styles/techniques for the next ad to be produced. "

### '*If you want to succeed, don't ever give up*'
Jan Newbold's advice to aspiring art directors:

"Persevere. Persevere. Persevere.

Although the industry is even more competitive than when I first started out and there are fewer places to fill, it is a rewarding and fun profession.

Team up and put a portfolio together with a copywriter.

Be prepared to have your work criticized and, on occasion, in no uncertain terms.

If you're a woman, be prepared and be able to handle certain forms of sexual discrimination (in, thankfully, only a few agencies). In creative departments, there are still fewer female art directors than male. You need to be 'one of the lads'.

Whether male or female, you generally need to be more gregarious and be able to fit in. You will be working closely with all kinds of personalities during your career. It is very much a sociable industry. You need to be a team player.

Arrange interviews with as many creative teams/group heads/creative directors as is possible, for them to advise you on your portfolio.

You will receive conflicting advice on what is good/bad in your portfolio. Take it all in and then decide which work you need to improve on, which needs binning, which to keep in your portfolio.

Go back to the interviewers, if you can, and show them your amendments/new concepts. This shows your determination to get it right and your desire to work at their agency.

Be prepared to work for nothing in order to get your foot in the door and prove yourself.

Keep improving your portfolio, even if it means working through the night. If you want to succeed, don't ever give up. "

## Silly ways to promote yourselves

The industry is full of stories (most of them true) of how creative teams got their first breaks.

### Our book is too hot to handle
One creative team sent a pair of oven gloves to the creative directors of their choice. They got seen – and yes, they got the job.

### Sandwich board man
The story goes that once an arts graduate stood outside the ad agency Abbott Mead Vickers, BBDO, with a placard that read, 'Please give me a job'. He did this day after day – whatever the weather. Eventually, David Abbott, the Creative Director, took pity on him and called him in for a chat. He wasn't given a job there and then but was advised to try and gain experience in smaller ad agencies. He took

that advice and in time returned to Abbott Mead Vickers, BBDO, where he worked successfully for many years. He built a reputation as an excellent creative – and eventually became the agency's Deputy Creative Director. The fairy story doesn't end there – he was recently named as Abbott's successor. We're talking, of course, about Peter Souter, the Executive Creative Director of AMV BBDO (Welch, 1998).

### Bright ideas

This one is a bit corny as it has been used so many times. A creative team sent a light bulb. Another creative team sent an onion representing the many layers of their creativity.

### Qwertyuiop

In the days when people were still using typewriters, someone sent broken bits of keys to creative directors with a letter saying that they had sent out so many letters that they had broken their mum's old typewriter.

### Bribery

If you can find a creative director's personal passion, you could try sending something to show that you've done your homework on their interests. For example, a bottle of really good wine was sent to Malcolm Gluck (the wine writer), when he was a creative director, by two students wanting a work placement. It worked.

## Don't underestimate yourself

Don't think, 'I shouldn't bother sending my book to that agency. They're too good.' All people are subject to low self-esteem and I think creative people are particularly prone to it. I can think of several people in our creative department who didn't think they were good enough, but sent their book in on a lark and we took them up on it.

*Luke Sullivan (1998)*

## How much will you earn?

Pay and conditions are good but the real buzz comes from hearing people talk about your work.

*Andrew Fisher (1998), Saatchi & Saatchi*

"A creative team on placement at Saatchi & Saatchi may receive £150 per week after the first two weeks. After three months it has been known for teams to get hired." (Fahn, 2001).

Saatchi & Saatchi are an exception – most agencies don't pay you at all while you're on placement, or they might offer to cover your travel expenses. However, if your placement is for longer than two weeks, the agency has to pay you the minimum working wage. It does get better – a copywriter can earn £50,000 a year after a few years in the business and top creatives get six-figure salaries.

According to a recent IPA survey (2001), the *average* salary for a creative team in a medium-sized to large London agency is up to £17,500, though you would expect to earn less outside London if you were working for a smaller company.

## Recommended routes

- Work experience/work placements (Chapter 15).
- A postgraduate, diploma or short course (Chapter 13).
- Direct marketing (Chapter 9).
- Sales promotion (Chapter 9).
- Interactive advertising (Chapters 8 and 9).

D&AD Workshops – see chapter 13.

British Design and Art Direction (D&AD)
9 Graphite Square
Vauxhall Walk
London SE11 5EE
020 7840 1123
Fax: 020 7840 0846
www.dandad.org

Recruitment Agency for creative teams and 'Book Club':
Kendall Tarrant
56–60 Hallam Street
London W1W 6JL
020 7907 4444
Fax: 020 7907 4477
www.kendalltarrant.com
Contact Sam Pooley:
sam@ktlondon.co.uk
info@ktlondon.co.uk
Kendall Tarrant New York
41 East 11th Street
11th Floor
New York 10003
001 212 645 8433
info@kt-ny.com

How to put together your first book (www.admentor.com and www.kuraoka.com).

Jobs for creatives (www.artjob.com and www.CreativeCentral.com).

*Campaign* (www.campaignlive.com).

## Recommended reading

No book can teach you how to write copy or art direct, but the following will give you some insight into the process:

Brierley, Sean (1995) *The Advertising Handbook*. Routledge.
Crompton, Alastair (1996) *The Craft of Copywriting*. Century Business.
De Bono, Edward (1993) *Serious Creativity: Using the Power of Lateral Thinking to Create New Ideas*. Harper Business.
Essinger, J. (1996) *How to Write Marketing Copy That Gets Results*. Pitman.
Evans, Robin (1988) *Production and Creativity in Advertising*. Pitman.
Gettins, Dominic (2000) *The Unwritten Rules of Copywriting: How to Create Better Press, Poster, Radio and TV Advertising*. Kogan Page.
Sullivan, Luke (1998) *'Hey, Whipple, Squeeze This'. A Guide to Creating Great Ads*. John Wiley & Sons.
Yadin, Daniel (1998) *Creative Marketing Communications*, 2nd edn. Kogan Page.

*Campaign Portfolio* (1999). Haymarket Publications.
*Creative Review* (www.creative-review.co.uk)
*Adline* (monthly journal).
*SHOTS* (CD-ROM and video).
*Communication Arts Magazine* (www.commarts.com)
*Advertisers Annual*. Reed Information Services.

All D&AD publications:
*D&AD Annual* (2001).
*D&AD Showreel* (2001).
*Student Annual* (2001).
*The Commercials Book.*
*The Copy Book.*
*The Art Direction Book.*
*Design and Art Direction Annuals* – these contain award-winning creative work and will certainly give you a good idea of what makes a good ad and what doesn't. Included with every copy is a DVD and a CD-ROM.

# 7 Advertising media – planning and buying

Media is an exciting/dynamic/creative ever-changing area to be in. You can get to the top via a career in media.

*Sally Paterson (1998), The Stevens Company*

It's a tremendously exciting time for those of us working in the industry.

*Graham Duff (1998), Chief Executive, Zenith Media*

## What do we mean by media?

Say media to most people and they immediately assume you're talking about jobs in *the* media. Many students choose media studies in the mistaken belief that it will help them get a job in advertising, when in fact they're more likely to be learning about soaps, film noir and sitcoms. Media, in advertising terms, means any of the following:

- *Media planning/buying*: people who work in the media department of an advertising agency or in a media independent company – choosing and strategically planning the appropriate medium or media for an advertising campaign and then negotiating for and buying space in that media on behalf of their client.
- *TV buyers*: specialize in negotiating TV time and space with TV media owners – for example, Carlton.
- *Sales assistants* working for media owners or within sales houses. Their job is to negotiate and sell advertising space to media buyers and to generate new ideas for using media space.
- *Researchers, analysts and statisticians*: they use quantitative research to analyse data in order to provide audience profiles, viewing figures, competitive data and market information.
- *Work in new media*: web/online advertising, CD-ROM, interactive kiosks, etc.

Media, in terms of advertising, means the selection and purchase of the media (newspapers, magazines, radio, TV, posters, cinema – every type of media) for an advertising campaign. This is usually the role of the media planner and buyer in a 'full-service' advertising agency or in a media 'independent' – a company which specializes in handling the media side of advertising. Once the media has been chosen, its price has to be negotiated, and that's the job of the media buyer.

> Quality media thinking can and does make a significant difference between an advertising campaign's success or failure.
>
> *The Media Planning Group (2001)*

Advertising agencies deal directly with the media owners (companies who exclusively sell space in their own product, such as a specific newspaper or magazine) and sales houses (independent companies who may sell space or airtime for a number of media owners).

## The digital age

With the advent of new technology, we're moving into a digital age – the whole way in which we communicate is going to be different. Digital TV is revolutionizing advertising and opening up a whole new world of opportunities for reaching consumers.

In the UK we currently have almost 300 TV channels. Interactive audio channels give people the opportunity of receiving audio through their TV which is set to revolutionize direct response advertising. Online shopping is set to reach £3.1 billion by 2003 in the UK (*Market Monitor*, 1998). Using the home-shopping channels, people can order goods from the comfort of their home and also arrange travel, financial, leisure and other services. The new buzz word in media is 'relationship marketing' – establishing a one-to-one relationship between seller and customer through 'interactive' media.

> These are times of unparalleled change in European television and media markets. The adoption of digital broadcasting technology and the merging of the internet with television will pose huge challenges to traditional broadcasters . . . unrivalled opportunities for individuals . . .
>
> *Digital Broadcaster (1999)*

## A new world of media opportunity

The areas traditionally associated with advertising have grown, developed and are rapidly changing. Consumers now have a far greater choice in their reading, watching and listening than ever before. Today we spend 70 per cent more of our time using the internet than reading newspapers or magazines (*MediaWeek*, 2001).

Traditional media is still going strong. Cinema audiences this year reached a record high with the largest monthly attendance figure for 32 years (*MediaWeek*). With 18.1 million people visiting the cinema in August 2001, it's the fastest-growing advertising medium. Interestingly, more young people today are listening to the radio. According to Julian Sampson of the Radio Advertising Bureau, 'new media has changed the way people spend their time. Many consumers are switching off their televisions in the evening and switching on their computers – and their radios' (*MediaWeek*, 2001).

> The fact is that, for many years to come, the new media we are becoming familiar with will be complementary to the old media we are already familiar with. People are coming to expect different qualities from different parts of their media repertoires.
>
> *Mark Girling (2001), Managing Director, Quantum New Media*

> If the medium doesn't exist, we'll invent it.
>
> *Optimedia (1999)*

Traditional media is just one of the options open to media planners and buyers. Today, everyone involved in advertising and media is having to think of more interesting ways of doing things. Anything can now be used as an advertising medium. Ads have appeared in all kinds of unusual places – so-called 'ambient media'. For example, on eggshells ('eggverts'), lids from take-away meals, supermarket floors, petrol nozzles, golf holes, videos ('vidverts') and tube tickets.

> If you can stick an ad on it, someone will.
>
> *Alan Morgan (1999), recruitment consultant*

> Lateral thinking is at the heart of creativity.
>
> *Simon Sadie (1998), Director of Innovation, MPG*

You now need to be able to think more laterally in order to reach people. As a result, jobs in media have become much more creative. Digital media is going to make a huge impact. With the tremendous growth in media and the opening up of new media opportunities, there couldn't be a better or more exciting time to embark on a media career.

### Top ten UK media specialists*

| | |
|---|---|
| 1. Carat | 6. Starcom Motive Partnership |
| 2. Zenith Media | 7. MediaVest UK |
| 3. MediaCom Group | 8. PHD |
| 4. MindShare Media UK | 9. OMD UK |
| 5. Initiative Media London | 10. Universal McCann UK Group |

* ranked by accounts handled on a media-buying basis
AC Nielsen MMS

Campaign Report *(February, 2002)*

**Top twenty media specialist companies worldwide***

| | | |
|---|---|---|
| 1. | MindShare (London) | 12. MediaCom (New York) |
| 2. | OMD Worldwide (New York) | 13. Carat North America (New York) |
| 3. | Initiative Media (New York) | 14. PhD (New York) |
| 4. | Universal McCann (New York) | 15. Horizon Media (New York) |
| 5. | Starcom Worldwide (Chicago) | 16. CIA USA (New York) |
| 6. | TN Media (New York) | 17. Empower MediaMarketing (Cincinnati) |
| 7. | MediaVest (New York) | 18. KSL Media (New York) |
| 8. | Media Edge (New York) | 19. R. J. Palmer (New York) |
| 9. | Zenith Media Services (New York) | 20. Camelot Communications (Dallas) |
| 10. | Optimedia (London) | |
| 11. | SFM Media/MPG (New York) | |

* ranked by US billings/revenues

*Advertising Age (2000)*

## Media planning

Your agency is working on an advertising campaign for a new product. Where it will be advertised will depend on how much the client has to spend and who the target audience are – that is, the people considered to be in the market to buy your product.

A media planner will have an understanding of all the media available and will be able to work out what medium or media will reach the most people in the target audience at the most cost-effective price. They will then draw up a media plan showing the time span of the advertising and the media selection in detail.

For example, a client wants to advertise a new shower gel. This could simply be advertised in women's magazines. But which magazines? *Vogue* or *Woman's Own*? *Cosmopolitan* or *The Lady*? They are all very different and have a very different readership.

Perhaps TV would be more appropriate for the launch of a new product? Or maybe it should be a poster campaign? The media planner will decide not only which magazines to use but also what spaces to buy and where in the magazine the ads should appear.

If it's a TV ad, the media planner will decide not only what channels to use but also what time of day the ads should appear. In consultation with the account team, decisions will be taken as to the most appropriate programmes for the client's advertising. Do the prospective buyers of the shower gel watch breakfast-time TV or late-night programmes? Do they have cable TV? Perhaps the client wants to send a sample of the shower gel to specific people? In that case, direct mail will be chosen as another medium.

Do retailers need to know about the new shower gel? If so, advertisements will be needed for trade publications such as *Checkout* (a supermarket publication) and *Chemist and Druggist*. Media planning, therefore, is a complex job requiring in-depth knowledge of all the media available, coupled with analytical skills.

## Media buying

Media buyers work very closely with media planners. Their job is to buy media space in whatever medium the ads are to appear. They try and reach the highest number of people in their target audience at the lowest possible cost.

### 'A thorough understanding of the client's business'

The first step in any media process is the gathering of information. Everything starts with the brief. Media strategy requires a thorough understanding of the client's business, the communication objectives and the characteristics of each medium. Strategic planning has become a way of making media more creative. You should feel confident that you are answering all the objectives and that *all* the media can work together.

After we've come up with the strategy, we negotiate the deals. A buyer is a strategist as much as a buyer. You get involved with the process at the earliest possible stage with the planner – it's a joint effort.

*Andrew Canter (1998), Broadcast Director, MPG*

## Training on the job

You'll probably start off as a media assistant joining a team of senior planners and buyers, working on a portfolio of accounts and learning on the job. You'll get to understand the basics of how media works and, if you are working for a large agency, you'll be sent on media training courses to learn about planning and buying.

A lot of training is on the job. 80 per cent of the buyer's work is done on the phone. You need to get a deep knowledge of the business. You will need to be able to think on your feet and have a considered view. It is crucial to build a relationship with the client.

*Andrew Canter (1998)*

### A TV buyer's day

"The morning is the busiest period of the day. The station sales houses close the airtime for that night between twelve and one in the afternoon, so the hours prior to this deadline are spent negotiating to move airtime into or out of that night depending on your requirements.

The afternoon involves booking in new airtime schedules, updating spreadsheets, checking that spots have gone out when they should have gone out and generally talking to the station sales executives in order to improve a campaign. I might also have to carry out some work for a client, which would usually involve looking at competitive activity."

*Simon Prindiville, Universal McCann*

### A day in the life of Andrew Canter, Broadcast Director, MPG

"I normally arrive at the office around eight in the morning. I spend an hour planning the day ahead or doing some spreadsheet work. It's usually quiet, so I tend to do the work that needs the utmost concentration with no distraction at this time.

Once the team has arrived we'll meet up for half an hour to discuss the work in progress and any issues that may arise.

I spend the next half an hour discussing specific client issues with the TV managers – all outstanding issues from the previous meeting. We'll then look to set up meetings with the relevant TV companies to talk about current business.

I may look to devise a strategic solution for a particular client, which would be an ongoing project. At certain times of the year we could have as many as ten different strategy documents to write. We would spend some time brainstorming ideas and involving other members of the company who may not work directly on those clients, adding an extra dimension.

Some of my time may be spent on the phone, negotiating deals or making sure that the deals that have been negotiated are being delivered.

I will normally have a couple of client meetings to attend – to review a campaign or to talk about future business. Or a meeting at one of the agencies to discuss general issues and future plans of certain clients and brands.

In the afternoon I may write a presentation for a specific client, responding to a brief that I have received from the agency. This may have to be 'turned around' straightaway and probably presented the next day.

Later on we could have a presentation from a media owner that looked at certain opportunities for one or several of our clients. This would normally be at the end of the day, followed by some sort of social gathering afterwards.

If nothing social is occurring and once the phones have stopped ringing, it's time to get back to the work that needs peace and quiet. On some days (usually Friday) I might do some filing, a necessary evil in this business.

After all that I'll probably leave the office around 7.30 p.m. (sometimes it's 6 p.m., other times 10 p.m.) ready for another day tomorrow."

## Media sales

Selling ads is no different from selling anything else. It's a people business.

*Jane Emma Peerless (1998), Advertising Manager,* Financial Times

> Forty per cent of board directors in media agencies started off in sales.
>
> *Alan Morgan (1999)*

Many media planners and buyers begin by working for a media owner selling space or time.

Every medium (whether it's a publication or a TV station) has its own advertising sales department. Their job is to negotiate, sell and book advertising space in their particular magazine, newspaper, radio or TV programme. These are the people who negotiate with the planners and buyers from the advertising agency.

The hours are more routine and, arguably, the job is possibly less demanding because you are only dealing with one medium – your own – whereas your opposite number at the ad agency is negotiating with all the media available. However, in media sales you are working under a lot of pressure. You have non-stop deadlines to meet. You are dealing with clients who may not want to speak to you, so you have to be persistent. Negotiating becomes easier once you know your clients well and have built up a relationship of trust and honesty.

### Why work for a media owner rather than an ad agency?

- More jobs available, so easier to get into than an ad agency.
- Well paid – and you get commission.
- Great perks – lots of corporate entertainment and lunches.
- You can move from media sales into working for an ad agency – e.g. from TV sales into TV buying.
- Many media owners employ their own in-house planners.
- Opportunities for research positions – e.g. to research people's perceptions of a particular publication.

## What are media employers looking for?

Agencies are all very different, as are the media owners. Working in the sales department of Capital Radio, Carlton or Virgin is very different from working for a large media independent such as Zenith or in the media department of an advertising agency. However, they are all seeking similar skills from applicants.

Your qualifications and relevant work experience are important. But so is your ability to demonstrate the following:

- excellent communication skills
- enthusiasm for the business
- motivation
- confidence
- strategic thinking
- negotiation skills
- common sense

- knowledge of the media industry
- commitment to media as a career
- tenacity
- sociability
- intelligence – logical thinking
- listening skills
- persuasive skills
- computer skills
- energy
- ambition
- numeracy – you need to feel comfortable with numbers
- analytical skills
- the ability to think on your feet
- team player
- adaptability
- sense of humour
- ability to work under pressure and to deadlines.

## A desire to succeed

'The most essential skill (among many) is the ability to convey trust.' So says Andrew Canter (1998), Broadcast Director at MPG. He goes on to suggest what he considers are the skills required for a successful media career:

> "You must be able to build relationships and gain respect among your peers and, in particular, your clients. A degree of calm and control is necessary. There must be a desire to succeed and this should be shown in your passion and enthusiasm.
>
> You must have the ability to show a thorough understanding of the client's business and work in a team environment. Self-presentation is important. You need to have good social skills and be personable. You should also be comfortable with numbers. You must not be fazed by being put on the spot and being expected to come up with considered answers. Good computer skills are essential.

### How to get into media

The old adage: You never get a second chance to make a first impression. *The first interview is only the beginning, not the end.*

Be focused on what you want to do and stick to it. Find out as much as you can about your chosen career. Even ask if you can be interviewed over the phone, as most of your time will be spent on the telephone.

Only apply to the jobs you really want to do. You are not only wasting your own valuable time but that of other people.

Be extremely honest and ask as many questions as you feel necessary to make a qualified decision. If you accept a job then take up the offer, do not dwell. **"**

## Work experience

A work placement is not only valuable in giving you on-the-job experience but also you are more likely to get a job offer at the end of it. Companies are more likely to employ people they know. Most media owners will pay travel and a basic allowance for food. Agencies may sometimes pay expenses. Information about work experience is given in Chapter 15.

## Recruitment consultants

> A vast majority of media jobs are got through recruitment agencies. Media agencies don't do 'milk rounds' so they need to use recruitment agencies to do the job for them.
> *Alexandra Botting (1998), Recruitment Consultant, The Stevens Company*

Specialist recruitment agencies such as The Stevens Company will help graduates find jobs in media and media sales. You need to be able to sell yourself to a recruitment consultant. It's important that you are sure that you want to work in media and that you know what the job entails.

### Why use a recruitment consultant?
- Ninety per cent of agency positions are filled by recruitment consultants.
- Gives you access to a wide variety of job opportunities.
- You receive a thorough briefing on the job specification, interviewer and agency, so you know what to expect.
- Many recruitment consultants offer interview practice beforehand.
- You receive constructive feedback on your interview so you can learn from your mistakes.
- Consultants offer salary advice and negotiate a starting salary for you.
- It doesn't cost you anything – fees are paid by whoever employs you, so you have nothing to lose.

## Graduate training

If you're a young graduate and you want to work as a media planner or buyer in an ad agency, you can apply to join a graduate training scheme (see Chapter 12).

## Do your homework

Read *Campaign, MediaWeek, Revolution* and other journals so that you have an industry view on all the issues. See the Directory at the end of this book for details of media publications.

## What area of media is right for you?

There's a blurring of the lines between agencies and media owners – both have planners, executives and researchers.

*Alan Morgan (1999)*

Think about whether you want to work for a large or small company. What training is on offer? Some companies offer formal in-house training or will send you on a training course. Many companies expect to throw you straight into the job, although you are usually under close supervision at the start.

What kind of clients would you like to work with? Is there an area you are particularly interested in? For example, if you are a sports fanatic you could work on the advertising side of a sporting publication. If you like jazz, you could work for a magazine specializing in music.

Could you cope with working to deadlines? Would you enjoy being on the phone most of the day? How good are you at working under pressure? Can you cope with stress? Where do you want to be in five years' time?

You must be prepared not to stay in one job for too long. Recruitment consultants say that it's quite normal to make three or four moves in your first ten years of a media career.

## How to apply

Your covering letter should specify what area of media you are interested in. You need to show that you have thought about what you want to do and know where you are going. Unless a handwritten letter is specified, word process your letter and CV. Some companies prefer a handwritten letter because it shows you have made an effort and gives them a good idea of whether you can write and spell. Information about CVs and job applications can be found in Chapters 11 and 12.

## The media interview

You are always presenting yourself.

*Recruitment Consultant*

The first interview will often be conducted by more junior members of the agency team. The second interview is more likely to be with a media director. You need to be fully aware of and have opinions on current media issues. At the interview you will be tested on your toughness.

They will keep coming back at you, challenging you. The more rigorous the interview, the better you're doing.

*Recruitment Consultant*

See Chapter 12 for general advice on how to handle interviews.

## Learning on the job

This was the experience of Harriet Bruce when she was an international media trainee at BMP DDB Limited:

"I got my job through media recruitment consultants. I was one of twenty people being interviewed. It was a totally friendly interview with no media questions. I was asked about my greatest achievements but very little about advertising. My second interview with the media director was more difficult. I was asked about the course I'd been on at Watford and what I felt about advertising.

I was given on-the-job training. Since I'd done advertising at Watford the usual 'Media Circle' course for graduates wasn't seen as necessary! The agency gave me a client straightaway, but I was closely overseen – I worked closely with my boss. I was thrown in at the start and given things to do including filing.

It's been a gradual thing – they've given me responsibility as I've been ready for it. There is such a volume of work that you have to prioritize and be able to say no. The real downside of the job is the pressure. A usual day was from 9 a.m. to 7 p.m., although I did often stay later.

A year at BMP has given me a lot more confidence, improved presentation skills and helped me become better organized. The postgrad course at Watford gave me good grounding, but there's nothing like being in the job for getting the experience.

### *Don't be put off by anything*

Media, in particular, is quite an aggressive environment. There are 70 of us in one big open-plan room divided into planners and buyers. You mustn't be put off by anything. A lot of shouting goes on over the telephone – people get angry when they can't get the rates they want. You need skills like diplomacy – so much of the work is based on goodwill. You need to be someone who is easy to get on with and to be good at keeping up relationships.

For my job you need to be genuinely interested in the international side. I'd advise potential applicants to ask as many relevant questions as you can think of at interview and in the job. You learn by your mistakes and by listening to other people."

*Harriet Bruce, Media Planner/Buyer, CIA Medianetwork, Edinburgh*

## 'Media is more than just sales'

"Anything young media professionals can do to set themselves apart is good and in a sense quite a lot of their marketing skills are going to have to go (transfer) from selling themselves to becoming multi-talented and flexible.

The whole business will require a lot more effort and deep thought than in the past. Media is more than just sales.

You have to understand the brand, the client's strategy for the brand, and the competitive environment; it's not just flogging an advertising campaign. "

*Kathryn Jacobs (2001), Commercial Director, Virgin Radio*

## What can you earn?

According to a recent IPA survey (April 2001) of medium-sized and large London advertising agencies, the average starting salary for a media assistant (i.e. not necessarily a graduate position) would be up to a maximum of £15,000.

In media sales, starting salaries range from £12,000 to 15,000, although with commission this could rise to £16,000 to 20,000 and you could get as much as £18,000–24,000 in your second year. Media sales has a fast career path – you can reach a managerial role in three to five years. If you're working in media sales you can also expect commission on top of your salary.

A trainee media planner or buyer would start at £15,000–£17,500. However, you need to bear in mind that these salaries apply only to London ad agencies. If you were working outside London or for a smaller company, you could expect a lower rate of pay.

### Average media salaries (UK)

- graduate: £15,000
- assistant: £18,000
- junior planner/buyer: £23,500
- planner/buyer: £26,000
- senior planner/buyer: £31,000
- manager: £36,000
- group head: £57,000
- client director: £73,000

*The Davis Company (MediaWeek, 6 July 2001)*

### Average media salaries (USA)

In the USA there appears to be a sizeable gap between the earnings of men and women working in media. Men seem to earn considerably more. The average salary for a media director (male) is $80,000, whereas it's only $68,300 for a woman in the same position. The current (2001) average salary for men and women working as media directors is $77,896. (*Source: Advertising Age* survey prepared by Irwin Broh & Associates.)

### 'Must be fun and hard working'

Here are some typical media recruitment ads taken from the advertising trade press:

Media Assistant – Direct Response Media
Salary negotiable – up to £19K

Are you a graduate with experience of the media industry? Perhaps you have a media-related degree or were lucky enough to get media work placements during your summer break? If so, I'd like to speak to you. A fantastic opportunity has arisen for someone to gain his or her first step on to the media ladder, specifically direct response. You will be responsible for supporting two planners/buyers who will provide you with a continual learning curve and you'll work across media with a TV leaning. The agency is fun, friendly and growing. A great opportunity. Call . . .

*MediaWeek* (September 2001)

Econometricians/Statisticians at all levels
Salary negotiable
Our clients are looking for talented econometricians/statisticians to work for leading media consultancies and advertising agencies within their research department. If you're looking for a move into the media industry, where you can be analysing audience figures, forecasting advertising effectiveness and dissecting sales figures and if you relish a fresh challenge, call . . .

*MediaWeek* (September 2001)

Media Information Provider
£15–18,000 + excellent commission + benefits
Young and vibrant company providing essential information to the media and marketing industries for fourteen years. Could be your first move into media, but you must be fun and hard working. Call . . .

*Campaign* (2001)

## Recommended routes and reading

New media recruitment (www.majorplayers.co.uk).
See the end of Chapters 8 and 9.

# 8 New media

The medium REALLY IS the message.
*Dave Katz (2001), Senior Planner/Buyer, i-level*

It is difficult to predict what advertising will be like even in the near future. What is clear is that it will be different.
*Donald Parente, (2000)*

The global interactive network of the internet does present marketers with a wonderful and yet serious problem: how do you sell to the entire world?
*Matt Freeman and John Young (2001), DDB Digital*

The advertising industry is undergoing a transition to a 'Direct Age' in which the consumer will have more power than ever before. Conventional channels of marketing sales and distribution are being challenged by more direct and unmediated access to the customer.
*Archie Pitcher (1999)*

## The new media age

New media is the means of communication that has been made possible with the onset of the digital age. It's an industry in its infancy. And, like all infants, it's had its share of tottering and falling over. However, despite some teething troubles, it's growing rapidly and is most certainly one you should consider for employment opportunities.

## Interactive advertising and new media

This is the name given to any advertising that uses the new technology. It includes web, CD-ROM, electronic commerce (ecommerce), interactive kiosks, intranet/extranet, email/direct marketing, online advertising, digital TV, electronic catalogues and new media PR. It uses the telephone, television, magazines, fax, mail, internet and email – any medium, in fact, that allows the advertiser to enter into a dialogue with, and elicit a response from, the consumer. In other words, *interactive advertising*.

## What makes new media 'new' media?

According to Dave Katz, who is a senior planner/buyer for i-level, the characteristic differences between new media and traditional media are that the new media are those forms of advertising media which are interactive. Although the term is usually applied solely to online advertising (internet, websites, emails), he feels that the term applies equally to digital TV and mobile platforms (e.g. WAP): 'I would include any form of interactive digital media as new media.' The largest and fastest-growing interactive media are the internet and digital TV.

## TV or not TV?

According to Parente (2000) and many others, 'in the future, the distinction between a television set and a computer screen will get somewhat blurred'.

With interactive TV, viewers of *Friends* or *Ally McBeal* might be able to chat while watching the action, or take part in real-time surveys for quiz shows such as *Family Fortunes*. According to Chris Harrison of Grey Interactive TV, interactive TV will inspire more and more creativity in advertising (*Revolution*, 2001a).

> If projections for digital TV penetration are on target, the audience should reach 69% of households by 2005 from the 21% it is now.
>
> Revolution *(2001b)*

## The internet

New research from analysts Jupiter UK shows that the internet is a mass market medium, with the majority of consumers in the UK now logging on. Sixty per cent of Britons now use the internet – and most of them do so from home.

According to *Internet Monitor*, people claim to spend 70 per cent more time using the internet in an average week than they do reading magazines or newspapers. What's more, a third of all internet users listen to the radio or watch TV while they surf the net. The younger the user, the more likely they are to do this. Only 9 per cent of internet users are currently using interactive services via a TV, although a further 20 per cent say that they intend to do so during the next twelve months (*MediaWeek*, 2001a). Jupiter UK predicts that by 2005 half of UK households will be connected to the internet from their TV (*Guardian*, 2001). However, as Parente (2000) points out, people who use the internet are not passive viewers and will actively tune out content that does not interest them. This means that those responsible for advertising on the internet have to strive to be even more creative in order to gain attention. The key to advertising effectiveness on the internet is to *involve* consumers so that they interact with the advertising, because today, it is the *consumer* not the seller who is in control.

Consumers initiate contact with the seller. They want information the way they want it, when they want it, where they want it. They want customized content. They want relationships and a sense of community. And they want it now.

*Andrew Salzman (2001), Siebel Systems*

According to Foley (2001), 'the principles of traditional advertising hold true online. The most effective advertisements are the most creative. They don't need to be complicated, just catch our attention.' She goes on to ask:

"Will online advertising survive? Yes, because we need it to. All popular media exist because advertising pays the bills. More importantly, it will survive because it is now big business. As *Business Week* recently pointed out, US advertisers spent $8.2 billion online last year, in comparison with $1.8 billion on outdoor (billboards) advertising and $11.2 billion on cable TV advertising. There is plenty of room for it to get bigger."

Currently only 1 per cent of advertising budgets in the UK and USA are spent on online advertising.

## One-to-one marketing

Interactive advertising includes any method of selling which establishes a one-to-one relationship with the customer. It allows advertisers and ad agencies to know how many people saw their advertising, how long they looked at it and what kind of people they were. This helps them target their advertising even more effectively for the future.

The web epitomises the capabilities needed to practice one-to-one marketing: it is an immediate and highly cost-efficient interactive channel; it can be customised to individual visitors; it can dispense complex product or service information, qualify sales leads, complete product transactions, and perform customer service tasks.

*Gray (1999)*

## Project management

Salim Fadhley is a digital project specialist at OgilvyOne, *the* leading interactive advertising agency. He used his initiative and exploited the new media technology to email himself into a job (see Chapter 15). Here's how he describes a 'typical' day:

"Perhaps 10–30 per cent of my day will be spent in meetings, another 10–30 per cent on the phone chasing up suppliers and client teams. When I am not trying to come up with creative technical concepts I'm managing an interactive project or researching a new one."

### Campaign's top twenty new media specialists*

Although only UK-based work was included in order to compile this list, it is clear that international presence plays a strong part in building a company's reputation. Many of these agencies would not be where they are today without the support of international networks. Of all the agencies featured in this book, this is the one area most likely to change. According to *Campaign*'s Bonello (February 2001), 'the next twelve months will be a make or break year for many of the players in the new media industry'.

| | | | |
|---|---|---|---|
| 1. | AKQA | 11. | Rufus Leonard |
| 2. | Agency.com | 12. | Quidnunc |
| 3. | Wheel | 13. | Victoria Real |
| 4. | Razorfish | 14. | Global Beach |
| 5. | Modern Media UK | 15. | Traffic Interactive |
| 6. | Revolution | 16. | Zentropy Partners |
| 7. | Hyperlink Interactive | 17. | Tenten Digital |
| 8. | Outrider | 18. | Syzygy UK |
| 9. | Seven Interactive | 19. | E-Marketing |
| 10. | Circle.Com | 20. | Grey Interactive |

* ranked according to declared new media income. Only those agencies with 50 per cent or more of new media work are included.

Campaign *(2001)*

## AKQA know-how

AKQA is *the* top new media agency – the 'runaway winner' (*Campaign*, 2001) in this year's new media league. Application – not surprisingly – is made online.

### Does AKQA hire recent graduates?

We've hired some of the best talent from colleges and universities. Many of our technology, creative, client services and strategy, consulting and project management staff joined AKQA as their first job since leaving college . . . AKQA have a mentor system – new employees are given the necessary guidance, direction and feedback to help them get up to speed.

*AKQA.com (2001)*

### Passion for great ideas and technology

According to AKQA, the company is looking for

"a burning desire to succeed and achieve success for our clients and our teams. We want to hire and keep people who get excited about the impact that they will have on a client's business, or by being the first to market with a new innovation or idea. While many companies are concerned about how long it takes to hire a new employee, AKQA is focused on hiring quality people."

These are the qualities AKQA seeks in a new employee:

- A passion for great ideas and technology.
- Commitment to AKQA's values of innovation, collaboration, quality and thought.
- The ability to adapt to change.
- The ability to seek out, learn and apply new knowledge.
- The ability to work as part of a team.

*AKQA.com (2001)*

### Top twenty US interactive ad agencies*

| | | | |
|---|---|---|---|
| 1. | Sapient | 11. | Answerthink |
| 2. | TMP Worldwide | 12. | Xpedior |
| 3. | iXL | 13. | Euro RSCG Worldwide Interaction |
| 4. | Razorfish | 14. | Luminant Worldwide |
| 5. | MarchFirst | 15. | Modern Media |
| 6. | Grey New Technologies | 16. | OgilvyInteractive |
| 7. | UX Design | 17. | Organic |
| 8. | Agency.com | 18. | Rare Medium |
| 9. | Digitas | 19. | US Interactive |
| 10. | Proxicom | 20. | Zentropy Partners |

* based on interactive revenues only

*AdWeek.com (2001)*

## An 'interactive' day

Dave Katz went straight from the Watford Postgraduate Diploma in Advertising course to a job at i-level – *Campaign*'s New Media Agency of the Year in 2000. Here's what he has to say about his work as a senior media planner/buyer:

"At the moment I am running a campaign that has been 'live' for the past four months – this is quite unusual, as most business is up for several weeks and then down for a few days at least. My client has had a permanent presence on various websites since March. So my average day is quite pro-active – sorting out problems with websites, 'adserving', planning for new activity, talking to sales reps, avoiding sales reps, buying media, negotiating deals . . ."

*Dave Katz (2001)*

## Web opportunities

The internet as a new medium is revolutionizing the advertising industry. There are plenty of employment opportunities for people with the imagination and skill to design, create and manage websites. Interactive agencies are particularly looking for people with a real grasp of information technology. Typical new media recruitment ads are looking for project leaders, systems developers, account managers, sales and marketing personnel, art directors, web designers, web programmers and online journalists/copywriters. See Chapter 6 for more information on writing copy for the internet.

*Revolution*, the magazine for new media marketing, is the monthly must-have journal if you're interested in working in this area.

## What skills do you need to work in new media?

Everything that you would need for traditional media plus the patience to deal with other people's incompetence and a high degree of assertiveness in order to achieve what you want to achieve without it being messed up.

*Dave Katz (2001)*

ICT literate with the ability to work on your own and in virtual teams 24 hours a day, seven days a week. Get proper training on both the technology and methods of use. Have an understanding of marketing and advertising processes.

*Vic Davis (2001), media/IT consultant*

## What kind of jobs are available?

The job covers all those in mainstream media, but with much more emphasis on the analytical and research skills.

*Vic Davies (2001)*

- planners/strategists
- buyers
- assistants (at all levels)
- new business people
- traffic managers
- project managers (account executives)
- web programmers
- webmasters (technical directors)
- interactive directors
- interactive developers
- interactive account supervisors
- interactive designers

- interactive art directors
- interactive copywriters.

## How does someone go about getting a job in new media

The internet – this time the medium REALLY IS the message . . .

*Dave Katz (2001)*

## What can you earn?

Starting salaries are from £15,000. However, interactive advertising/web advertising/marketing is one of the highest paid and fastest-growing areas. If you have what it takes, it's possible to earn as much as £26,000 after your first year.

## Recommended routes

Consult the new media websites, such as akqa.com, i-level.com, mad.co.uk, agency.com, media.com, circle.com, or any of the agencies in the above league table or in the Directory (Chapter 17). In addition, browse the new media trade press – see below for details.

- New media recruitment agencies (see Directory)
- *E-commerce Times Weekly* (www.ecommercetimes.com)
- The American Association of Advertising Agencies (www.AAAAdvertisingjobs.com)
- UK-based site for ecommerce job-seekers (www.E-job.net)

## Recommended journals

*Admap* (journal for marketing, research and media)
NTC Marketing Department
01491 411000

*Creative Review* (www.creative-review.co.uk).

*MediaWeek*
Subscription department
Tower House
Lathkill Street
Market Harborough
LE16 9EF
Subscription enquiries: 01858 438872
www.mediaweek.co.uk

*New Media Age*
Centaur Communications
020 7970 4000
www.nma.co.uk

*Revolution*
Haymarket Publishing
PO Box 270
Southall
UB1 2WF
Subscriptions: 020 8606 7500
www.uk.revolutionmagazine.com
www.revolution.haynet.com

*Guardian* Media (Mondays)
*Guardian* Online (Thursdays)

## Recommended reading

Bonime, A. and Polhmann, K. (1998) *Writing for New Media*. John Wiley &
    Sons.
Davis, M. and Zerdin, D. (1996) *The Effective Use of Advertising Media*.
    Century Business.
Grusin, R. and Bolter, J. (2000) *Remediation: Understanding New Media*. MIT
    Press.
*New Media Showcase* – a showcase of American media (1993).
Pedersen, M. B. (2000) *Advertising Annual 2001*. Graphis Press.
Redman, S. (1999) *Taking the Leap into New Media*. North Light Books.
Reedy. J., Schullo, S. and Zimmerman, K. (2000) *Electronic Marketing
    (Integrating Electronic Resources into the Marketing Process)*. Harcourt
    College Publishers.

Also, see Chapter 9 for recommended media and marketing communications
publications.

# 9 Marketing communications – direct marketing, public relations, sales promotion (the marketing mix)

Marketing communications is the name we give to the whole marketing mix, as follows:

- direct marketing
- sales promotion
- public relations.

## Direct marketing

> The best career move I ever made.
>
> *Kate Woolf (1999),*
> *Institute of Direct Marketing*

Advertising is mainly about building awareness of brands. Direct marketing is about highly targeted communications using a database to reach your target audience. It is advertising that calls for a response from the consumer and can include all or any of the following:

- TV advertising
- newspaper advertising
- magazine advertising
- telephone
- door-to-door leaflets
- inserts
- the internet
- direct mail.

> The distinctions between ad agencies and direct marketing agencies are increasingly blurring. While advertising can change people's attitudes through generating brand desire, direct marketing can change people's behaviour, turning them into active, rather than passive, consumers.
>
> *Eleanor Trickett (1998)*

### Direct mail

The best-known form of direct response is probably direct mail – often called 'junk mail' (although advertisers would only consider it to be junk mail if it had been incorrectly targeted). Direct mail is advertising which is personally addressed, sent through the post and targeted to a specific person. Its main advantage is that it is personal and its success can be evaluated by the number of responses received, so the advertisers are able to know which approaches have been the most successful.

### Relationship marketing

> Direct mail is advertising that elicits a response and starts a relationship. It is about targeting and talking to individuals . . . and listening. I like to think of it as the corner shop reborn. We are rebuilding personal relationships with customers using modern technology.
>
> *Kate Woolf (1999)*

Many advertisers use direct marketing as part or even all of their advertising budget and many more ad agencies are offering direct response/interactive advertising to their clients as a media solution. With the current revolution in digital media there is now a huge growth in agencies specializing in direct response, which means that there are more job opportunities than ever before because direct marketing uses all the new media.

### Top ten direct marketing agencies worldwide

| | |
|---|---|
| 1.  Digitas | 6.   Brann Worldwide (Havas) |
| 2.  Draft Worldwide (IPG) | 7.   Aspen Marketing Group |
| 3.  Impiric/Wonderman (WPP) | 8.   Harte-Hanks Direct |
| 4.  Rapp Collins Worldwide | 9.   Carlson Marketing Group |
|     (Omnicom) | 10.  Grey Direct Marketing Group |
| 5.  OgilvyOne Worldwide (WPP) |      (Grey Global) |

*Advertising Age (2000)*

### Job opportunities in direct marketing

- account executives
- planners

- creative
- marketing executives (on the client side)
- media roles (in media agencies and for media owners)
- computing/information technology – analysts, statisticians and programmers
- consultants – opportunities for working freelance and for starting your own company once you have had some experience.

**Skills needed for direct marketing**

- working to deadlines
- attention to detail
- lateral and analytical thinking
- computer literacy
- creativity and imagination
- problem-solving
- people-focused.

## What's it like working for a direct marketing agency?

Ajay Shah, Smith Bundy Carlson:

" A typical day as an account handler in a direct marketing/advertising agency can include a mixture of the following:

- Checking artwork and briefing the studio on changes required.
- Writing a creative brief for a new mail pack/press ad/direct response TV ad.
- Discussing media options with the media planning department – agreeing a new media proposal in response to previous results and current costs.
- Selecting images for the next mail pack. For example, for UNICEF – one of my accounts – it could mean scanning publications/images supplied by the client.
- Briefing the print department to source quotes for the next mailing or to send an approved job to print.
- General day-to-day administration – call reports for client meetings (operational meetings are held at least once a month).
- Receiving client briefing material and rationalizing it to be of use to the creative team.
- Working with the client to analyse results and looking at new opportunities to recruit donors. For example, a new insert or perhaps an adaptation of current creative work.
- Sometimes meeting the occasional celebrity. For example, Trevor McDonald to record a Sight Savers radio ad, an ex-Brookside star to record a voice-over for a direct response television ad.
- Assessing creative work prior to presentation to the client and suggesting amendments to resolve issues that may arise.
- Constant liaison with the client – rationalizing creative decisions etc. "

### Direct marketing apprenticeship scheme

If you're interested in finding out more about direct marketing, see Chapter 12, which gives details about the Institute of Direct Marketing's graduate programme. The IDM also operate a graduate job register which is a free service open to all graduates. You can register by mail or online.

## Sales promotion

Sales promotion (sometimes known as below-the-line advertising) is one element of what's called 'the marketing mix'. It's the name given to any activity or any incentives – usually short term – that encourage people to buy a product or service. A sales promotion offer is usually only available for a specified period, so its effects can be measured. Incentives can include money-off coupons, on-pack competitions, vouchers which can be collected and exchanged for goods, air miles and loyalty cards such as the Tesco Club Card or the Boots Advantage Card. Whereas an advertising campaign can take nine months to develop, a sales promotion campaign may have to be conceived, developed and implemented within a matter of weeks.

Sales promotion agencies or consultancies are agencies which specialize in creating, developing and implementing sales promotion ideas and campaigns. Many are part of existing ad agencies (either in the same building or on a separate site), while others are separate specialist companies offering sales promotion expertise.

### What skills are they looking for?

> Energy, passion, enthusiasm – detail and flexibility. Good presentation skills – both written and verbal. Good people skills and a creative approach to problem-solving. Tenacity – the ability to bounce back when projects do not go as well as hoped.
>
> *Louise Wall (1999), Managing Director, EHS Brann*

As an account executive working in sales promotion you will need to have a good eye for detail, have excellent organizational skills, be able to work to deadlines and take responsibility for every aspect of a campaign from start to finish.

Here's what one director of a sales promotion agency said she was looking for in a junior account executive: 'A definite interest in working in a below-the-line agency, combined with good writing skills, enthusiasm, commitment and a willingness to learn is of as much interest to us as actual experience.'

### Working in sales promotion

Karl Perry, Managing Director of the Promotional Campaigns Group, Manchester, describes a typical day:

"Thankfully, no two days are the same. Arrive at the office and inject coffee.

Start opening post. As various team members arrive, they wander into my office for a quick chat. Invariably, there is a 15–20 minute catch-up with somebody who has been out of the office the day before – client, supplier or new business.

The morning could consist of one or two meetings:

- Production meeting: overview of all jobs going through PCG Manchester, resources required, workload, whether freelancers are required, print/production problems, new creative briefs to be issued or expected. Account handlers argue for creative/design time, jobs are prioritized and resources are allocated.
- Status meeting: account director, manager and executive meet with me to review the current status on all clients' jobs and to plan the next stages that need to be covered during the coming week.

Lunch is usually around the corner for a take-out sandwich to eat at my desk (unless it's a Friday or we've won some new business, in which case *The Grapes* or *Hogshead* benefit from extra custom. I finish looking at the post over lunch and flick through the marketing press.

Afternoons are usually spent developing projects: new business briefs or approaches to new business prospects, new briefs from clients or reviewing creative proposals from the creative director.

As a board director, there are invariably other company level tasks or projects that I may be working on that have to be shoe-horned into the day.

Pepper the day with phone calls to and from colleagues at our other offices, the odd request from the financial director, an ex-Watford College buddy on his latest scuba dive exploits and, of course, clients and the day becomes rather full.

At about 4.30 we review the workload in the office to see what still has to be done that day. If an account handler looks as if they may have to work very late, where possible we try and reallocate some of the tasks to spread the load.

Usually, the last thing I do is complete a time sheet for the day and scribble myself a few reminders for the next day. **"**

## A multitude of tasks

Wendy Milne describes a day in the life of an account executive for the sales promotion company PCG Manchester:

**"**I normally arrive in the office at 9.15 a.m. Once the various phones have been diverted, I set about my role as account executive by switching the kettle on. I then spend two minutes reading the various post-it notes which have been glued to my desk as a form of reminder to myself or message from a colleague to call someone. I then begin to follow up issues which have been carried over from the previous day's work.

I blink and suddenly it is lunchtime and when I stop to draw breath I realize that I have completed a multitude of tasks which most people wouldn't complete in a day's work. Such tasks include attending various production meetings, status meetings and creative meetings where your mind is expanded to its limits.

Throughout the course of the morning I also deal with suppliers who can't find the right order number, who don't know what a proof is or even find it difficult to grasp the fact that various clients can't afford to pay £100,000 for a couple of branded T-shirts.

I have also sourced various vital research reports from associations as far fetched as the Association of Football Statisticians to the Ministry of Agriculture, who can tell me how many people eat muesli between 7 and 8 a.m. at the weekend. I have also run to the local printing shop, which is located down the road from our building, so by lunchtime I have lost a couple of pounds and am ready to go to the local café for my midday energy boost lunch.

Lunch normally takes place between 1.30 and 2.00 and can often involve a quick sandwich run for everyone in the office if the workload is extremely high. Yet on Fridays we often spend a few hours in the pub (purely on a professional basis, of course) to reflect on our working week.

Returning to work in the afternoon, I find that I have six telephone messages to answer. Although there is no such thing as a typical day when you work in a marketing agency, time in the afternoon is often used to liaise with creatives and clients, or to develop new ideas or expand on existing ones.

Due to the fact that I come from a strong research background I spend a great deal of my time researching these ideas or gathering and preparing information in response to client briefs. The afternoon is also dedicated to sending out requests (which change by the minute) by courier.

My working day never ends at the same time – it depends on the level of work or crisis level which exists. We have recently introduced a new system in the office in which any member of staff can raise alarm bells at 4.30 p.m. if their workload is too much to bear. At this point we all chip in to help each other out. At around six o'clock we tend to begin rounding off our day by tying up loose ends and filling out time sheets.

I thoroughly enjoy the variety in my job, the team spirit that exists and the adrenaline rush which is required in certain demanding situations. **"**

## In search of a solution in sales promotion

Paul Alexis, Creative Director, PCG Manchester:

**"**9.30ish. Arrive at work. If I'm lucky, coffee will be waiting at my desk. Today I'm unlucky.
- 10 a.m. Production meeting. We plan who does what, when and at what time. I organize the production sheets and hand them out in the meetings. The account handlers give it the once-over. We make decisions.
- 11.15 a.m. I'm well into my first job. The idea is to find a solution.

- 12 noon. I'm thinking crack backs, scratch cards, warm reveals, cold reveals – but I'm not thinking solutions. I need a coffee.
- 1 p.m. Lunch. Should I go or should I stay? I go because I need to start thinking solutions.
- 2 p.m. Coffee. Phone calls (returning them).
- 2.15 p.m. I think solutions. Good, bad, indifferent solutions.
- 4 p.m. I need brain food. I eat a Kellogg's Rice Krispie Squares Bar, while desperately trying to inculcate fresh ideas through various magazines. *Loaded, Arena, Daily Mirror, GQ*, etc. – the really educational stuff.
- 5 p.m. Coffee. More phone calls. More briefs.
- 6 p.m. My brain will fall through a sieve – no problem. Still in search of solutions. **"**

## A day in the life of 'a human sponge'

Working in sales promotion, as described by a number of account executives at Triangle Communications Limited, who were asked to list the tasks they did in a typical morning and afternoon of a 'typical day':

### *Morning*
- Start the day off with status meeting with line managers and have a plan of action for the day ahead.
- Artwork and creative briefing sessions.
- Progress current projects – pack-shot chasing from third parties, artwork approval and sign off from client, constant contact with print production department to ensure that all is running according to plan.
- Speak to clients to run through what they expect to see from us and what we may need from them. For example, spec confirmations, legal approvals to copy, etc.
- Write creative briefs for scamps (concepts), gather reference material, timing plans.
- Attend brainstorms.
- Briefing sessions with studio.
- Artwork returned from studio – distribute internally and gather comments and approval.

### *Afternoon*
- Brief catch-up with line manager re day's progress and any new developments – re-evaluation of priority tasks for the afternoon.
- Compose status reports to be distributed internally and sent to client.
- Attend client meetings.
- Check finances are up to date.
- Filing.
- Write contact reports on conversations carried out during the day with client or third parties.

- Wrap packages to be sent out for a next-day delivery.
- A 'human sponge' – from first thing until the end of play, an executive is constantly observing and learning from those around.
- Relax with colleagues – go to the pub!

## Creating promotional campaigns

Michael Bartman, promotional marketing consultant:

"I work for client companies and sales promotion agencies creating promotional campaigns which are communicated on-pack, in-store or through the media. All types of media (including direct marketing) are considered. All the promotions I have ever handled have been the direct result of my own creativity, including business from clients such as Bass Taverns, General Foods, Lyons-Tetley, Diners Club, Crown Paints, Qualcast, Hoseasons and many others.

A typical day would involve mailing or phoning potential clients, having sent them a mailshot. Creating promotions involves coming up with a cost-effective response to the brief. Often negotiating with third parties (film-makers, other products, field forces, printers, studios, etc.) can take several days. Client liaison takes up the rest of my time.

### Skills needed to succeed as a sales promotion consultant
- awareness of what's going on in the world
- an eye for detail
- a sense of business
- a willingness to work hard
- an open and extrovert personality
- a sense of humour
- a thick skin
- the patience to wait for the right chance to come along and then the belief in oneself to go for it."

### 'Be capable of listening as well as talking'
Job application and interview advice from Louise Wall (1999):

"Present a really clear, comprehensive CV. Write an excellent covering letter with a point of difference as there are so many letters. Ensure you find out about the company you are being interviewed by. Do some research. Know their client list and be able to name some of their work. Always be on time. Never turn up late – it sends out the wrong signals.

Follow up the interview with a thank-you letter. Always seem pro-active and interested. Be confident and presentable face to face. Ensure you prepare questions prior to the interview. Always know why you have selected the agency you are visiting. Be capable of listening as well as talking in the interview."

*How to cope with interviews*

"Look them in the eye and smile when you enter a room or approach an interviewer. Look up the company's background. Who are their clients? What's the current big issue in the marketplace?

Have an answer to the inevitable question you will be asked, 'Have you any questions for us?'"

*Michael Bartman*

## Opportunities for graduates

Many sales promotion agencies, such as The Marketing Store Worldwide, have their own graduate training schemes. Training lasts for a year, beginning with a four-month placement working on different accounts – including three one-week placements within each client's in-house marketing department (Pandya, 1999).

Successful graduates are given training in IT skills and presentation techniques. Each trainee also receives sponsorship for the Institute of Sales Promotion's Diploma (see below and the Directory).

Perspectives (a sales promotion and marketing communications agency) also runs its own graduate training course for those interested in working in sales promotion:

Perspectives
Swan Court
Swan Street
Old Isleworth
Middlesex TW7 6RJ

## The Institute of Sales Promotion

The ISP is the only professional body representing the whole of the sales promotion industry. Its aim is to protect, promote and further professional and effective sales promotion. The ISP provides in-house training and advice for promoters and agencies, and provides in-house training for people working in the sales promotion industry. Information about courses run by the ISP is given in Chapter 13.

To receive a membership pack from the ISP or for details of recommended courses, write to:

The Institute of Sales Promotion
Arena House
66–68 Pentonville Road
London N1 9HS
020 7837 5340

### Graduate clearing for sales promotion

The Sales Promotion Consultants Association (SPCA) has set up a graduate clearing scheme that provides information on sales promotion agencies that take on graduates, along with guidance on training opportunities (Pandya, 1998). The phone number is 020 7580 8225.

#### Top ten sales promotion agencies worldwide

| | | | |
|---|---|---|---|
| 1. | Carlson Marketing Group | 6. | Gary M. Reynolds & Associates (Omnicom) |
| 2. | Bounty SCA Worldwide (Havas) | | |
| 3. | Jack Morton Worldwide (IPG) | 7. | SPAR Group |
| 4. | CommonHealth (WPP) | 8. | Aspen Marketing Group |
| 5. | Alcone Marketing Group (Omnicom) | 9. | Momentum Worldwide (IPG) |
| | | 10. | Frankel (Publicis) |

*Advertising Age (2000)*

#### Top twenty UK direct marketing and sales promotion agencies

| | | | |
|---|---|---|---|
| 1. | OgilvyOne Worldwide | 12. | The Marketing Store Worldwide |
| 2. | WWW Rapp Collins | | |
| 3. | BHWG Proximity | 13. | Holmes & Marchant Group |
| 4. | Claydon Heeley Jones Mason | 14. | Colleagues Direct Marketing |
| 5. | Mosaic Group Marketing Services | 15. | Clarke Hooper Momentum |
| | | 15= | 141 Communications |
| 6. | Tequila | 16. | GGT Direct Advertising |
| 7. | Draftworldwide | 17. | McCann-Erickson Manchester (MRM) |
| 8. | ehsrealtime* | | |
| 9. | IMP | 18. | Triangle |
| 10. | Joshua | 19. | Interfocus Network |
| 11. | KLP Euro RSCG | 20. | Lowe Direct |

* now EHS Brann

*Marketing Report (2001)*

## Public relations

> Rule one of good public relations is to tell the truth. Rule two is to have credibility as a spokesperson.
>
> *Julia Hobsbawn (1998)*

Public relations is yet another aspect of 'the marketing mix' that goes to make up an advertising/marketing campaign. PR is an integral part of the whole marketing process. An important aspect of the work of PR consultants is to persuade and convince the media of their point of view. As consumers become more advertising literate, the role of the PR practitioner has gained in importance – in particular, their role of representing the company behind the brand.

The Institute of Public Relations (IPR) describes PR as 'the planned and sustained effort to establish and maintain goodwill and mutual understanding between an organisation and its publics' (IPR, 1998).

## What does working in PR involve?

- producing well-written press releases to the appropriate press
- arranging press launches
- organizing news conferences
- preparing and making presentations
- public speaking – press conferences, presentations and interviews
- liaising with journalists
- organization of PR activities such as exhibitions, trade fairs, sponsorship, corporate hospitality
- producing corporate literature, e.g. company magazines
- crisis management.

## Skills needed to work in PR

- excellent communication and presentation skills
- a smart appearance
- superb organizational skills
- an eye for detail
- writing ability
- a good telephone manner
- ability to communicate with people at all levels
- unflappability
- an outgoing and friendly personality
- confidence
- tact and diplomacy.

## 'Always different things to do'

Brad Abrahams (2001) describes his work as an intern at Rhea & Kaiser Marketing Communications in Naperville, Illinois, USA:

"My job consists of assisting the senior account executive and vice president. At Rhea & Kaiser Marketing Communications, I am the assistant account executive. However, because we are a smaller agency (for now), we do not operate like the big agencies where everyone has different job functions. Here, we all work together to get everything accomplished for the client, whether it be writing, planning, pitching or monitoring.

The best part of working for a 'smaller' agency, in a starting position, is that I feel I have more hands-on experience than I'd get in a bigger agency. My position allows me to be more a part of what's happening and enables me to learn faster.

There is no typical day in public relations. Public relations moves so quickly: there are always different things to work on day in and day out. Most days, however, consist of media monitoring, talking to the media, writing, planning, developing and basically going through the PR plan to get everything done. **"**

**Top ten US PR companies**

| 1. | Fleishman-Hillard | 6. | BSMG Worldwide |
|---|---|---|---|
| 2. | Weber Shandwick Worldwide | 7. | Ketchum |
| 3. | Burson-Marsteller | 8. | Porter Novelli International |
| 4. | Hill & Knowlton | 9. | Ogilvy Public Relations |
| 5. | Edelman Public Relations | | Worldwide |
| | Worldwide | 10. | Golin/Harris International |

*Advertising Age (2000)*

## What will you earn in media and marketing communications?

The funkier the job, the less it pays. Once you've proved yourself, the money goes up very quickly. They're putting time and effort into you – they want to know you're going to stick it out.

*Alan Morgan (1999), recruitment consultant*

In the ad industry you are rewarded on performance and your salary can rise very quickly. The following will give you some idea of what you can expect in terms of salary in the first year or two:

- Sales promotion and direct marketing: starting salaries about £15,000.
- Public relations: in the USA, a typical starting salary would be around $30,000.

## Working in market research

All advertisers use research in one form or another. 'Quantitative research' is the name given to the collection of data by mail or by personal interviews with a sufficient number of individuals to enable statistical analysis. In media planning, for example, this refers to the numbers of copies sold or read of any given publication or the coverage received within a particular viewing or listening audience.

'Qualitative research' is more to do with feelings and emotions and is often used in consumer research to find out people's perceptions of a brand and its advertising. In advertising planning, for example, you might want to evaluate the effect of your agency's latest advertising campaign.

Researchers and planners seek to discover people's perceptions of a brand or an advertising campaign and to assess the changes in these perceptions throughout an advertising campaign – from start to finish.

A market researcher might be involved in conducting house-to-house or street questionnaires or with the data resulting from a discussion group – a 'focus group' – which is organized by an agency for its clients. People considered to be in the target audience of a particular product are brought together to discuss a brand's attributes or its advertising. What is their opinion of the advertising campaign? Do they understand the advertising message? What do they think it is trying to say?

## Skills needed to be a market researcher

- an ability to gather data
- an aptitude to interpret data and draw conclusions
- the ability to combine strategic planning with creative skills
- excellent interpersonal skills
- a good listener
- a good communicator
- to be able to get on with people at all levels
- tact and diplomacy
- an eye for detail.

## Jobs available

Market research is used for all aspects of an advertising campaign – from the concept stage to post-campaign evaluation. Therefore, there is tremendous scope for jobs in this area. You can work for a market research company, conducting consumer research or as a researcher for a media owner such as a television company.

There are jobs in media research and research jobs with companies such as Mintel or the British Market Research Bureau (BMRB), which publish the Target Group Index (TGI). BMRB recruits researchers to cover particular districts of London. Pay can vary from the minimum hourly wage to daily rates plus expenses. Many local and national research companies will provide training for inexperienced researchers, and it's a good starting-point for those of you who want to follow a career in market research or move across to working as a planner in an advertising agency. If you're interested in a career in market research, you might like to contact the Market Research Society, which organizes regular courses and seminars.

## 'Show up-to-date knowledge and understanding'

One of the best ways of showing a passion for this industry is in an interview to show up-to-date knowledge and understanding. The best way to fill your mind with this knowledge is by reading the trade press and reference books.

*Scott Knox, recruitment consultant*

## Recommended routes

- Recruitment consultants.
- Work experience (see Chapter 15).
- Institute of Direct Marketing and Institute of Sales Promotion courses (see Chapter 13).
- Further education and higher education courses (see Chapter 13).
- GAP scheme – Institute of Direct Marketing Graduate Apprenticeship Scheme.
- Media sales.
- Market research.
- IPA and IPA Factfile.
- The Market Research Society.
- The Institute of Direct Marketing.
- The Institute of Sales Promotion.
- Graduate training (see Chapter 12).

## Recommended journals

*Admap*: advertising effectiveness and evaluation.
*Campaign*: weekly advertising publication.
*Digit*: monthly new media publication.
*Direct Response*: journal of direct marketing.
*Marketing*: general weekly marketing journal.
*Marketing Week*: comprehensive marketing coverage.
*Media World*: comprehensive media coverage.
*MediaWeek*: weekly media coverage.
*Marketing Direct*: direct marketing coverage.
*Precision Marketing*: weekly coverage of direct marketing.
*Promotions & Incentives*: monthly publication on sales promotion.
*Revolution*: weekly magazine for new media marketing.
*Sponsorship News*: monthly round-up on sponsorship.

## Recommended reading

Baines, A. (1995) *The Handbook of International Direct Marketing*. Kogan Page.
Bird, D. (1993) *Commonsense Direct Marketing*, 3rd edn. Kogan Page.
Brassington, F. and Pettit, S. (1999) *Principles of Marketing*, 1st edn. Pitman.
Brown, C. (1993) *The Sales Promotion Handbook*. Kogan Page.
Carter, D. (1999) *Branding: The Power of Market Identity*. Hearst Books.
Cummins, J. (1989) *Sales Promotion: How to Create and Implement Campaigns that Really Work*. Kogan Page.
Harrison, S. (1999) *Public Relations*. Thomson Business Press.
Hart, A. (1991) *Understanding the Media: A Practical Guide*. London, Routledge.
Hart, N.A. and Waite, N. (1994) *How to Get on in Marketing*. Kogan Page.

Haywood, R. (1984) *All about Public Relations*. McGraw-Hill.

Jefkins, F. and Yadin, D. (1997) *Public Relations*, 5th edn. Pitman.

Jefkins, F. (1990) *The Secrets of Successful Direct Response Marketing*. Heinemann.

Nash, E. (1995) *Direct Marketing Strategy, Planning and Execution*, 3rd edn. McGraw-Hill.

Lancaster, G. and Reynolds, P. (1999) *Marketing*. Macmillan.

Lancaster, G. and Reynolds, P. (1999) *Essentials of Marketing*, 3rd edn. McGraw-Hill.

McCorkell, G. (1990) *Advertising that Pulls Response*. McGraw-Hill.

O'Malley, L., Patterson, M. and Evans, M. (1999) *Exploring Direct Marketing*. Thomson International Press.

Pearson, S. (1996) *Building Brands Directly*. NYU Press.

Peppers, D. and Rogers, M. (1994) *The One to One Future*. Piatkus.

Pringle, H. and Thompson, M. (2001) *Brand Spirit: How Cause-related Marketing Builds Brands*. John Wiley & Sons.

Shimp, T. (2000) *Advertising Promotion (Supplemental Aspects of Integrated Marketing Communications)*. Harcourt College Publishers.

Stone, M., Davies, D. and Bond, A. (1995) *Direct Hit*. Pitman.

*The Direct Marketing Guide* (1998). Institute of Direct Marketing.

Toop, Alan (1994) *Crackingjack!: Sales Promotion Techniques and How to Use Them Successfully*. Gower.

*Top Marketing and Media Companies in the UK* (2001) Corporate Research Foundation.

Watson, J. (1996) *Successful Creativity in Direct Marketing*. WWAV Rapp Collins.

Williams, J. (1996) *The Manual of Sales Promotion*. Innovation Licensing.

See the previous chapter for new media publications.

BMRB (British Market Research Bureau):
BMRB International
79–81 Uxbridge Road
Ealing
London W5 5SU
020 8566 5000
www.bmrb.co.uk

AC Nielsen: media expenditure and analysis (www.acnielsen.com).

Office for National Statistics
1 Drummond Gate
Pimlico
London SW1V 2QQ
020 7533 6262

World Advertising Research Centre (www.WARC.com).

Freelance marketing links (www.knowthis.com).

Advertising/PR (www.hotjobs.com).

Advertising and media careers (www.nationjob.com).

Media and marketing communications journals (see Directory).

# 10 Creative services

We make things happen – on time, on budget and make the end result look great.

*Production manager, Saatchi & Saatchi*

Production is responsible for the reproduction of clients' ads to the highest possible standard.

*Brian Herron (1999), WCRS*

Creative services (sometimes called production) is the agency department that is responsible for all the day-to-day coordination and organization of the production of ads from concept to completion.

It is one of the few areas in advertising where you can start off at the bottom and work your way up. Many of today's top production managers started off at a very junior level, perhaps as messengers or delivering the post. And many TV producers and heads of traffic started as secretaries or students on work experience. It's an excellent place to start, because the production department interacts with everyone in the agency, so you get a good understanding of all aspects of agency life and a real insight into how an ad is put together from start to finish.

If you want to work in production, it helps if you're computer literate and comfortable with the new technology. Virtually all ad agencies now work with digital data – digital proofs are produced by scanning images on to computers.

Nothing works now without a Mac. All our typesetting and concepts are produced on one.

*Production manager, Saatchi & Saatchi*

## 'A new type of creative services person'

There's a shortage of trained people coming into creative services . . . we want to develop a new type of creative services person who is keen to learn.

*Jason Rowe (1998), Creative Services Director,*
*Duckworth Finn Grubb Waters*

Creative services is an area of advertising that has been more or less ignored by graduates in the past – mainly because of a lack of awareness of the job opportunities available. Agencies are now trying to attract graduates and a new Creative Services Association will provide training, education and a social diary for creative services staff. It's being headed by Jason Rowe, the Creative Services Director of ad agency Duckworth Finn Grubb Waters.

## The creative services director

The control and flow of an agency's work is the specific responsibility of the creative services director. Duncan Stokes describes his job heading the creative services department of OgilvyOne, an interactive ad agency:

"I look after the creative services department – eighteen people. I also have additional responsibility for the IT department, mobile and static phones, faxes and photocopiers.

Mondays are always a planning day. We start the week with a 'control meeting'. The main aim of this is to discuss issues with all the other main departments – discussions normally relate to work flow and the amount of work that needs to be processed during the week. With my type of job it's normally reacting to situations. For example, 'I've lost my mobile phone', 'I need a laptop computer' – basically requests for services.

I see a lot of suppliers. I believe it's important to keep abreast of what's going on in the market. One of the best ways of doing this is to see people who are selling the products, asking them questions and 'digging'. Better reporting of information leads to better reports being produced, which in turn gives you concrete information to act upon.

I also get involved in process. We are always looking at new ways of working. This usually has an IT angle to it in one form or another. I'm very involved in the digital production area at the moment – a very exciting process, using cutting-edge technology. Modern technology has revolutionized our work. Things that used to take weeks or hours now take minutes – or even seconds – to do.

### 'A bit like the stock exchange'

Friday afternoons usually go completely mad as we are preparing ads for the weekend press. Media buyers leave it to the last moment to get the best deal and we still have to supply the final copy. Phones are constantly ringing. Working in production is a bit like the stock exchange – very pressurized but exciting. It's a very varied week and that's what makes it so interesting.

### Skills needed for the job

You need to be able to multi-task, be gregarious, be relatively good with figures, a lateral thinker and enjoy team work."

## The creative services team

1. Traffic.
2. Art buying.
3. Production.

The creative services team works on a large number of ads and projects that will all be at different stages of completion. Within the department there will be traffic people, art buyers and production assistants. Each week a list of work is prepared and it's the job of traffic/production to check that not only all the work has been done but that all the agency's ads have been produced to deadline and on budget. The list will include all new work, who's doing what, who's busy and who's not.

# I. Traffic

We need to find out what's in the creatives' heads. We need to know what they want as much as they do themselves.

*Olga Budimir (1998), Head of Production, Burkitt DDB*

It's the role of traffic (sometimes called progress chasers or project managers) to fill the communication gap between client services (account handlers) and creatives – to 'traffic' the work through the creative department ensuring that all the deadlines are met.

### Working to deadlines

Things may change but the date never changes.

*Agency production manager*

It's not a 9 to 5 job. We don't have lunch hours. We work hard and we play hard.

*Phil Penn, Head of Production, Saatchi & Saatchi*

Traffic produce a timing plan of all the production processes and approval dates for all the different stages of the production process. For example, photography, artwork, retouching. Everything must be planned down to the last detail and all those concerned have to ensure that enough time is allowed for everything that needs to be done. It's their responsibility to ensure that all the dates are met and that the budget is adhered to. Competitive quotes are obtained for all the work and all the costs are estimated down to the last penny.

### Traffic meetings

In many ad agencies it's the head of creative services or 'traffic' who decides, in cooperation with the agency's creative director, which creative team is going to work on what creative brief. She or he will know everyone's workload and who is available to do the work when it comes in. Traffic set up all the meetings related to the ongoing work and check that all the work is approved by everyone concerned in the ad agency.

## Traffic/production assistants

You could very well start off as an assistant in the production department, either as part of graduate training or as a job in its own right – production is one of the few jobs in advertising you can still do straight from school. Most production assistants still learn on the job, although some agencies now offer training programmes.

You'll work on a number of different accounts, liaising with the production team and the creatives. You'll keep a record of each ad and a daily check of its progress. Once the final ad has appeared in a publication, it's the responsibility of traffic/creative services to ensure that the ad has appeared correctly – for example, that it's the right size, colour and that all the type is legible.

Working in production, you'll learn about paper, type and printing. You'll need to brief external suppliers such as paper suppliers, printers, designers and photographers about what is required for each ad and ensure that they all deliver on time according to requirements. You'll also be expected to do a lot of running around chasing up work, which may be why traffic people are sometimes called 'progress chasers'.

You get to work very closely with the creative teams. You'll see how ads are put together and really get into the creative process by seeing how an ad progresses from an idea in someone's head to the finished advertisement that appears in print.

## Traffic advice

Recognize people are different and treat them differently. Treat people fairly.

*Olga Budimir (1998)*

## How to get into traffic

You can write a speculative letter to the head of creative services (see Chapter 11) and enclose it with your CV. Some may prefer a handwritten letter as it shows you can write and spell. It's also worth contacting the recruitment consultants who specialize in the creative services area of advertising.

## Network

Try and find work experience in the creative services/traffic department of an ad agency. Don't expect to be paid, although you may very well get reimbursed for the cost of travel to and from work. If you're working at an agency for more than two weeks you should receive a minimum wage as it's now a legal obligation.

While you're in the job, network as much as you can. That way, you'll get to know a lot of people, including production companies and suppliers. With any luck, you'll hear about a job through the grapevine.

## 2. Art buying

Art buying is one of those jobs that no one outside advertising has usually heard of, yet art buyers play a vital role in the creation of an ad. They are the people who are generally responsible for choosing the illustrations or photographs which are used in advertising, not only in the finished ads but also in helping to convey ideas to the client at the start of the campaign. Together with the creative team, you are responsible for everything related to the 'look' of the ad.

Your work will involve spending time with the creative team, helping them select the most appropriate artwork (photography and illustrations) to fit in with their ideas. You'll recommend the photographer who will take the pictures for a press ad and the model (or models) who will appear in the ad – maybe the picture will comprise one model's face and another's hands or legs – and then estimate all the costs for the photographic shoot.

You may be briefed to source images on a wide variety of topics for a number of different campaigns. For example, a jeering football crowd, a teenage mother holding a newborn baby, a barren moonscape or maybe a lively bar scene. Most creative teams don't have the time to look at photographers' books and therefore much of your time may be spent searching through the work of photographers and artists in order to source appropriate material. You'll use books, catalogues, image banks and photo libraries to help you and you'll be responsible for building up a database of useful sources. It's helpful to have a knowledge of photo libraries; they can arrange to supply you (for a fee) with the pictures of the people or places you want without the expense of a photographer.

You will also arrange for 'clearance' for all the work the agency uses in its advertising – it's your job to get permission for people's pictures to be used and to arrange for the agency to pay any costs involved in the process. Just mentioning someone's *name* in an ad can cost the agency thousands of pounds if you haven't previously arranged clearance for its use.

### Getting into art buying

It's a difficult area to get into because very few ad agencies have art buyers – those that do tend to hang on to the ones they have, so positions don't become available very often. In many agencies, art buying is handled by the people in the traffic department, an art director or a TV producer.

Many art buyers start their careers by working as a secretary or as an assistant to an agency art buyer. Some begin by working as personal assistants to photographers or as picture researchers for an image bank or photo library. Others start in traffic and move across to art buying. A few stumble across art buying by accident. Although there are no courses specifically available in art buying, some graduates have discovered a liking for the area while on a postgraduate advertising course or during work experience. If you're fortunate enough to obtain a work placement, it could lead to something permanent if you demonstrate that you're capable and determined (see Chapters 15 and 16).

### Skills needed to be a successful art buyer

It's useful, but not necessary, to have an art background. It doesn't necessarily follow that just because you have studied fine arts, the history of art, graphic design or been to an art school that you will have an understanding of artistic concepts. The kind of skills that make a good art buyer – such as a sound artistic judgement – can probably only be learned over a number of years on the job.

You need to have a good eye for detail, be well organized, be able to arrange meetings with creatives and outside suppliers and also to have excellent interpersonal and communication skills. A good understanding of the money side is also helpful – it's essential to be up to date on the latest guidelines for usage and to be able to question quotes. As with most of the jobs discussed so far, it's important that you have the ability to get on well with and be able to communicate with people at all levels. You need to be outgoing and sociable with a good sense of humour. Above all else, you must have a real enthusiasm for art – as part of your job you'll be expected to visit art and photographic exhibitions, galleries, museums and private views on a regular basis.

## 3. TV production

A TV producer working in an ad agency is responsible for all aspects of the production side of an ad – except the actual making of the ad, which is done by a production company or freelance film director, chosen by the TV producer and the ad agency team.

The TV producer helps choose the director, is responsible for the budget and the day-to-day organization of all aspects of making the TV ad. This includes everything to do with pre-production, such as casting, set design, location and post-production – editing, recording and approval by client and advertising clearance. He or she organizes all the pre- and post-production meetings and ensures that everything is kept strictly to budget.

One of the most important attributes a TV producer needs is a cool head – 'unflappability'. The job demands serious organizational skills and a strict eye for detail. Although you need to understand the business of advertising, much of your time is taken up with day-to-day administration.

Your first task, usually, is to ensure that the ad (while it is still in the concept stage) can actually be made – that it is viable. You must be objective and diplomatic in your dealings with everyone with whom you come into contact and be able to get on with people at all levels.

The great thing about the work, like many jobs in advertising, is that no day is ever the same. You are meeting new people every day and you are not, as a rule, tied to the office – the day-to-day administration is normally handled by a production assistant, who is usually someone in training to be a TV producer.

## How to become a production assistant

You need to have at least a year's experience of being a production assistant before you can be a producer because there's so much you need to learn. If you haven't got the knowledge behind you, you can't do the job.

*Lara Richardson-Hill, TV producer, Publicis*

A production assistant is the TV producer's right-hand person. Production assistants are very often female, as many begin their careers by working as a temp or a secretary in the TV department of an ad agency. If you want to get into TV production, you'll need to make it clear from the start that you intend to further your career and don't want to remain a secretary for ever. If you're keen to learn and are liked, you will receive help and maybe promotion.

Don't be under the mistaken impression that the job is glamorous. You are more likely to be tied to the office than spending time on shoots (and these cease to be glamorous very quickly – usually after the first few hours waiting around in the cold!). Job progression usually depends on how keen you are – you can stay as a PA or move up to be a producer, although competition is fierce.

As a TV production assistant, your work will involve attending meetings to discuss work in progress. Much of your time will be spent on the phone – ringing directors, requesting show reels, chasing estimates, arranging auditions, booking rooms, etc. As well as providing admin support to the TV producer on a day-to-day basis, you may also be involved in post-production (editing and dubbing) and ensuring that the ads are finished to plan and on time. If you can be spared from the office you may get to go on a shoot, but you're more likely to be working behind the scenes and helping to make life easier for the TV producer.

### Skills needed for work in TV production
- a genuine enthusiasm for TV ads
- able to cope with working under pressure
- able to get on with people and respect their ideas
- patience and understanding
- communication and negotiation skills
- the ability to listen
- very well organized
- able to 'juggle' – you may have to work on six productions at any one time
- one step ahead at all times
- a team player
- able to handle budgets and timetables
- computer literacy.

### Work experience

Write to the creative services director or TV producer of the ad agency of your choice with your CV and covering letter. Demonstrate that you are all of the above.

If you're lucky enough to get work experience, make yourself useful, work hard and make as many contacts as you can. If you're unable to find work in an ad agency, you could approach an independent production company.

### Advice for would-be production assistants

"Talk to anyone you can and go and see them if they will let you. It will put a face to a name.
- Give them your CV. Ask their advice about what to put on your CV (being a prefect at high school is not as relevant as it used to be).
- See if you can do a placement. Even a week is better than nothing. It's good experience, looks good on your CV, gets you contacts, lets you know if you actually like the job and the place.
- Be interested in *all* media. Keep up to date with new film directors etc.
- Ask anyone you meet who else they could introduce you to. Always get another contact if possible. Then they can all be looking out for a job for you.
- Enjoy it. It's hard work but worth it. It's interesting and you get to work with great people."

*Lara Richardson-Hill*

### Advice to people wanting to work in production

"Have an interest in some form of art – typography, photography, colour, etc. Show knowledge in a subject without bragging. Be polite and honest. Don't be afraid to ask. Use others' experiences to learn. Learn when and where to say no and not to panic. Keep a good address book. A lot of this comes down to experience and just as importantly, attitude."

*Duncan Stokes*

## Progression

Traffic people can move on to account handling – they understand the process.
*Duncan Stokes*

Some people start in creative services with the idea of moving on to other areas of advertising. It's certainly an excellent way of finding out what goes on in an ad agency – who does what, when, how and where. By working in creative services you will get to know people in other departments and also outside suppliers to the agency, so you will be making useful contacts all the time. However, you may very well find that you want to stay in creative services and make a career for yourself in that area.

**Start as a runner for a production company**

A runner is exactly what it sounds like – someone who does all the running around. Many people now working in the film industry began in this way, and it's a great way to start if you have the stamina and can cope with the low pay. On the plus side you get to go on 'shoots' and can make good contacts. Working as a runner for a film production company is a good way of obtaining experience on the production side if you are willing to start at the bottom and work very hard.

**What can you earn?**

- production/traffic assistant: up to £15,000 (not necessarily graduate intake)
- graduate level: starting salary on average £15,000–17,500
- traffic controller: £18,000–24,000
- traffic manager: £25,000–35,000+
- print production controller: £20,000–30,000
- production manager: £30,000–35,000+
- TV production assistant: £24,000
- TV producer: £36,000+.

These are *average* salaries in a medium-sized to large London agency. If you are working in a smaller agency or outside London, you could very well be paid at a lower rate.

## Recommended routes

- Work experience (see Chapter 15).
- Temping.
- Secretarial.
- Despatch department/post room.
- Photo libraries and image banks.
- Agency traffic/production departments.
- A direct approach to ad agency heads of creative services/production departments.
- A vocational course (see Chapter 13).
- 'Runner', receptionist or administrator for a film production company.

## Recommended reading

Brierley, Sean (1995) *The Advertising Handbook*. Routledge.
Evans, Robin (1988) *Production and Creativity in Advertising*. Pitman.
Any of the recommended books in chapters 4–9.
*Audovisual, Televisual, Broadcast* and other film/TV/audio production journals.
*Campaign* and the advertising trade press.
*Creative Review*.
*SHOTS*.

# 11 Selling yourself – how to get the job you want

## How to keep your CV/résumé off the reject pile

### The WPB factor

WPB stands for waste-paper bin – where you don't want your application to go. Remember that an agency can receive 3000 applications for one graduate trainee position. How are they going to whittle these down so they don't have to sift their way through all of them? Your CV or résumé may be rejected before it's even opened because you used the wrong envelope or sent it second class instead of by first-class post. Here are some tips gleaned from my experience in talking to agency recruiters to ensure that your CV/résumé doesn't end up in the bin.

### First appearances are vital

Make sure you know who should receive your application. Are they Mr, Mrs, Miss or Ms? Spell their name correctly – even if it means phoning up the agency to check that you've got it right. What is their function? Are you writing to the human resources manager, the head of recruitment, an account director or supervisor? Check it out and get it right. Make sure you address the envelope correctly. You can write or type the address. Use a normal font or typeface.

### Don't throw away your chances

This could be the week that they are throwing out all the pink or vellum envelopes. Don't use coloured or fancy paper. A white or manilla A4 envelope is recommended. Keep it simple, clean looking and accurate. Don't throw away your chances before they even get to your CV/résumé.

### Dos and don'ts of a successful CV/résumé

- Word process or type your CV – do *not* send a handwritten CV.
- Do *not* fold your CV – keep it flat. Use A4 paper so that you can slide it into your A4 envelope. Some agencies throw away folded applications without even opening them! You may also like to use a stiffened envelope so that your precious CV/résumé doesn't arrive crumpled.
- Use plain white paper.
- Use a clean, clear, normal font or typeface. Just because your PC has twenty

different typefaces doesn't mean that you have to use them all. Choose one and stick with it.

- Do not mix capitals, bold, italics, underlines. Adopt a clear style and keep it consistent throughout.
- Aim for a clean layout. Don't feel that you have to use up all the space.
- Use only one side of each piece of paper – the recipient should not have to turn the page.
- Use a maximum of two sides A4, a minimum of one side A4.
- Don't try to be witty or clever.
- Send only the original – never a copy. (And remember to keep a copy for yourself.)
- Tailor your CV/résumé to each job.
- Use action words to describe your abilities and achievements.

## Examples of action words to use in your CV/résumé

| | | | |
|---|---|---|---|
| Acquired | Discovered | Launched | Redesigned |
| Advertised | Displayed | Led | Reorganized |
| Analysed | Distributed | Liaised | Researched |
| Approved | Edited | Maintained | Restructured |
| Arranged | Encouraged | Managed | Revised |
| Assessed | Established | Marketed | Rewarded |
| Awarded | Exhibited | Motivated | Saved |
| Collated | Expanded | Negotiated | Scheduled |
| Completed | Formulated | Obtained | Selected |
| Conceived | Founded | Organized | Serviced |
| Consolidated | Generated | Originated | Sold |
| Consulted | Identified | Performed | Solved |
| Controlled | Illustrated | Pioneered | Supervised |
| Coordinated | Implemented | Planned | Supplied |
| Created | Improved | Prepared | Taught |
| Defined | Increased | Presented | Tested |
| Delivered | Initiated | Produced | Trained |
| Demonstrated | Innovated | Promoted | Transformed |
| Designed | Instructed | Proposed | Translated |
| Determined | Interpreted | Provided | Uncovered |
| Developed | Introduced | Recommended | Verified |
| Devised | Invented | Recorded | Widened |
| Directed | Investigated | Recruited | Wrote |

### Highlight your name

Most people write 'curriculum vitae' at the top of the page. Most people get the spelling wrong. The person reading it knows that it's your CV, so you don't need to tell them. Instead, use that space to highlight your name. Write it in the way you want it to be known. You are not applying for a passport or choosing the words for your degree certificate. If your friends know you as Amanda Elizabeth Brown, then by all means put that at the top of your CV. Otherwise, simply write Mandy Brown and put your telephone number (i.e. where you can be contacted for most of the time) underneath.

All the other personal details which usually take up so much unnecessary space at the start, can go at the very end of the second page. After all, they are only going to need them if they decide to contact you. And they won't know that when they're only at the top of page one.

### Make them want to know you

Most people do not have the time to read résumés/CVs – they skim them. You need to make yours stand out – not by using red paper or fancy lettering, but by what you say. You need to make yourself sound so interesting that they will want to meet you to find out more.

### Be yourself

Just be you. Let yourself come across to the reader so that they can get a feel for the kind of person you are.

### Be honest

Always be honest in a CV/résumé. You must tell the truth about yourself. If you don't, these things have a way of being found out. That doesn't mean that you have to tell them everything. You can leave out things as long as you account for all the dates between leaving school and your application. For example, you may not have done brilliantly at GCSE and may not want to tell them your results. Although it is generally better to give your grades, you can if you wish write 'seven passes at GCSE' or 'three A levels' without mentioning your grades. Your qualifications don't have to feature on page one of your CV or résumé – they can go on the second page. Obviously, if you did extremely well, flaunt it on page one. If you have had a year out between school and university, make sure you account for that time. It is unwise to leave gaps, as it could arouse suspicions.

### Be single-minded

Angle your application and résumé/CV towards the job you want to do. For example, if you want to work in account handling, your CV/résumé should point towards an account handling career.

## Have a goal

Make it clear from the outset what career you have in mind. Some people like to have a heading at the top of the first page, such as 'Career Goal' or similar wording. For example:

Career Goal: Account Management

## Personal statement

Some CV/résumé writers like to summarize their skills and put them at the top of the first page in a personal profile statement. There are no rules about this. Play around with the layout and see what suits you best.

## Focus on your experience

It's a good idea to have a heading on the first page to follow on from your career goal. For example, if your aim is to work in media, your next heading could be 'Media Experience'. Then, you need to dredge your brain to discover what experiences you have had that could fit your heading. If you have been on a media or advertising-related course, then you will have plenty to say. Make sure you highlight any work experience you have had in advertising or a related field.

## Achievements

CVs are sales documents – they need to say what's good about you.
*Alan Morgan (1999), recruitment consultant*

You can turn anything into an achievement. It doesn't just have to mean academic and other achievements at university. Try and use incidents from your life that have been character forming or demonstrate that you have leadership qualities. An example of an achievement could be working as a nanny, looking after three children under five. (Think of the skills gained from coping with the demands of three small children and translate those to the skills needed in a demanding job.) Maybe you've played in a team or won a debating prize. Don't just list your achievements, write about them. Bring them to life.

There may be aspects of your life that you might have put under other headings (such as interests or travel) that could transfer to achievements. Fund-raising for charity. Telephone sales. Working for a pressure group. Acting or directing. Chairing a committee. Climbing a mountain. Deep-sea diving. Learning a new language. Learning to swim, drive, ride a bike. Playing in a band. Winning a prize. Door-to-door selling. Running a club. Leading a movement such as the Scouts. Captaining a team. Running a student union. Getting into print. And so on. It's how you describe the effect and impact on your life that turns it into an achievement. If you really can't think of anything that amounts to an achievement, simply don't include an achievement heading. Maybe focus on your skills instead.

## Highlight your skills

Bring out the skills that are necessary for the job. Don't just list them – give evidence. Don't say that you have good communication skills. Demonstrate that you have them in the way that you write and structure your CV or résumé. If you are fluent in another language or have relevant computer skills, let them know.

## Skills employers want

- computer literacy
- languages
- information-gathering/analysis
- presentation
- business/financial management.

*Gareth Morgan, Marketing Manager, London Taxis International*

## Be interesting

Put down interests that show you to be a lively, interesting and sociable person. Avoid listing solitary hobbies such as reading or stamp collecting. Don't expect anyone to believe you if you say that one of your interests is looking at ads – it just sounds so corny. Treat this as an opportunity to demonstrate your independence, enthusiasm, competitiveness and character. Show that you are a team player.

Agencies like applicants who have a passion for something – it doesn't matter what. There are no rules about what you should or shouldn't put down as an interest, although most people would agree that it's a good idea to avoid the subjects of politics and religion unless they relate in some way to your achievements. My advice is not to put anything on an application that you are not willing to discuss or demonstrate, if necessary, at interview. For example, somebody was once asked to demonstrate their tap dancing in front of an interview panel. If you can't do it or aren't willing to talk about it, don't put it down.

## Education and qualifications

Always start with the most recent. Give all the dates. You don't need to give any addresses. Simply state the university and the degree you achieved. If your work included a dissertation, only include it if it's relevant to your application. You need go no further back than A levels and certainly no further than GCSEs. Some people recommend only putting in GCSE grades if you have grade C or above.

Don't forget to include any extracurricular activities, such as computing and desktop publishing courses. If these haven't led to a qualification, you can create a new heading for them, or put them under skills. Examples might be a course in counselling skills or photography.

## Employment

Start with the most recent and put in reverse chronological order. If you have had many part-time and vacation jobs you can sum them up in a sentence. For example, from 1996 to 1999, summer vacation work included babysitting, retail work, telephone selling and helping in a children's summer camp. However, the latter two – telephone sales and work with children – could possibly warrant their own paragraph. They could, with a bit of work from you, become achievements in their own right and be moved into another heading. If you have had real work over a long period, you will need to list the jobs, but you do not need to go into any detail about them (unless you think they are relevant and will be of interest) and you certainly should not say why you left them. You can, if you wish, write a line or two about each job you held, explaining the skills you have gained from doing them. You are not expected to give employers' addresses and telephone numbers.

## References

Unless references are specifically asked for, it's often enough to say that references are available and have people standing by just in case. If you do give references, don't use relatives. The ideal referee would be someone from an ad agency – maybe where you've had work experience. If you have a contact in an agency, ask if you can use their name. Most people use one academic or work-related referee and in addition someone who knows them well who can provide a character reference. Don't forget to ask permission of the person you are giving as a referee and to let them have a copy of your résumé or CV and information about the job you're applying for.

## Personal details

At the end of your CV/résumé, put your name and telephone number again, your address and age or date of birth (no need to put both). You don't need to say you have a driving licence. We can safely assume that most people today know how to drive and you are not applying for a job as a truck driver. Don't emphasize typewriting or shorthand skills – you are not applying for a job as a secretary. You don't need to mention your marital status. It's up to you whether or not you wish to mention your nationality. Make sure that you give the address and telephone number where you can be contacted. If you are a student, give your term-time and your home address. Don't forget to include your mobile phone number and your email address.

## Be accurate

If people can't pay attention to detail when they're trying to get a job, how will they cope with the pressures of the job?

*Olga Budimir (1998), Head of Production, Burkitt DDB*

## Letters of application

> If your letter's no good, they're not going to look at your CV.
>
> *Alan Morgan, 1999*

Always send an accompanying letter with your CV/résumé (unless specifically asked not to do so). Your covering letter is your advertisement for yourself. If your résumé/CV is the bone, your letter is the meat on the bone. It fleshes out what you've written and tells the reader why you are worth interviewing. *Think of it as a sales letter.*

### To type or not to type?

A handwritten letter shows that you have made an effort. However, if you are in any doubt about the excellence of your handwriting, the letter should be word processed. Many recruiters prefer a word-processed letter, claiming that it is quicker and easier to read. All the same rules apply as for the CV/résumé in terms of paper, typefaces, layout, structure and accuracy. Always enclose a CV/résumé with your application (unless you have been specifically asked not to do so).

### Do your homework

You *must* do your homework first. Research the agency or company you want to work for. Read the advertising press so that you are aware of the latest accounts and the most recent developments. You would not, for example, apply to an agency that in the same week had lost a major account or made staff redundant. However, if you should read in *Campaign* that there's a new agency starting up, that could be a good time to apply for a job or work experience. If an agency has taken on a new account, it's probably going to need more people. And, if it's a brand-new agency, they may very well welcome – and possibly even be flattered by – your approach.

### What to say

A letter of application should begin by saying why you are writing to that particular ad agency. You need to say what it is you are looking for – a job or work experience – and in what area. Be specific. Remember to be focused and goal oriented. Explain in your letter of application why you think you might be suited to that particular job area – what do you have to offer? Your letter of application is your opportunity to say all those things that you did not have space for in your résumé/CV. There may be something you can say that is so intriguing that they will want to meet you in order to get the full picture. Remember that the covering letter is your sales letter.

### Size matters

You need to sell yourself and make them want to meet you – at the same time it pays not to be too verbose. It is hard to strike the balance of writing just about enough without saying too much (and boring them to death) or too little.

### Know to whom you are writing

Do not write 'Dear Sir or Madam'. And never put 'To whom it may concern'. Write to a named person. For example, 'Dear Mrs Brown'. Again, you will need to do your homework, phoning up the ad agency if necessary to find out the correct form of address and how to spell their name. Each letter you send out will need to be 'tweaked' in order to be angled towards a particular person, job or ad agency. Don't forget to alter your letter each time!

You might like to say something about why you have chosen that particular ad agency. It's a good idea to show that you know something about the company and the work that they do. For example, it could be that you admire their latest ad campaign or their creative work.

### Test the market

You can send out test letters. Try some witty ones, some straight. Play around with what you write and how you write it. If you get a response with version A, you will know it's worth using again. Don't send all your letters out at once. Send them out in batches of ten or so at a time. Work your way through your top twenty favourite ad agencies, then your second twenty and so on. You may need to send out fifty or more letters before you get any response.

### Keep it straight

Don't send them a light bulb or your name headlined on a mock-up of the front page of *Campaign* or *Admap*. They have seen them all before. My advice is to keep it straight unless you are applying for work as a copywriter or an art director (see Chapter 6). Avoid clichés, jokes, swear words and jargon.

### Stand out from the crowd

Keeping it straight doesn't mean that you have to be dull. Write a thought-provoking letter that's different from the thousands of others they're likely to receive. Make yours stand out by being interesting and memorable.

### 'First impressions count'

I've binned applications from people with a typo or a spelling error in their CV. First impressions count and the first impression you are making is with your CV and your cover letter.

*Louise Wall (1999), Managing Director, EHS Brann*

Spelling, punctuation and grammar have to be perfect. If in doubt, check it out. Use a dictionary/spell check and ask someone you trust to proofread your work for you.

### Signing off

Always use 'Yours sincerely' if you have addressed someone by name, not 'Yours faithfully'. Never 'Yours truly'. A lot of people make the mistake of writing 'sincerely' with a capital S – use the lower case 's', or 'f' for faithfully.

Don't forget to let them know how they can contact you. Do they have your phone number? Don't be so pushy as to ask them to call you or tell them that you'll be seeing them on a certain date.

### Follow-up

If you are sending an application form for graduate training, you will have to be patient. Do *not* phone the agency. This will only serve to irritate them and put you in the reject pile. However, if you have sent a speculative letter or an application in response to an ad, you can – after a reasonable interval – give them a ring to check. Some people even write in their letters that they will be phoning on a certain day. You'll find a section on how to phone an ad agency in Chapter 15.

### Persevere

Whatever you do, don't give up. If you do get rejected, don't take it personally. Somewhere, there is an agency to suit you. It's just a matter of persevering.

## Summary of CV/résumé tips from two advertising professionals

"Do your homework – research agency background, current clients, work produced, key personnel.
- Be yourself.
- Be specific about your skills, experience and knowledge.
- Tailor your CV/résumé and application to *their* needs – what is relevant to the prospective employer.
- Ask for help and advice."

*Gareth Morgan*

## 'Make sure your CV or résumé sells you'

"Your application will probably be one of hundreds. Ensure your CV or résumé is concise and clear. The covering letter should also be concise, with the reasons why you want the job.

- Try to fit your CV/résumé on to two pages maximum.
- Use an easy-to-read font/typeface.
- Aim for a clear, simple layout.
- No spelling mistakes.
- Tailor your CV/résumé to each job.
- Send only an original copy – not a photocopy.
- Don't try to be clever or humorous (you don't know your audience).
- Summarize your key capabilities and strengths in a 'core skills' and/or 'profile' section.
- Highlight any major achievements or successes.
- Give a brief, business-like impression of your attitude and personality.

- Make sure your CV/résumé 'sells' you as best as possible.
- Enclose a specific customized covering letter which should show your enthusiasm for the job. **"**

*Bob Lampon, Director, Making Waves*


## Recommended reading

Bolles, R. N. (2001) *What Color Is Your Parachute? A Practical Manual for Job-hunters and Career-changes.* Ten Speed Press.

Bolles, R. N. (1999) *Job-hunting on the Internet.* Ten Speed Press.

Fox, J. (2001) *Don't Send a Resume: And Other Contrarian Rules to Help Land a Great Job.* Hyperion.

Gibson, N. and Gibson, P. (1993) *Excuse Me . . . Your Rejection Is Showing.* Sovereign World.

Hansen, K. (2000) *A Foot in the Door (Networking Your Way into the Hidden Job Market).* Ten Speed Press.

Higham, M. (1983) *Coping with Interviews.* New Opportunities Press.

Nicholson, J. (1991) *Good Interview Guide.* J. Rosters.

Root, W. A. (1996) *The Joy of Failure.* Summit Publishing.

Savage, E. (1997) *Don't Take It Personally.* New Harbinger.

Sjodin, Terri L. (2000) *New Sales Speak.* John Wiley & Sons.

Yate, M. (1989) *Great Answers to Tough Interview Questions.* Kogan Page.

# 12 Graduate training and interviews

It's knowing how to play the game to give yourself a head start.
*Rachel Burrows (1999), recruitment consultant*

Enthusiasm is 70 per cent of the message you must get across.
*Andrew Hyde, Head of Strategy, BT Communication Products*

## Where are all the good graduates?

In the past few years there have been endless articles in the industry journal, *Campaign*, bemoaning the dearth of 'good' graduates in the industry. In times of recession ad agencies have tended to cut back on their graduate intake. Of course, once the economy has recovered they desperately try to make up for lost time. And up comes the inevitable cry, 'where are all the good graduates?' Agencies then start recruiting with a vengeance. As Ted Goater (2001) of the IPA put it: 'Agencies are concerned about getting the right calibre of people and retaining them.'

Every year at the start of October, the IPA, publishes its Graduate Factfile. This is an online listing of all the ad agencies looking to recruit a new intake of graduates. In 2001, for example, 39 IPA ad agencies recruited at graduate entry.

Agency training schemes are considered to be one of the most desirable ways of finding employment in account handling, planning or media. It is regarded as an incredibly competitive and difficult entry route and should only be attempted by those who are really determined to succeed.

Remember that ad agencies do not offer graduate training for positions in the creative department – see Chapter 6 if you want to find work as a copywriter or an art director.

## 'We do not hire graduates to pigeonhole them'

One useful thing you can do when researching ad agencies is to look at their websites. Lowe's is one of the better ones – it's very informative and gives you a good idea of what they have to offer if you're thinking of applying to their agency.

On their web page, Lowe suggest you might like to ask the following questions if you're thinking of graduate training. You can see their own answers to them if you look at their website. Here are mine:

- *How important is work experience in marketing, advertising or production companies?* Work experience is one of the best ways of finding a job in advertising (see Chapter 15). If you've got relevant work experience on your CV, it will help you get an interview because it shows that you're seriously interested in working in advertising.
- *Does the subject of my degree matter?* No. See Chapter 13 on advertising and marketing communications courses.
- *How will I know which agency is right for me?* By doing your homework and by experiencing work placements/interviews at as many agencies as possible. Finding the right agency is like clicking with the right person. When it happens, you'll just know that it's the right one for you.
- *How many agencies should I apply to?* As many as you possibly can. Agencies prefer it if you have also applied to other agencies – they expect you to do so. Therefore, if they ask you, and you have, don't conceal the truth.
- *Is it best to apply during my final year at university?* Applications normally have to be in by the end of December, so you have to apply in the autumn. The IPA publishes its Graduate Factfile at the start of October every year. If you get accepted for a trainee position, you will start work the following September so you will be able to enjoy a long, lazy summer. If you're planning to take a gap year, apply to agencies in the autumn that you return. If an agency offers you a place, they expect you to be able to take it.
- *What's the difference between first- and second-round interviews?* This is explained to you later on in this chapter.
- *What kind of preparation would be valuable for a first interview?* Reading this book for a start – and then taking up some of its suggestions.
- *What's special about the Lowe training programme?* According to information on the Lowe home page, their training programme is probably the longest and most comprehensive of any of the agencies. It lasts around eight months compared to others which, they say, last around three months or even days. Lowe's believe that it's important that you have a complete picture of how an ad is made and how an agency is run. Therefore, they say, if you're a graduate trainee at Lowe you will spend time in every agency department and in their sister companies dealing with PR, direct marketing, new media and other below-the-line activities.

The six-month training scheme at Lowe is broadly split into three areas:

- Hands-on experience in all areas of Lowe and sister agencies.
- Internal and external seminars/workshops in conjunction with the agency's

training consultant and the IPA.
- Preparing work on a variety of live or purpose-built advertising projects from presentations probing issues to actually writing ads.

*(www.loweuk.com)*

## Career progression in account management

This describes a fairly typical career progression in a large advertising agency:

graduate trainee (or junior executive where there is no graduate training)
account executive
account supervisor/manager
account director
group account director
board director.

## Typical qualities of a graduate trainee

- graduate
- often (but not necessarily) under 25
- energetic with a passion for advertising and other things in life
- an interest in people and in what makes them tick
- a degree in *any subject*
- self-confident
- excellent presentation and interpersonal skills
- determined to succeed in an advertising career.

## How to apply for graduate training

In order to apply for graduate training, you must follow the rules exactly as laid down in the IPA Factfile (available from ipa.co.uk). Some agencies will ask for a CV and covering letter, others rely on their own application forms. Agency application forms are designed to be off-putting so that the faint-hearted are dissuaded from applying.

Unfortunately, graduate training application deadlines tend to be at the busiest time of the year for students, when you are coping with a heavy load of college work. Interviews are often conducted around February, when undergraduates are taking their finals, so it is only the most determined students who bother to proceed. Nevertheless, competition is fierce – the average ad agency receives about 3000 applications for every graduate training position.

# The application form

You might think that given the skills you have developed during your time at university that you should be able to cope with a normal application form. However, there is no such thing as a normal or typical agency application. Over the years each ad agency has developed its own style and aims to reveal this to some extent in the information that it passes on to prospective applicants.

No expense is spared in producing stunning application forms which set each agency apart from its rivals. Since they are all competing for the same bright graduates, the agency is as much selling itself to you as you are selling yourself to them.

Each application form differs from the next and on average takes about a day to complete. Although it is time-consuming, you should aim to apply to as many different ad agencies as possible. The more you apply to, the better your chances of succeeding in getting an interview.

## The Saatchi & Saatchi application form

The 1996–7 graduate trainee application form for Saatchi & Saatchi consisted of a black 'briefcase' which opened to reveal acetate pages representing a real presentation to a prospective client, including the proposed creative work. This showed a 'rough' for Club 18–30 holidays and the headline 'Beaver Espana'.

The final acetate revealed that the client was a born-again Christian and asked how you, as a prospective advertising person, would sell this idea to the client. You were asked to say how you would set up the preliminary meeting with the client, how you would present your point of view and how you would overcome the client's objections to the advertising idea.

Applicants were given a maximum of 150 words for each part of their presentation and asked to send it with their CV and a covering letter to the agency's personnel officer. Multiply this by at least ten other similarly complicated applications and you can see what a difficult and time-consuming task it is. Most university students I have spoken to consider agency application forms to be the most demanding and challenging of all the forms they complete.

There's no real knack to filling them in. Sometimes, the one you spend the least time on can be the one that achieves a positive response. If you like doing them and have fun answering the questions, there's a good chance that someone will enjoy reading your responses and that you will be invited for interview.

The 1997 Saatchi & Saatchi application form consisted of a black package. On the front it read, 'One advertising agency will always be remembered for famous words and pictures.' Inside it said, 'In 400 words and pictures will it remember you?' Applicants were given a roll of film to use. It went on:

> "A few snaps. And approximately one side of A4. What could be simpler? You don't even have to create ads. (So please don't try.) This is your opportunity to make us want to meet you.
>
> Just make yourself famous. With us. Something you won't do with clichéd

ideas and hackneyed expressions. Our agency is built on originality. Not just the work we produce, but the whole approach of our people. Some of the same people who will be judging your submission. And hundreds of others of course.

Easy. So, four photographs . . .

1.  An existing ad. Any existing ad. 50 words on why it deserves universal acclaim. 50 on why it deserves universal condemnation.
2.  Somewhere, anywhere. But explain why it is a place of significance for you. 100 words.
3.  Something that makes you angry. What can you do to change the general public's attitude? 100 words.
4.  A picture of you. Tell us what your best friend sees in you and what you look for in your best friend. 100 words. **"**

The 1998 application form from Saatchi & Saatchi was not a form at all but a large empty envelope. On the outside it read, 'What comes out of the world's most famous agency depends on what you put in.' It went on to say:

**"** Saatchi & Saatchi is famous for extraordinary ideas. But to create extraordinary ideas you need to have extraordinary people looking for extraordinary careers. This is exactly what we have. This is also where you come in. Or rather, this is where you 'put' in.

Because we want to get an idea of what you could put into the agency. So we would like to hear about some of your ideas. But this doesn't mean we want you to send us a load of essays. (You've probably done enough of those already.) We want you to bring your ideas alive. In any way you like. Ready?

1.  *Your idea of you.* Send us a 'visual' simile of yourself and explain how this demonstrates what you will contribute to us.
2.  *Ideas on a postcard please.* What's the most important journey you've made in your life? Send us a postcard.
3.  *Your best ever idea.* What was it and how did you make it become a reality?
4.  *Exploiting ideas.* Take one of our ads and show us how you would exploit it further. Four ideas. Each accompanied by 100 words. **"**

Applicants are then asked to put everything into the envelope provided, together with their CV, a covering letter saying why they want to work for Saatchi & Saatchi and a passport photo.

### Some typical tasks and questions

Ammirati Puris Lintas (now Lowe Lintas), another successful international ad agency, asked applicants for their graduate trainee scheme to complete a form that contained a number of different tasks. Under the heading 'Lonely Hearts Club', applicants had to sell themselves to their ideal mate in no more than 50 words. They were also asked to answer such questions as, 'What is the biggest mistake you've made? What is your worst nightmare? What words or phrases do you most over use? What do you consider to be the most overrated virtue? What is your most treasured possession?'

Some of the questions on their 1997 application form included:

> **"**In your opinion, which is the best advertising campaign you have seen this year and which is the worst?
> - Which is the best piece of direct marketing or sales promotion that you have seen this year?
> - Should Alcopops be advertised? Discuss in no more than 150 words.
> - Who would you invite as star guest to your last meal and why? (30 words) Sell something in a classified ad in no more than 35 words.**"**

The 1998 application form for Bates Dorland asked, 'If you had £60,000 and six months to spare, what would you do?' The 1998 DMB&B (now D'Arcy) application form asked, 'How would you persuade someone to give up all their worldly possessions? If you could go back to one period or event in time, what would it be and why? And, what advice would you now give to yourself as a ten-year-old?' They are not expecting the literal truth. For example, they're not expecting to hear that you wished that you'd worked harder at school so that you could have done better in exams. You are not talking to your therapist!

## Be original and memorable

Don't feel that you have to fill in all that white space they have given you. If you can say what you want to say in just a sentence or a short paragraph, then do so. You can use humour – with care. The first idea you come up with is probably not the best one. If you thought of it quickly, others will too. Don't state the obvious – try to be original and memorable.

You should always check your spelling, punctuation and grammar. Make sure your writing is legible. It's a good idea to make a few photocopies and practise on those first, before you fill in the real thing. Do not send an accompanying letter or CV, unless it is asked for. And, whatever you do, do not phone the ad agency to enquire about what has happened to your application. Be patient. They will contact you in due course – either with a letter of rejection or a letter asking you for interview.

## What kind of person are they looking for?

> I don't think they'd interview you if they didn't think that you had the right sort of personality.
>
> *A student applicant*

Agencies say that they have no fixed opinions of what kind of person they are looking for or what kind of background they come from. What matters to them is that you love ads and want to be involved in producing them. The application forms are designed to demonstrate your personality, aptitude and individuality.

There are no set answers that will guarantee you an interview. If you enjoy completing the application forms, there is a chance that someone will enjoy reading what you have written and want to meet you as a result.

## The first interview

I think you've got to be matched to the agency.

*A student applicant*

You have been fortunate enough to have been invited for a first interview. The following section deals with interviews – in particular, those related to graduate training – and offers some advice, help and tips on what to expect.

### The basics

Look smart. Check you've got the right date, time and place. Know where you're going and how to get there. Whatever you do, make sure you arrive on time – or even early – so that you can relax and get the feel of the place.

It's essential that you have researched the background of the ad agency well in advance of the interview – its accounts (clients), ad campaigns, key personnel – and that you have read recent issues of *Campaign* so that you are informed about current events. Have they lost or won any accounts recently? Won any awards? Merged with another agency? Taken on a new creative team? And so on.

If you are going for a specific job – perhaps one that you have seen advertised – you need to have researched it beforehand as much as possible. Find out what accounts you are going to be working on – brands, account history, what the account is worth and where the money is spent (i.e. in what media), what your duties will be when you're working and who you will be working for.

### Nice and nasty

Most agencies have two rounds of interviews for graduate trainee positions. At the first visit you may be interviewed by one or more people. An interview is only going to be as good as the person conducting it. An experienced interviewer will generally try to put you at your ease, although a tactic might be to deliberately say something controversial to see how you will respond. Sometimes, you might get a Mrs Nice and a Mr Nasty (or vice versa). The atmosphere will probably be quite relaxed, but you should never let your guard slip. Always remember that you are on show, that you are being interviewed and do not relax too much!

### What do you do in your spare time?

You may be asked questions about what you have written on your application form, or you may be surprised to discover that your interviewer does not seem to have read your application form. This is not unusual, as the person interviewing you is rarely the person who originally read your application. Be prepared to talk about your interests and leisure pursuits. Let them see that you get involved in things happening around you and that you have an interest in what's going on *outside* of advertising. A successful interview often does not feel like an interview but more like a chat. If you can turn the interview into what feels like a conversation, so much the better.

## Just a chat

This was Natasha's experience at her first interview:

> "My first interview was really strange because they didn't actually ask me a single question. It was really odd. I didn't know quite how to take it at all. We were just chatting over a cup of coffee and having a laugh. At the time, I thought it could either go really well and be a positive thing or it could just be that they weren't interested and that's why they didn't ask me any questions. As it turned out, I went back a second time, so it must have been OK. And I ended up getting the job!"

This is what happened to Steven when he went for his first interview:

> "When they said which ads do you like and which campaigns have you admired, I said I liked being stretched and being pushed in a business situation. They asked me then if I would get impatient if I was working on a detergent or something similar and I said no, that would be fine. They then said that there would be a lot of repetitive work to do on some of their accounts, so I think I knew I wasn't suited to them."

The mistake Steven made here was to contradict what he himself had said. On the one hand, he said that he liked to be 'stretched and pushed', and on the other, he said that he wouldn't get impatient if he was working on a detergent account.

## What kind of things will they ask?

A graduate describes her first interview:

> "The first interview I went to was at JWT, which was quite intimidating, because it was in this really posh hotel. I was quite nervous but it was really quite relaxed. They didn't ask anything tricky – it was all really obvious stuff you knew they'd ask, like why you wanted to go into advertising, what did you do in your degree, what adverts did you like, don't like, the sort of thing that you kind of prepare for. It wasn't too tough really."

## What ads do you love/hate?

Do your homework before you go so that you know something about the agency and the work they do. Have an opinion on their ads and on ads in general. It's a good idea to prepare a good ad and a bad ad to talk about in case you are asked.

You may be shown a specific advertisement and asked to comment on it. There is no right or wrong point of view but you must be able to defend what you say. If your interviewer disagrees with your opinion, don't feel that you have to agree with the interviewer's point of view. Agencies want people who have opinions and who can stand their ground under criticism. One aspect of the interview is that it's designed to discover if you will have the ability to 'sell' ads to clients in the future.

### What are your interests?

*Never* put anything on your application form that you are not prepared to follow up at interview. For example, if you say you like reading, be prepared to talk about books. If you have said you love the cinema, make sure that you have seen a film recently and that you are able to talk about it. If you put origami down as an interest, be prepared to demonstrate your skills!

### Do you have any questions?

Always have questions ready to ask: these should be questions about the job not about pay, lunch breaks or holidays. A good question might be something like, 'What kind of things can I expect to be doing in my first week at work?' Ask about the training they are going to give you. Remember that they are competing for you against other agencies. If you have other interviews lined up, let them know – but not in a way that makes you seem arrogant or complacent.

### Three key questions

According to Alan Morgan, a recruitment consultant, 'You need to convince the interviewer you want the job – for the right reasons.' He suggests that you prepare for the interview by asking yourself these three key questions:

- What do I want?
- Why do I want it?
- Why will I be any good?

> Enthusiasm and confidence accounts for 60 per cent of interview success. Be lively, be sparky, be positive.
>
> *Alan Morgan (1999), recruitment consultant*

## What happens at the second interview?

If you've been successful at the first round you are asked to return for a second interview. You may have to compete with other candidates by taking part in team games and presentations. Sometimes you are put up at a hotel for a weekend so that the ad agency can make an accurate assessment of your abilities, aptitude, behaviour and interpersonal skills.

## Ice-breakers

A graduate who recently went through the process describes her experience:

"First of all they played some games where they broke the ice. You had to get together in a team and make whole pictures out of these little jigsaw pieces and haggle with the other teams. It was all about interrelating and how you bargained, dealt with one another and that sort of thing. There were a lot of tests and also group work going on all the time.

I didn't think I'd got through at all. They kept calling you up for interviews at the spur of the moment. I just felt that the interviews hadn't gone well. I was sent to my room for an hour on my own to do a test. I didn't think I'd done very well on that. It was just a gut feeling. I just didn't think I'd got it."

Asked what she thought the agency was looking for, she responded:

"They said that they weren't paying much attention at that time – it was an ice-breaker. However, I am sure that they were looking for the way people related to each other, because they were there taking notes constantly."

## Under pressure

Another graduate trainee describes her experience at second interview:

"The second interview was tough. It was over three days and very intensive – up at seven and through till four in the morning. It was held in a hotel in Mayfair – two nights in this rather salubrious hotel with a fluffy dressing gown, double bed and satellite TV. I didn't get to appreciate it because I only slept for about three hours a night. They deliberately kept us up so that they could see what we were like under pressure. They put you in teams and they were there every single minute taking notes the whole time, which was really quite wearing after three days."

## What do agencies want?

Various agency directors were asked what they looked for in a graduate. Here is their response:

- Agencies want people who can think and communicate, have an enquiring mind and know how to relate to people. They should have an interest in people and what makes them tick. They need to be intelligent and understand about advertising and marketing.
- We want interesting people. Individuals who are strong characters in their own right. People who have their own opinions with a passion that goes beyond advertising and who can think imaginatively.
- We want people who can learn quickly and accept responsibility. People who take the initiative and don't wait to be asked to do things.
- Motivated, ambitious, bright, enthusiastic, business-minded and sociable

individuals – people with that extra spark, those who have demonstrated initiative and self-starting.

- We want people who are open to our influence. We don't want people who think they already know all there is to learn.

## How do agencies select?

Here's what happens at Saatchi & Saatchi:

"The first interviews are held in December and January and you will be seen by two senior directors with one other candidate. During the one-hour interview you will be asked about advertising among other topics.

The second interviews are held in late January/early February – over one and a half days (Friday and Saturday). The finalists are given a presentation and tour of the agency by graduates from the previous year – they also meet our management and senior directors. During the final round you will be divided into groups working on different exercises.

When you've been with candidates for a whole day you do get to know them fairly well. A decision is made by the end of the second day. We inform the successful applicants the following day.

### What to expect in your first few months at the agency

The graduate intake starts in early September. You receive comprehensive training until the end of December. You are allocated to a group from day one.

We take great care to invest in our graduates and are looking for future management in years to come.

We like them to have applied to other agencies – not just to us. We're looking for team people who are also individuals – we look for examples of leadership roles in their application. They must be persuasive and have a passion for the industry."

*Corinne Fahn (2001), Personnel Assistant, Saatchi & Saatchi*

## How I got my job at Saatchi & Saatchi

A Saatchi & Saatchi account executive:

"I applied from Oxford on the 'Milk Round'. We had to complete Saatchi's usual nightmare application, which involved 'presenting' the Club 18–30 work. After that, an interview with two account directors (one of whom I ended up working for) was followed by a two-day marathon session at Saatchi's. By this time there were around 30 people left out of 1800. We completed a series of pre-set tasks, discussions and presentations, in groups of five people. We were called the next day with offers."

## We look at every CV

A recruitment director describes the process at her agency:

" An account planner and an account manager look at every CV. We have six different people looking at the CVs of prospective candidates – three of them are account planners and three account managers. They reduce 3000 applications to 120. Each one marks each application as either a possible to see, a definite interview or a definite rejection. We may look at possibles again if we don't have enough definites.

We do two rounds of interviews. If we get a lot of applications from Oxbridge we might go and interview there (as well as at the agency). We're looking for people from two different disciplines. Each candidate is interviewed for half an hour with an account planner and a separate half-hour interview with an account manager. In this way, the agency can decide in which area the candidate is better suited – planning or management.

We interview one-to-one. We don't like aggressive interview techniques. We ask them why they want to work in advertising, what they like, what ads they like. It's an informal, friendly chat. They're interviewed in one of our offices so that they can see the agency is not glamorous. If that's what they want, that's not us. It helps them to see where they want to be – they might be better suited to another agency. "

## Do your preparation

The more interviews you have, the better you will become at them. Do your homework beforehand, as discussed earlier in the chapter. Think about the kind of things you might be asked and practise answering them. Ask someone you know to give you a mock interview and be prepared to listen to his or her feedback.

## Do your homework

Find out as much as you can about the company. Look them up on their website. If your interview is for graduate training with an IPA agency, you can arrange to make an appointment to visit the IPA and see the agency's show reel.

The Advertising Association has a library where you can find information on ad agencies. You will need to phone them up beforehand to make an appointment before you visit.

## First impressions are crucial

Be aware that some people hold the view that your job prospects are decided within the first *fifteen* seconds of an interview (Freeman, 1998) – about the time it takes you to walk in, shake hands and sit down, and certainly before you open your mouth. Therefore, how you present yourself can be crucial.

Start off by arriving on time and unharrassed, looking smart, smiling and with a firm, friendly handshake. (If you think your hands are going to be damp and sweaty, rinse them under cold water before your interview. But make sure you dry them thoroughly – otherwise they will be damp and sweaty!)

## What should you wear?

There are no real rules about what to wear. But there are rules about what *not* to wear. Don't go along to any interview looking scruffy and unkempt – even if it's for a creative position. Those interviewing you will simply think that you don't care enough about the job.

Andrew Croft (1999) from Agency3 advises would-be account executives to 'dress the part'. For example, carry a briefcase rather than a carrier bag. Alan Morgan, recruitment consultant, suggests that men wear a suit and tie and that women dress smartly – though not necessarily in a suit.

Some people actually suggest visiting the ad agency beforehand and hovering around outside to see what the staff wear, so that you can follow the company's dress code. If in doubt about what to wear, dress smartly and wear the clothes you feel comfortable in. Above all, be yourself – don't put on an act.

## Be yourself

At your interview you need to be able to observe, speak and question openly. You can't do this hiding behind some sort of mask. If you pretend to be what they're looking for by acting the part (whatever that may be) you will end up disappointed.

I'll always remember the graduate who had an interview lined up at Saatchi & Saatchi. She got as far as the second interview and was then rejected. When she asked why, she was told that she had not been assertive or outgoing enough. At her next interview for another agency, she was determined to show them her personality and to act assertively. She didn't get the job. When she asked why, she was told, 'You're too assertive for us – you should try Saatchi & Saatchi!'

## How to behave at interview

- Practise a good, firm handshake.
- Smile at the start but not all the time.
- Be aware of body language. For example, don't cross your arms. Don't cross and uncross your legs.
- Gestures – in moderation – are fine. Try not to touch your clothes, skin, face or hair during the interview.
- Use plenty of eye contact but not a fixed stare.
- Be aware of how you are sitting. Once you've made yourself comfortable, sit still and don't fidget. Relax.
- Don't smoke at the interview or chew gum!
- Be ready with some intelligent questions – about the job you'll be doing, not the pay you'll be getting.
- Have opinions but don't be aggressive.
- Be prepared to answer any of the following questions: 'Why advertising?' 'Why this particular agency?' 'Why account handling/planning/media?' 'What ads do you love/hate?'

## An opportunity – not a test

Show them you want the job.

*Alan Morgan (1999)*

Think of the interview as a chance to show how good you are. No one is trying to test you, trick you or trip you up. Set out to enjoy the interview – whatever the outcome.

## Match yourself to the agency

Every agency is a brand in itself with its own personality. You have to match the brand in order to be what they're looking for. Only by doing your homework and going for as many interviews as possible can you find out what the agencies are really like. And, only by being yourself can they find out what you are really like and if you are suited to their agency – and vice versa. Remember that they are just as concerned about selling themselves to you as you are about selling yourself to them.

## Ask for feedback

A number of years ago a TV documentary programme was made following the progress of graduates during their second interview stage at the advertising agency DMB&B (now D'Arcy). The programme aroused a lot of criticism of the industry and the way it handled the interview process. As a result, the IPA (1996) published a document for ad agencies on best practice for recruitment. It contains advice to ad agencies on how to respond to applicants. For example, they are now recommended to give feedback to candidates on interview outcome.

An agency should always acknowledge your application and respond to your request for feedback. They might, for example, tell you that they think you're well suited to an advertising career – even though you may not have been right for their agency. If you don't get the job but were very close to getting it, you will probably be told.

If you get a rejection letter or don't hear at all, you have nothing to lose by giving the agency a ring and asking for feedback. This will help you to improve your technique for the next time. Remember that if you don't get a particular job, it may simply be a mismatch – you were not suited to that particular agency. You will find a job somewhere else.

## Ask for work experience

If you find, when you receive feedback, that you came very close to being chosen, then it's worth asking if you can have some work experience. Sometimes this can lead on to a job with the company – once you've 'proved your worth'.

## Always say 'thank you'

Always follow up an interview with a thank-you letter. If your interviewer has asked you to keep in touch or to contact them again at a later date, take them at their word. They are not just being polite. It pays to follow up if you have been asked to do so and it could lead to a job in the long term.

A graduate remembers her own experience:

"One thing I appreciated was that they rang everybody the next morning. It finished at about six o'clock on Friday night and they'd rung every single person – both those who had got jobs and those who hadn't. Some agencies only ring the ones who get the jobs, which is not so nice. "

### Getting into planning as a graduate trainee
Advice from an ad agency planner:

"I applied to all the agencies listed in the IPA Factfile with vacancies in planning. I wrote to all eleven agencies and after a series of interviews I was offered a place on the graduate trainee scheme of my current agency as a trainee planner.

### 'Planners and account handlers are worlds apart'
Bear in mind that rejections from agencies more often than not mean that you do not fit in with the agency atmosphere rather than not being capable of the job. Start by finding out the agencies which you would feel the most comfortable working with. Beware agencies which have a very strong creative department – they often impinge on traditional planning space and the job becomes more like that of a brand manager.

Dual roles (account manager/planner roles) are useful for getting an overview of the industry but it is far better to specialize in one field – it improves your chances of future employment. I also believe that planners and account handlers are worlds apart – one is essentially a thinking role, one a business position.

### 'Believe in yourself'
Keep going – never be disheartened. There are more ways into the industry than graduate schemes – for example, through media, research agencies and the client side. The most important thing is to find out if this area is right for you and to believe in yourself. No one expects you to be a rocket scientist when you first start – it takes two years to gain the basic experience you need to be a good planner, and your employers know that.

### 'Don't tie yourself in knots'
In interviews, prior research into the agency is crucial. Find out recent ads – work out which ones you love and hate and why. Don't be afraid to criticize an award-winning ad.

Above all, don't panic if you don't know the answer to a question. Be honest. Ask for more info or clarity – don't tie yourself in knots. It is better to suggest how you might go about finding the information you need for a good answer than to guess.

They want problem-solvers, people who find new routes. As long as you point them in the right direction, it doesn't matter if you don't take them to the solution.

*At the end of the day, agencies are looking for people who can make a campaign even better, not one who loves it as it is.* **"**

## Ten top tips for interviews

1. Be confident and arrive in a positive state of mind. It should be a two-way exchange of ideas.
2. Research the agency or company and try to get a clear understanding of the role.
3. Be ready to discuss the agency's advertising/products and how you think you could fit in.
4. Arrive at the interview on time.
5. At the meeting use positive body language and look them in the eye. Be dressed appropriately.
6. Try role-playing with a friend to try and focus your mind.
7. When responding to questions make your point immediately and don't waffle. If there is more than one person interviewing, direct your answer to the questioner.
8. Work out beforehand how to introduce your 'plus points' naturally into the conversation if not asked the right questions.
9. Highlight what you can do rather than what you can't. If you have no experience in a particular area, try to respond by mentioning your capabilities in a similar area. Be enthusiastic.
10. Make sure you listen (two-way communication) and understand what is being said. Don't fidget or yawn.

*Bob Lampon, Director, Making Waves*

## 'Try to have a little passion and flair'

Postgraduate student Carolyn Park describes her job application and interview experiences:

**"**I applied to BMP, DMB&B (now D'Arcy), Abbott Mead Vickers, Euro RSCG, WCRS, Lowe Howard-Spink (now Lowe), M&C Saatchi, Publicis, Leagas Delaney and Leo Burnett.

BMP and Leagas Delaney simply asked for CVs and covering letters and left the content up to the applicant. WCRS was by far the worst and would have taken days if I hadn't rushed it. They wanted everything: a biography, a headline for yourself, how you had achieved something. All this and more due in just before the new year.

Publicis and M&C Saatchi were the most enjoyable and most creative forms. Publicis asked for a day in the life of a five pound note, M&C for a Christmas card for the agency. DMB&B (D'Arcy) was also quite creative, asking for a favourite song lyric and how you would persuade someone to give you their worldly possessions as well as asking you to talk about good and bad adverts.

Lowe's offered me an interview. Their form was quite diverse, with questions on the Smirnoff ads and 100 words on anything you feel strongly about. They also wanted to know your favourite ad and the most interesting thing you've ever done – it was the same form as they had used last year!

### Why my application was successful in obtaining an interview

Lowe seemed quite down-to-earth and so I think they were looking for a good and intelligent all-round form. I linked my favourite ad to an experience I had had travelling and I spoke about the exercise we did on my course at Watford to rebrand the Tories. I wrote, 'I've never felt so passionate about the Tories before!' and I think this caught their attention. I don't think they wanted pushy people, and I think they wanted to hear intelligent, informed opinions.

My first interview was one-to-one with a recruitment consultant who told me she'd done a lot of recruiting for Lowe. She was very friendly and the interview took place in a small room at Lowe's office in Knightsbridge. First I was shown a show reel of their ads. The first question was intended to blow me out of the water: 'So what would you do next with the Smirnoff campaign?' It didn't really put me off but I couldn't answer it very well.

Later on in the interview, however, I made sure I returned to the question and gave her a creative idea but obviously to no avail. The next questions were about good ads/campaigns I liked (I had to tell her about three ads) and bad ads (I had to tell her about two). This part was quite easy and she seemed to like my choice of an obscure ad for BSM by Lowe.

At the end of the interview she asked me to give an autobiography. So I was busy trying to push everything I hadn't conveyed into it. Perhaps I said too much. It seemed strange to me that she was writing stuff down as I said it.

Then I went to meet a graduate trainee for an off-the-record chat. She was really friendly, down-to-earth and seemed to be doing in her training exactly what I am on my postgrad course. When I told her about the Smirnoff question she said that it was an awful question and that she couldn't have answered it! I left thinking that, whatever the outcome, it was good to meet such nice people in the industry and find that they are actually on your level.

### What I've learned from the experience

I think I may not have been successful at the interview because I was very chatty – I wasn't persuasive or direct enough, though it seemed to go well and the interviewer said that I was 'obviously a person with many interests'. It might have helped at interviews to think about what they were trying to gain from the question, not in order to change your answers completely and lose your personality but in order to be more focused and persuasive in your answer. "

## Postgraduate student Charlotte Middleton describes her interview experiences

"I applied to Lowe and BMP DDB. BMP asked for 'a letter about yourself as if you were writing to a friend'. The application form for Lowe asked for personal details and opinions on the first page: 'Describe yourself. Write 150 words about anything you feel strongly about. What's your favourite ad and why (in about 30 words – very little space given). What's the most interesting thing you've done?' Again, with a small amount of writing space.

On the second page you had to write a critique of the Smirnoff campaign:

a) On the print ad which was shown on the form.
b) Show awareness of other Smirnoff campaigns at the cinema and link them to the press ad.

### *Why my application was successful in obtaining an interview*
I thought about the questions before writing anything on the form. I didn't rush to complete it in one night. Some good ideas/phrases would come at different times, so I just scribbled ideas on a rough scrap of paper. I think they were looking for sharp, focused opinion which got to the point – fast! They made this clear by the fact that such little space was given.

### *The interview process*
I didn't meet any other candidates while waiting. I think they deliberately spaced out the interviews so that we wouldn't feel intimidated by anybody else we met. The atmosphere was very friendly, right from the start. The receptionist was very welcoming and excellent at putting me at my ease. I was interviewed by a consultant brought in by Lowe who has a very close working relationship with the agency and has been conducting interviews for them for years.

There was a very relaxed tone to the interview. I was offered a drink and then asked to watch the agency show reel. The last ad shown led on to the interviewer's first question: 'Where do you think Smirnoff should go next with their campaign?' I discussed some of the answers on my form and talked about the Royal Mail campaign I had said I liked. I was asked to name five of my favourite ads in quick succession.

The interview lasted 50 minutes but seemed much quicker. Afterwards I was taken to meet one of the graduate trainees in an informal capacity to ask them about their experience of the training scheme and the agency. The girl I spoke to had been a teacher for two years before applying to Lowe. In her year they took four graduates – three girls and a boy. I was actually in the agency for nearly two hours.

### Rejected but not dejected

I'm not sure why the interview wasn't successful. It was so informal, it was actually difficult to gauge because of the friendly tone. I think that perhaps I didn't have the right background or experience. 'Graduate trainee' can refer to anyone who has a degree, whether or not they have just completed it. I didn't realize that a lot of people go into advertising as a career change rather than as an initial career decision. I received a very friendly rejection letter which said that the standard of applicants was higher than expected this year – they were only taking twelve candidates down to the next (and last) interview stage.

When my postgrad course has finished I plan to try and get some more work experience and write speculative letters. Hopefully, I will have heard from the International Advertising Association about possible placements in the USA. **"**

*Charlotte is now working as an account manager for an advertising agency.*

## One graduate's experiences of three different interviews

It's quite rare to get people who find a job at their first interview. It normally takes two or three goes to get it right.

*Alan Morgan (1999)*

Jamie Maker, postgraduate student:

### 1. J. Walter Thompson: 'Putting me under the microscope'

Length of interview: 30 minutes.
Interviewed by a senior account director and a previous graduate trainee.
Applications received: 4500.
First interview: 180.
Second interview: 40.
Graduate trainee positions: 6.

**"**I was first greeted by the receptionist along with two other interviewees. The three of us were taken upstairs, where two more receptionists offered us drinks before we were interviewed. In the waiting room there was a television showing the TV ads JWT were responsible for.

I was the last to be taken to my interview. A suited senior account director greeted me with a smile and a firm handshake before taking me into a room, where I was introduced to a previous graduate trainee. They both put me at my ease and offered me drinks.

They then asked me why I had chosen advertising as a career and what I thought advertising was. They asked me what skills I thought were needed for an account manager. This was followed by asking me if I saw the show reel in the waiting room and which of the ads I liked. After choosing an ad, I then had to discuss who I thought it was aimed at, whether I thought it was successful and what the ad said about the brand.

I was shown a recent Boots print ad which was in among many other JWT print ads scattered on the table. I was given time to read it and then I was asked who I thought were the target audience, whether it was successful, what it said about the brand and in what paper or magazine I would have found the ad. They then put me in a scenario where I was the account manager on the Boots account and the client had phoned me to say that he didn't like the print campaign and that I didn't understand Boots at all. How would I deal with it? Finally, they showed me the recent RAF TV campaign and asked me the same questions again. I was then asked if I had any questions.

Overall, I thought the interview went quite well, even though I hadn't really expected the questions they asked. The senior account director asked most of the questions and was really putting me under the microscope, which didn't really put me at my ease. The female executive, who had been a graduate trainee three years before, was friendly and was making notes most of the time.

I received a letter the following Monday telling me that they would not be inviting me to a second interview. I believe I wasn't asked back because I was not suited to JWT. **"**

### 2. Duckworth Finn Grubb Waters: 'The friendliest agency in the world'

Length of interview: one hour. Two twenty-minute two-on-two interviews with two account managers/planners, followed by a tour of the agency by previous graduates.

Applications received: 1000.

First interview: 40.

Second interview: 10.

Graduate positions: 3.

**"**This is the friendliest agency in the world. Everyone seemed really happy to be meeting me and was interested in what I had to say.

We were first greeted by the secretary, who took the three of us upstairs, where we waited to be interviewed. The first interview concentrated on my advertising knowledge. What is advertising? Why have you chosen advertising? What skills are needed for an account manager?

I was then asked four marketing/advertising questions, which was just to see if I had an understanding of brands, target audience, media, etc. I have to point out that these were quite tough questions but, as I am always told, there is no right or wrong answer – they were just interested in what you had to say.

I was asked before the interview date to bring in what I thought was a good ad and what I thought was a bad ad. In the first interview I was asked to show my good ad. They asked me about the target audience, media placement and why I thought it was good. They finished by asking what career interested me within the advertising business and where else I had applied.

The second interview was with two other account managers/planners, and they were concentrating on my CV and activities not involving advertising. I then had to show my bad ad and give them my reasons why it was bad. I then had to act as an account manager for the product and sell the ad (which I had just criticized) to the client. Finally, they asked me four difficult questions. How would I persuade my friends to go to church? How would I persuade my friends not to take Viagra? They had a big list of questions and picked them out at random.

After both interviews we were shown around the agency by the graduate recruits from last year, who were really friendly and answered any questions we had.

A week later I received a letter telling me that I was not to be invited for a second-round interview, which really surprised me because I thought it went really well and would have been the ideal place for me to work. I was asked in the letter to phone them back for feedback, which I did. It was explained to me that they thought I'd be better suited to media which is why they were not offering me a second interview. The account manager I spoke to then sent my CV to media agencies in London recommending that they should interview me. As a result I got three interviews at media agencies. **"**

### 3. Saatchi & Saatchi: 'A really enjoyable interview'
Length of interview: one hour. Interviewed by two senior account managers/ planners.
First interview: 300.
Second interview: 29.
Graduate trainee positions: 6–8.

### *First interview*
**"**Everyone was really friendly and greeted me with a smile even though it was the end of the day. I was taken into a room with one other interviewee, where we were met by the two interviewers, who explained what would be happening at the interview.

The first one-to-one concentrated on my CV, achievements, leadership skills, organizational skills, etc., and I was asked for examples.

The second one-to-one was more about advertising – what I wanted to do, why advertising, my favourite ad and why it was my favourite. It was very similar to the other two interviews. They also asked me what accounts I would like to work on if I worked for them.

We finished off with both lots of interviewers and interviewees in the same room. We were asked to select a poster/print ad from a pile on the table and sell the ad to the other interviewee. After this we were invited to ask questions.

Less than two weeks later I received a phone call inviting me to a second interview, which would take place over two days, a Friday and a Saturday.

*Second interview*

This began at noon on the Friday and ended when the meal finished in the evening. We were first given name badges and a pack that contained all the information for the next two days – except what you would be doing on the Saturday.

All 29 of us were taken to a room where personnel, the graduates from the year before and one of the 'top guys' – Adam Crozier – talked to us about being a Saatchi graduate and about Saatchi & Saatchi.

We then had to complete a short personality profile and a written test, after which we were separated into our groups and sent to a room.

I was a member of a group of six. Two senior guys watched our presentations and then gave us group exercises. Throughout the rest of the day and all day Saturday, we were observed performing the team exercises that they gave us to do.

This was a really enjoyable interview. It never felt as though they were trying to catch us out or trick us. The people there were great, easily approachable and eager to talk to you.

The next day I received a phone call from Saatchi & Saatchi offering me a job, which I was pleased to accept. **"**

*Jamie has been working at Saatchi & Saatchi since this book was first published.*

## 'It's a temptation to want to sell yourself' – some last word advice

To students I'd say, by all means pass your course but do other work as well – such as work experience and job applications if possible. Despite the questions on the forms, try not to write in a stuffy, textbook way. Try to let a little passion and flair come through the writing.

*Carolyn Park*

To be oneself. Not to succumb to the psychological restrictions such things put on people. Have fun!

*Liam Cronin (former advertising student,*
*now working as a media planner/buyer for a media independent)*

Go for as many application forms as you think you can possibly do *well*. It's the most frustrating experience to spend time on something just to receive a standard rejection letter some weeks later.

Don't be afraid to *listen* at interviews – it's a real temptation to want to sell yourself and talk continuously. They want to see evidence that you can take in information and give a considered, thought-out response – they don't try and catch you out with trick questions.

*Charlotte Middleton (former advertising student,*
*now working as an advertising agency account manager)*

First, when you get to an interview, prepare well. Do your homework. Understand the agency, its clients, its culture and familiarize yourself with its brands. Take examples of advertising you really like, explain why and second-guess the brief. Best of all, choose one of the agency's campaigns. Remember that agencies are full of egos that enjoy a vigorous massage.'

*Gareth Morgan, Marketing Manager, London Taxis International*

Answer the questions you are asked. Elaborate but don't ramble. Ask *them* questions – the interview is just as much for you as it is for them.

*Alan Morgan (1999)*

I always try to look for the team player with personality. I am hoping that they are being true to themselves and not trying to play a part. I watch the body language and responses when talking about my company and the role. You can always tell if they're listening and understanding. Enthusiasm is the key – when talking about themselves, their experiences and the reasons they want the job.

*Bob Lampon*

Know your stuff – have an opinion on the company's advertising and advertising in general. Be professional at all times – dress, manner, speech, etc. Be personable – a lot of people say that the way you choose someone to work with is by asking yourself, 'Could I spend a five-hour train journey with this person?' Be yourself – all agencies have different types of people they're 'buying'. You just have to find the right agency.

*An account executive, Saatchi & Saatchi*

## Starting salary for graduate trainees

This varies from agency to agency. Saatchi & Saatchi appear to be at the top end of the market with their offer of £17,250 (2001). Some agencies offer much less. However, it's important to bear in mind that salaries are reviewed on a regular basis and will increase depending on your ability not on the length of time you spend with a particular agency.

According to a recent IPA survey of industry salaries (2001), on average, trainees working at medium-sized to large London ad agencies earn between £14,250 and £16,800 in their first year. You might expect to earn less outside London or if you were working for a small company.

## What next if you don't get accepted for graduate training?

It may feel like it, but it's not the end of the world if you don't succeed in finding a graduate training place. *There are many other routes into account handling.* It's only one of the many jobs in the industry – you may find you are better suited to one of the others. Think about taking a postgraduate course (Chapter 13) or finding work experience (Chapter 15). Remember, most people working in advertising today did not start out as graduate trainees.

## Ten things I wish someone had told me about job-hunting

1. You won't get the first job you apply for.
2. Or the second.
3. Or the tenth.
4. And maybe not even the 50th.
5. Having a degree – even if it's in something to do with media or communications – doesn't guarantee you an interview.
6. Angle each letter – and every CV you send out – to each job.
7. Sometimes any job – even if it's not where you really want to work in the long term – is better than no job at all, providing it's related to what you really want to do.
8. Don't get rejected by rejection – keep coming back. Show them you're hungry for it – but not starving!
9. An interview is just the beginning.
10. Use everyone you know and don't be too proud to ask for help.

## Recommended routes

- Postgraduate courses (see Chapters 13 and 14).
- Work experience (Chapter 15).
- Website for the American Association of Advertising Agencies (www.AAAAdvertisingjobs.com).
- John Hartman Center for US Advertising and Marketing History (http://scriptorium.lib.duke.edu/hartman).
- Advertising jobs in India (www.adjobz.com).
- Milkround Online (www.milkround.co.uk).
- Ogilvy & Mather (Worldwide) (www.ogilvyone.com/jobs).
- www.monster.com
- Prospects – information about postgraduate courses and universities (www.prospects.csu.ac.uk).
- www.careerbuilder.com
- Directory of Postgraduate Studies (www.postgrad.co.uk).
- Jobs Unlimited (*Guardian* newspaper online job search) (www.jobsunlimited.co.uk).
- Job-seeker information (www.aboutwork.com).
- CV advice (www.monsterboard.com).
- Employment Service Direct: 0845 6060 234 (www.employmentservice.gov.uk).
- *Campaign* Live (www.campaignlive.com).

- Ad Agency websites (see Directory)
- Graduate salaries and vacancies: IES (Institute of Employment Studies), 01273 678322.
- Association of Graduate Recruiters: 01926 623236.
- High Fliers Research: 020 7428 9000.
- The London Graduate Recruitment Fair (www.careers.lon.ac.uk).

For information on ad agencies and advertising, you can make an appointment to visit the library of the Advertising Association (AA). The AA also publishes its own guide, *Getting into Advertising*.

The Advertising Association
Abford House
15 Wilton Road
London, SW1V 1NJ
020 7828 2771
www.adassoc.org.uk

## Recommended reading

The IPA Graduate Factfile, which is available from their website: www.ipa.co.uk

Byrne, J. (1987) *The Headhunters: A Provocative Look at the Corporate Search Business*. Kogan Page.
Krechowiecka, I. (1998) *Net That Job*. Kogan Page.
Krechowiecka, I. (1999) *Using the World Wide Web to Develop Your Career and Find Work*. Kogan Page.
Perkins, G. (1991) *Snakes or Ladders? An Ambitious Executive's Guide to Headhunters and How to Handle Them*. Pitman.
Sarch, Y. (1999) *How to be Headhunted*. Random House.
CSU (n.d.) *Making Applications*. Higher Education Careers Service Unit (0161 277 5271).

# 13 The right course for you

> It's what you put into a course that determines how much you get out of it.
>
> *A postgraduate student*

## How to know which course is right for you

This chapter outlines information on HND, degree, postgraduate courses and – for those of you who know in what direction your interests lie – information about courses in sales promotion, direct marketing and brand management.

The details given here are by no means comprehensive and I recommend that you find out as much as you can about all the courses available in your own particular area of interest. Some of the routes you can use are given at the end of this chapter.

## Are qualifications really necessary for a job in advertising?

As you have seen from the previous chapters, work in advertising is highly sought after, very demanding and extremely competitive. Agencies receive hundreds of letters every week – and thousands of applications for graduate training. Companies, therefore, can afford to pick and choose their employees – so anything you can do that will give you the edge over other applicants is likely to be more helpful in getting you a job.

## What kind of degree do agencies favour?

> A good grade from a degree course – from any university – shows you've got discipline and that you can apply yourself.
>
> *Andrew Croft (1999), Director, Agency3*

> Although it is obviously important that they have reached a certain level of education, I am not biased towards the academic high achiever. The ability to communicate is my overriding criterion.
>
> *Bob Lampon, Director, Making Waves*

For certain jobs – graduate training, for example – a degree is an essential requirement. However, most ad agencies are not too concerned about what subject you have studied. It certainly does not have to be in an advertising- or marketing-related subject for you to be considered for a job in the industry. Sometimes an advertising degree can even be a disadvantage, as some employers seem to prefer candidates who have studied other subjects, or worked in a totally unrelated area, before choosing to work in advertising. As you have seen from earlier chapters, agencies tend to be more interested in you as a person – in your interests and your experience of life – and of course they expect you to be passionate about advertising.

Don't imagine that agencies won't be interested in you if you are a science, maths or law graduate. You have exactly the kind of problem-solving and analytical skills that employers are seeking. Don't assume either that agencies will be bound to be interested in you because you have some kind of advertising-related degree. Agencies look at the person as a whole – your determination, enthusiasm, personality and aptitude. You'll need to be able to convince them that you are worth employing – that you have something to offer *over and above your qualifications.*

> Too many people we see think that just by coming out of university and getting an interview means they've got the job. *The hard work has just begun.*
> *Andrew Canter (1999), Head of Broadcasting, MPG*

## What skills do I need?

Many courses today offer invaluable help in CV writing and interview practice, and give you opportunities to practise your presentation skills. These interpersonal skills are an essential requirement to all employers – and to you. They will help build your confidence and be an asset to you when you start job-hunting. In addition, computer literacy is now also almost an essential requirement for any job.

> Young people entering the business will need to be familiar with all aspects of new developments and have strong IT capabilities.
> *Archie Pitcher CBE (1999), President IAA UK Chapter*
> *and Past President Ogilvy & Mather London*

Most advertising employers say that they want people who can 'hit the ground running' – who are able to work without supervision from day one. Therefore, courses that are all theory may not be the best option. Ideally, you want a course that gives you insight into the advertising business and the practical skills to do the job.

> It's about handling pressure, stress and managing deadlines.
> *Andrew Canter (1999)*

## To specialize or not to specialize?

If your course is too narrow it may not give you enough scope when you come to look for a job. Many recruiters now say that they prefer all-rounders to specialists and that they would like to be able to employ people who have a knowledge of areas other than their own. It's quite useful to be able to employ a media planner who also knows about the creative side, or a copywriter who understands strategy, planning and media. Your colleagues and clients will certainly appreciate and respect you more if you understand their subject area and can talk to them with some knowledge about their specialism. Agencies also like you to have some understanding of business if possible.

If you choose a broad-based course, it not only helps you to discover what area you are interested in but also to realize what area you definitely do *not* want to work in! However, if you know that you are interested in a specific area such as sales promotion, copywriting or direct marketing, then you may like to choose a course that is focused on your specialist area.

If you want to work as a creative, the only qualification you will need is the ability to have ideas and be able to express them.

> The Academy of Life is where I've learned to do my job. There are no bits of paper for creatives. You've got to sell your uniqueness.
>
> *Paddy Hall, Art Director, Lowe Direct*

## Is it worth doing a postgraduate course?

Some students go on to do a postgraduate qualification and this can certainly enhance your chances if you have not been successful in finding a job straight from university. As one student put it:

> It puts you ahead so much in knowledge and in the jargon, but where it really does help is that people look at it . . . you've got something as opposed to someone who's just come out of college with, say, an English degree. It gives you the edge on other candidates. I've got friends who've just finished university who are going for the same kind of advertising jobs as me. They moan at me saying 'Oh yeah you've got this advertising course . . . you're going to be much more employable and they're going to interview you first.' That's the way they see it and that's how the employers may see it as well.

It is true that some employers value the extra layer of 'selectivity' – the fact that a student was selectively chosen to enter a postgraduate course and went through an assessment process to gain a successful qualification. It is also fair to say that some ad agencies do not perceive training courses, however good they are, as having the same value as the agency's own courses or the experience of employment in an ad agency. However, if you are unable to obtain work experience or get a place via graduate training, then a postgraduate course could be the answer. If you choose with care, it will also help you to gain those valuable skills you need to 'hit the ground running' – an essential requirement for most industry jobs today.

## What about media studies?

> More media studies graduates get jobs in management positions across a whole range of industries than other graduates in humanities or social sciences.
> *Peter Golding (1999), Chairman, Association for Media, Cultural and*
> *Communication Studies*

Many students take a course in media studies in the mistaken belief that this will lead to a job in an advertising agency, although, according to Golding and Kilgarriff (1999), 'a general media studies degree is not a surefire route to comfortable employment in a glamorous occupation'. A media studies course may help you in your analytical and interpersonal skills but it is unlikely to give you the knowledge and experience necessary for a career in advertising.

In the media industry, and also in advertising, there is general scepticism as to the value of college courses in media studies. As John Humphrys (1997) said when interviewed in the *Guardian* Media supplement about his career: 'If I were doing it again I'd go to university. I would not do a media studies course. Better, surely, to do a more rigorous degree and maybe a postgrad media course later.' Julie Burchill (*Guardian*, 2001) goes even further: 'Each year thousands of people with no talent for communicating whatsoever emerge [from university] with media studies degrees.' On the other hand, according to Richard Kilgarriff (1999), Head of Programming for Rapture TV: 'A good media studies course will give you some basic tools, although it can't prepare you for the cut and the thrust of the real world.'

## How important is technology?

According to the Open University (2001), '50 per cent of captains of industry say technology is the top skills requirement in 21st century business.'

New media degrees range from the highly technological to the mainly creative – some of the available options are listed later on in this chapter.

## Advertising sells

Advertising seems to be the new buzz word in universities. You only have to look at the UCAS clearing list (and some of the courses listed towards the end of this chapter) to see the proliferation of subjects now attached to the word 'advertising'. Without wishing to appear sceptical, I can't help wondering how much 'advertising' you're going to get with your English, Languages, Law, Psychology and so on. My advice would be to investigate the content of any course you're considering very carefully. Obviously, there are other factors to consider, such as how far you will be from home, the availability of accommodation and the kind of social life you can expect.

## Do your own 'SWOT' analysis

There are many considerations to be taken into account when choosing a course. You might like to conduct your own personal SWOT analysis – strengths, weaknesses, opportunities, threats – to help you decide which would be the right course for you.

Here are some of the questions you might want to ask yourself – or better still, the course tutor – when making your choice:

- Has the course been in existence long?
- What kind of reputation does the course have. Is it known in the industry?
- How long is the course?
- Is it full time?
- Do you want to study while you are working? If so, choose a part-time, weekend or evening course.
- Do you know that you want to work in a particular area? For example, direct marketing or sales promotion.
- How much of the course content is advertising specific?
- If the course is more general, does it cover enough advertising-related topics to be of use to you?
- Does the course have industry and/or professional recognition?
- Are there any exemptions from professional examinations in case you decide to go on to further study?
- Success rate – what percentage of the students on the course pass the examinations?
- Does the course lead to a job? What are the employment prospects? What percentage of students find work in the advertising industry?
- Are any of the former students working in places where you would like to work?
- What are the course fees and are there any additional expenses you need to bear in mind, such as the cost of living away from home?
- What is your preferred style of study? Lectures or hands-on? Individual work or group work? Examinations? Continuous assessment? Or a mixture of both?
- Is the course practical or theoretical? What percentage of the course has a practical component?
- Does the course offer a work placement or help you to obtain one?
- Do the lecturers on the course have any advertising-related experience?

- What links does the course have with the advertising industry? For example, visiting speakers and visits to advertising agencies.
- What facilities are offered by the course? For example, library, computer and internet access.
- Do you get help with job applications, CVs and interviews?

# Professional courses

## The Communication, Advertising and Marketing Education Foundation (CAM)

The Communications, Advertising and Marketing Education Foundation is the examining and awarding body for the CAM Diploma. Tuition is provided by colleges throughout the UK in a variety of formats:

- daytime courses
- evening courses
- intensive courses
- distance learning.

### Study at your own pace

The advantage of the CAM Diploma is that you can study at your own pace – many candidates do so while working full time. A CAM Diploma is no guarantee of a job in advertising, but it can enhance your chances.

Some students consider it a disadvantage that CAM do not offer their own tuition. It is up to you to find a college that offers CAM courses or to take some other study route, such as distance learning. Full details of fees, entry qualifications, courses, content and colleges are available from CAM.

### The CAM Advanced Diploma in Communication Studies

This is the first level of the CAM Diploma for school-leavers and graduates. Subject areas include: marketing, advertising, PR, media, research, consumer behaviour, direct mail and sales promotion.

### The CAM Higher Diploma in Advertising

Graduates of the Advanced Diploma can take further modules in:

- management and strategy
- consumer advertising
- business-to-business advertising.

**The CAM Higher Diploma in Integrated Marketing Communications**

You need to have successfully completed the Higher Diploma in Advertising (above) and, in addition, the Higher Diploma in Public Relations.

The CAM Foundation
Abford House
15 Wilton Road
London SW1V 1NJ
020 7828 7506
www.camfoundation.com
info@camfoundation.com

## The Chartered Institute of Marketing (CIM)

- The CIM Certificate
- The CIM Diploma.

### The CIM Certificate

Subjects studied are:

- fundamentals of marketing
- principles and practice of selling
- economics
- statistics (quantitative studies)
- business law
- behavioural aspects
- financial aspects of marketing
- plus either practice of sales management and Certificate of Sales Management or practice of marketing and Certificate in Marketing.

### The CIM Postgraduate Diploma in Marketing

You are examined in four subjects including the main marketing case study:

- international marketing communications
- international marketing strategy
- planning and control
- marketing management (analysis and decision).

The Chartered Institute of Marketing
Moor Hall
Cookham
Maidenhead
Berkshire SL6 9QH
01628 427500
www.cim.co.uk
registrations@cim.co.uk

## Direct marketing

- The IDM Diploma
- The IDM Certificate.

The two-year Graduate Apprenticeship Programme (GAP) offers you the opportunity to work for a direct marketing company and study at the same time for the IDM Diploma. Successful candidates are placed with direct marketing companies and receive a graduate salary while working and receiving training. The idea is to produce well-rounded graduates and put them on the fast track to a direct marketing career – 'the future managing directors and pioneers of direct marketing' (Kate Woolf, 1999, Institute of Direct Marketing).

During the two years of the course the graduates take part in live campaigns for real clients. You'll also spend about a week at six different placements under the guidance of a senior member of staff. During this period you gain experience in the skills you will be using in direct marketing, such as computing, telemarketing, negotiation, account handling, media and production.

> The course allows you to do an account executive's job without the experience.
> *Kate Woolf (1999)*

In order to be considered for the scheme, you need to show that you really want to work in direct marketing, although it is of course possible – once you have qualified – to transfer your skills across to work in an advertising agency or any related business.

The Institute of Direct Marketing produce a useful free student guide to all the undergraduate and postgraduate direct marketing courses – some of which are listed below. They also have a job register that offers a free service to graduates. Chapter 9 gives you more information on a direct marketing career.

### How to apply

For more information about the GAP, send your CV to the IDM (address below) with a covering letter explaining your idea of direct marketing and saying why you think you should be considered for the programme.

### The Graduate Job Register

This offers graduates free access to the full range of career opportunities in direct marketing – by post or through the IDM Job Register website. For more information contact the education manager at the IDM.

The Institute of Direct Marketing
1 Park Road
Teddington
Middlesex TW11 0AR
020 8977 5705
education@theidm.co.uk

IDM Job Register: kasumi.corpex.com/users/idm/

The Direct Marketing Association
Haymarket House
1 Oxenden Street
London SW1Y 4EE
020 7321 2525

The IDM Diploma in Direct Marketing is offered at the following colleges:

Kings College London
Strand
London WC2R 2LS

Imperial College of Science, Technology and Medicine
Exhibition Road
South Kensington
London SW7 2AZ

Leeds Metropolitan University
Business School
Leighton Hall
Beckett Park
Leeds LS6 3QS
0113 283 2600
course-enquiries@lmu.ac.uk

A full list of colleges offering direct marketing courses can be obtained from the IDM.

### Diploma in Marketing, West Herts College

The CIM Diploma is offered on a part-time basis to practitioners in marketing and sales management. The modules covered are:

* analysis and decision
* planning and control
* integrated marketing communications
* international marketing strategy.

01923 812525
www.westherts.ac.uk

## Sales promotion

* The ISP Diploma
* The ISP Certificate.

Through the Institute of Sales Promotion you can qualify for the ISP Diploma – a recognized qualification for those wishing to work in sales promotion. You don't have to take time off work to do it as it's a distance-learning course supported by a series of evening seminars and tutorials. The training begins in January each year and takes three months. It covers the full theory and practice of sales promotion, including the law and codes of practice. The final stage involves working to a sales promotion brief. See Chapter 9 for more information on a career in sales promotion.

The Institute of Sales Promotion
Arena House
66–68 Pentonville Road
Islington
London N1 9HS
020 7837 5340

## Public relations

### The PRCA Diploma in Public Relations, West Herts College

A practical, full-time, vocational course which trains graduates for a career in public relations. It includes varied work placement experience and a visit to Barcelona. Assessment is mainly by course work with an emphasis on team working. Course content:

- creating and presenting public relations programmes
- corporate communications
- writing skills
- media
- public relations workshops
- marketing and communication
- management and organizational behaviour.

Employment prospects

Students from the course usually find their first job in PR soon after graduating. Normally, all are working by October.

Career opportunities

Graduates tend to start as account executives or assistant account executives in public relations consultancies, or as assistant public relations officers in-house within a company.

> The Watford Diploma gave me the skills and confidence I needed to launch my career in public relations.
>
> *Tim Callington, August.One Communications*

How to apply

The majority of students on the course hold a degree, although those with work experience may be accepted. All students are personally interviewed. Commitment to a career in public relations is important.

The Course Director
PRCA Diploma in Public Relations
Watford School of Business and Management
West Herts College
Hempstead Road
Watford WD17 3EZ
01923 812585
www.westherts.ac.uk
wsb@westherts.ac.uk

Institute of Public Relations
The Old Trading House
15 Northburgh Street
London EC1V 0PR
020 7253 5151

## BA (Hons) Public Relations, Bournemouth University

The only sandwich honours degree of its kind in the UK, this four-year undergraduate course includes a 40-week work placement in a public relations consultancy or an in-house public relations department.

Bournemouth University
The School of Media Arts and Communication
Talbot Campus
Fern Barrow
Poole
Dorset BH12 5BB
01202 524111
www.bournemouth.ac.uk
prospectus@bournemouth.ac.uk

# Advertising courses

## The Watford Postgraduate Diploma in Advertising, West Herts College

Begun in 1971, this 30-week full-time vocational course trains graduates for a career in advertising. It is the only postgraduate advertising course in the UK and the only course accredited by the International Advertising Association, which gives it worldwide recognition. Developed with support from the IPA, it is recommended by the CIM, CAM and many leading ad agencies, including Saatchi & Saatchi.

> I chose this course because it has a sound reputation. It is extremely practical and gives a good solid overview of the industry.
>
> *Liam Cronin, graduate on the PG Dip Advertising, 1998–9*

Successful completion of the course leads to the Diploma of the International Advertising Association and the Diploma in Continuing Professional Development awarded by BTEC/EdExcel. Watford Advertising Diploma students receive complete exemption from the CAM Certificate and the consumer advertising paper of the CAM Diploma (the highest grade of exemption granted by CAM), plus exemptions from the CIM Certificate.

> Most students who come on the course don't know what they want to do at the outset, except that they are determined to work in advertising. The course helps them to focus on what they want to do and decide which area suits them best.
>
> *Course tutor*

The course modules are:

- Advertising organization and management (including brand management, advertising strategy and planning).
- Consumer behaviour.
- Creative strategy and execution – copywriting, art direction and workshops in video or radio production.
- Media communications – media planning & buying and new media.
- Marketing, market research and sales promotion.
- Advertising presentation – CV writing, presentation skills, interview practice and IT.
- Campaign planning – the planning, development, execution and presentation of ad campaigns to ad agencies and client companies.

The course is very practical and gives you hands-on experience in working on case studies, planning and presenting campaigns, writing briefs, creating and producing ads and putting into practice many of the skills you would need in an advertising environment.

A main feature of the course is campaign planning, where students role-play ad agency teams, work to briefs set by top ad agencies and plan, prepare and present ad campaigns to real clients. There is also a varied programme of visiting speakers and agency visits.

> The course is the best introduction to advertising without actually doing the job.
>
> *Steven Rennie, account executive*

Industry links

Members of the course advisory panel include representatives of the IAA, IPA and directors of leading ad agencies. Students on the course benefit from its excellent links with the advertising industry – many obtain work experience and jobs through contacts made on the course.

Employment prospects

The course has an excellent employment record – the majority of its students find work in the advertising industry and many are working for the top 30 ad agencies.

> One of the best things on this course that really helped was being able to get in touch with last year's students, because that did help me get my job. If I hadn't had the experience of the Watford advertising course, I would have been completely out of my depth.
>
> *Graduate trainee, D'Arcy*

Career opportunities

Students on the course obtain jobs in account handling, planning, media planning and buying, public relations, creative services, TV production, marketing, market research, sales promotion, direct marketing/interactive advertising, copywriting and art direction.

> The course is highly regarded in the industry and helped me to walk straight into a job.
>
> *Claire Harrison (PG Dip 1997–8)*
> *European Marketing Co-ordinator, Aspects Computing*

Course assessment

Assessment is based on 60 per cent course work, 40 per cent examinations. There is continuous assessment in all subjects and examinations in media, marketing/market research, advertising and consumer behaviour.

How to apply

Selection for the course is based on a written assessment test on application and further assessment at interview.

The Course Director
The Postgraduate Diploma in Advertising
Watford School of Business and Management
West Herts College
Hempstead Road
Watford WD17 3EZ
01923 812591/2
www.westherts.ac.uk
wsb@westherts.ac.uk

# The IAA Diploma in Marketing Communications

Multinational agencies are becoming increasingly global and one of the reasons why the International Advertising Association's Diploma in Marketing Communications is important to you is that it will become a passport to jobs across the world.

The IAA's network includes more than 5,300 members in 94 countries. Each chapter has a president and each committee organizes its own programme of events. In the UK, for example, the Associates run a series of evening lectures, a three-day course in an Oxford college tackling a real-life advertising problem set by a real client, an internship programme, quizzes, Christmas party, football matches, etc. They also participate in the full programme of the chapter, which includes a distinguished speaker – usually an advertiser giving a case study at a monthly luncheon – presentation training, a business management course, a summer ball, Christmas lunch, golf day, debating group and – perhaps most important of all – networking.

The IAA's global mission is the defence of the freedom of commercial speech and it works closely with other official bodies in this endeavour.

*Archie Pitcher (1999)*

For further information about the IAA Diploma and the work of the IAA and the IAA internship program, contact:

The International Advertising Association (UK Chapter)
12 Rickett Street
London SW6 1RU
020 7381 8777

International Advertising Association
World Secretariat
521 Fifth Avenue
Suite 1807
New York NY 10175
212 557 1133
www.iaaglobal.org

## BA (Hons) Advertising and Marketing Communications, Bournemouth University

A three-year, full-time undergraduate course that includes a six-week placement in your second year. This theoretical course studies the management of marketing communication, with a particular focus on advertising.

Bournemouth University
Talbot Campus
Fern Barrow
Poole
Dorset BH12 5BB
01202 524111
www.bournemouth.ac.uk

### BA (Hons) Advertising and Marketing, Lancaster University

A three-year undergraduate course focusing on managerial practice.

### BA (Hons) Advertising, Economics and Marketing, Lancaster University

A three-year undergraduate business course that studies advertising in the context of economic analysis and competitive strategy.

Lancaster University
Lancaster LA1 4YW
01524 65201

### HND in Advertising and Marketing Communications, West Herts College

This two-year full-time course combines business with advertising, which helps give students the edge in a competitive marketplace. There's also the opportunity to progress on to the Watford BA in Advertising and Marketing Communications.
    Course content includes:

- marketing
- business strategy
- management information systems
- managing financial resources
- organizations and behaviour
- advertising
- media
- copywriting
- art direction
- direct response
- public relations
- sales promotion
- campaign planning
- a four-week work placement in the second year.

Skills development includes computing, presentations, negotiating and interview techniques. Foreign language study is also available as an option.

A good overall understanding of business practices and basic advertising skills.
*HND student*

### How to apply

Entry requirements are two A levels (minimum ten points), BTEC National or Advanced GNVQ with merit profile. Mature students (over 21 years) with relevant employment experience will also be considered. The main criteria for entry is a demonstrable commitment to work in the advertising and marketing communications industry, together with motivation and enthusiasm.

Applications may be made through UCAS or direct to Watford School of Business and Management at West Herts College – address below.

## BA (Hons) in Advertising and Marketing Communications, West Herts College

Developed in association with the University of Hertfordshire, the Watford School of Business and Management offers a one-year modular degree course for students who have obtained a marketing/advertising-based HND or related qualification. The degree builds on the core and specialist subjects in the HND programme and is entirely based at the Watford campus.

The course is conducted over two semesters with examinations at the end of each. The programme includes modules in business strategy, integrated marketing communications, advertising effectiveness, brand management and a dissertation.

### How to apply

Applicants must have obtained a marketing/advertising-based HND and achieved the necessary grades for progression. Those with industry experience and other qualifications may also apply. All entrants must complete a preparatory assignment (by post) before commencing the degree year.

Watford School of Business and Management
West Herts College
Hempstead Road
Watford WD17 3EZ
01923 812591/2
www.westherts.ac.uk
wsb@westherts.ac.uk

## Brand management

If you are looking to work on the client side of the business, most established companies offer their own training schemes and graduate recruitment programmes. You can research these by surfing the web – just look up the name of the company you are interested in working for. For example, Marks & Spencer, Unilever and Procter & Gamble all offer graduate training schemes.

### Procter & Gamble

Procter & Gamble (P&G), for example, offer excellent courses in brand management or sales management. These are intended for undergraduates and are held in the winter vacation so that your studies are not affected.

The courses are based around real-life case studies and are heavily team-based to reflect the reality of working life at P&G. You will get the opportunity to meet a wide cross-section of people from the company – managers from every level are actively involved in the courses.

All the courses are held in first-class accommodation. P&G pay for all your meals, travelling expenses and accommodation.

### Brand management

You will learn about marketing strategy, product development, packaging, launching a new brand and running a business.

### Sales management

You will learn about marketing, finance, persuasive selling, handling customer objections, communication, negotiation and presentation skills.

### P&G brands

| | |
|---|---|
| Always | Pampers |
| Clearasil | Pantene Pro-V |
| Fairy Liquid | Pringles |
| Head & Shoulders | Sunny Delight |
| Hugo Boss | Tampax |
| Max Factor | Vicks |
| Oil of Olay | Vidal Sassoon |

### How to apply

Preference is given to final-year students, from *any* degree discipline. Shortlisted applicants will be asked to sit a short verbal reasoning and numeracy test. Successful candidates will be invited for an interview. More information can be found on the P&G website, or write to P&G for the management application form.

Corporate Recruitment Manager
Procter & Gamble
Box 63
The Heights
Brooklands
Weybridge
Surrey KT13 0XP
www.pg.com/careers

## The *Guardian*/Whitbread Student Marketing Programme

This programme, which is open to all students – not just to those studying marketing – was set up to give undergraduates a grounding in marketing theory.

The course, which is offered in association with the Cranfield University School of Management, lasts four days and takes place in the Cranfield Management Development Centre. A wide range of topics is covered, including market research, new product development, branding, media planning and buying.

You have to compete for entry by writing a thousand-word essay on a set topic. The deadline is usually at the start of February. If you're interested, email: marketing.dept@guardian.co.uk for more information (Pandya, 1999).

# Courses in media production and new media technology

### Perth College

- SCOTVEC National Certificate in Media Studies: a one-year, practical, full-time course.
- SCOTVEC Higher National Certificate in Media Production: a full-time, practical, one-year course (part-time option available) for those wishing to pursue a career in the media.

Perth College
Faculty of Arts
Goodlyburn East
Crieff Road
Perth PH1 2NX
01738 621171

### BA (Hons) Interactive and Broadcast Media, Manchester Metropolitan University

A practical course giving students the opportunity to investigate a wide range of media, delivery systems, content, applications and target audiences. All students follow a common first year, after which they can choose from either interactive media design or broadcast media, or a combination of both.

Manchester Metropolitan University
Department of Communication Media
Chatham Building
Cavendish Street
Manchester M15 6BR
0161 247 1293

### BA (Hons) Media Studies, University of Ulster

A three-year honours degree integrating theoretical, critical and practical approaches to the study of media. The syllabus includes opportunities for production in video, sound, photography and computer-based media. Students can undertake an industrial placement in the second year.

University of Ulster
Coleraine
Co. Londonderry
Northern Ireland BT52 1SA
01265 324196

### BTEC National Diploma in Design (Multimedia), Weston College

A two-year, practical, full-time course for those wishing to design for the internet and CD-ROM.

Weston College of Further Education
Creative Arts and Design Department
Westcliff Annexe
Kewstoke Road
Weston-super-Mare
North Somerset BS23 2ER
01934 411517/529

### BSc in Multimedia Technology, Leeds Metropolitan University

The course is 50 per cent technology, 50 per cent creative, and includes the following modules:

- computer programming
- computer technology
- video production
- 3D graphic design
- music.

The course allows students to be very creative, but also has the technological underpinnings you would expect of a BSc degree offered in a school of engineering.

*Nick Cope (2001)*

0113 283 3113

### BSc in Multimedia and Technology, University of Greenwich

- digital-image processing
- photoshop
- digital video production
- website design
- CD-ROM production

- animation
- composition and musical creation
- creation of virtual worlds.

0800 005 006

## BSc in Web and Multimedia, University of Central Lancashire

- audio recording
- filming
- editing
- generating computer images
- producing CD-ROMs
- website design
- advanced computer graphics
- animation.

01772 201201

## BA (Hons) in Electronic Media Design, University of Sunderland

- web design
- 3D modelling
- animation
- interactive multimedia
- desktop publishing.

0191 515 3000

## University of North London
- multimedia and digital media
- ecommerce.

020 7753 3399
www.unl.ac.uk

## University of East London
- IT
- media and communication technologies
- media studies
- multimedia studies.

www.uel.ac.uk

# Creative courses

### The Watford Diploma in Copywriting and Art Direction, West Herts College

This course is designed for those who want to find work as copywriters or art directors. Students work on advertising briefs and come up with ideas for advertising campaigns on a daily basis.

Students on the course build up a portfolio of work, which is assessed by the course tutor and visiting creatives from the advertising industry. At the end of the course most copywriters have found art director partners, and vice versa. They are then ready to seek work as a creative team in the advertising industry.

Many famous creatives began their careers on this course, including Jeremy Sinclair of M&C Saatchi, who was a student on the Watford copywriting course in the 1960s. He went on to become one of the founders of Saatchi & Saatchi in 1970, the Executive Creative Director of Saatchi & Saatchi Advertising Worldwide and Chairman of Saatchi & Saatchi Europe. He is now a founding partner of M&C Saatchi.

#### How to apply

Competition for the course is fierce. Students who apply have to complete a rigorous assessment test designed to bring out their creative skills, and then undertake a gruelling interview process.

The Course Director
Diploma in Copywriting and Art Direction
School of Creative Industries
West Herts College
Hempstead Road
Watford WD17 3EZ
01923 812578

### Buckinghamshire University College

The following courses are available:

- BA (Hons) Graphic Design and Advertising. Course content: art direction, copywriting, media, advertising and account management.
- BA (Hons) Graphic Design and Illustration. Course content: printmaking, life drawing, animation and photography.
- BA (Hons) Graphic Design. Course content: editorial design, multimedia, packaging, typography, retail and corporate design.

This three-year, full-time course includes a placement, either in the UK or overseas. Many former graduates are currently working in top London agencies.

How to apply

The college has regular open days. Phone for more information about the courses available.

Buckinghamshire University College
Faculty of Design
Wellesbourne Campus
Kingshill Road
High Wycombe
Buckinghamshire HP13 5BB
0800 0565 660
www.buckscol.ac.uk

## PG Diploma in Creative Advertising, Falmouth College of Arts

Collaboration and teamwork are key to the creative process in most areas of media communication, and nowhere is this skill more important than in the advertising industry.

*Falmouth (1998)*

The college's degree and postgraduate programmes are validated by the University of Plymouth. Assessment is by course work – there are no examinations.

The one year, full-time programme consists of a 30-week academic year with four study blocks, each composed of one or more units. There are thirteen key subject areas: agency structure, audience and media, business skills, collaborative teamwork, creative thinking, critical judgement, design skills, historical and cultural studies, marketing, production knowledge, research skills, technology and writing skills.

How to apply

If you have a BA in graphic design or a similar field, you are ideally suited to becoming an art director. You don't necessarily have to know how to draw – an ability to express ideas visually is required. A BA in English literature, creative writing or any of the humanities is excellent grounding for a copywriter. Or maybe you're from a science background and enjoy writing. International students need to have an IELTS score of 6 and a fluent grasp of conversational English. Applications to the college by 30 April in the year of entry.

Falmouth College of Arts
Faculty of Design Studies
Wood Lane
Falmouth
Cornwall TR11 4RA
01326 211077
www.falmouth.ac.uk

### HND in Graphic Design and Advertising. West Thames College

London Road
Isleworth
Middlesex TW7 4HS
020 8568 0244

### SCOTVEC HND in Graphic Design, Perth College

A full-time, two-year, highly practical course for those interested in a media career.

Perth College
Faculty of Arts
Goodlyburn East
Crieff Road
Perth PH1 2NX
01738 621171

### Diploma of Higher Education and BA (Hons) Combined Studies in Art and Design, University of Ulster

A modular programme with a practical component of up to 85 per cent.

University of Ulster
Faculty of Art and Design
School of Design and Communication
York Street
Belfast BT15 1ED
01232 267240

### BA (Hons) Advertising, The Southampton Institute

Faculty of Media Arts
East Park Terrace
Southampton SO14 0YN
01703 319000

### HND/BA (Hons) Multimedia, The Arts Institute at Bournemouth

Wallisdown
Poole
Dorset BH12 5HH
01202 363218

### BA (Hons) in Graphic Design, St Martins College of Art and Design

St Martins College of Art and Design
020 7514 7022
www.csm.linst.ac.uk

**British Design and Art Direction creative workshops**

The D&AD advertising workshops are a well recognized route to a job in advertising (see Chapter 6 for full details). The workshops are held four times a year and each individual workshop lasts for six weeks. Last year, 800 applicants competed for the 80 places on the four workshops that were held during the year. Entry is by competition as follows:

- All applicants work to a competition brief that will be sent to them.
- Successful applicants are invited to attend the course – the judges' decision is final.
- Unsuccessful applicants receive a feedback sheet in response to the work entered.
- Successful applicants pay a course fee.

How to apply

Register with D&AD (address below) by application and payment of the registration fee.

Education Officer
D&AD
9 Graphite Square
Vauxhall Walk
London SE11 5EE
020 7840 1123
Fax: 020 7840 0840
www.dandad.org
info@dandad.co.uk

# Undergraduate and postgraduate marketing communication courses

**Bournemouth and Poole College**
- A level Diploma in Marketing
- HND/C CIM Certificate in Marketing
- CIM Advanced Certificate in Marketing.

Bournemouth and Poole College
Faculty of Management and Professional Studies
North Road
Parkstone
Poole
Dorset BH14 0LS
01202 747600

**BA (Hons) International Marketing Management, Bournemouth University**

This undergraduate programme provides students with foreign language and marketing skills in preparation for a career in international marketing.

Bournemouth University
Department of Management and Marketing
Talbot Campus
Fern Barrow
Dorset BH12 5BB
01202 524 111

**MA courses at Bournemouth Media School**

* Interactive marketing
* Broadcast and film management
* Corporate communication
* Radio production.

www.media.bournemouth.ac.uk
bmspgrad@bournemouth.ac.uk

**Manchester Metropolitan University**

* IDM Diploma in Direct Marketing
* Postgraduate Certificate in Marketing Management
* Certificate in Marketing Communications.

Manchester Metropolitan University
Retail and Marketing Department
Aytoun Building
Aytoun Street
Manchester M1 3GH
0161 247 2000

**BA (Hons) Communication, Napier University**

This course, which has a 10 per cent practical component, includes the study of IT, media law, production studies, marketing, corporate communication, advertising communication, marketing and public relations.

Napier University
Department of Print Media, Publishing and Communication
New Craig
Craighouse Road
Edinburgh EH10 5LG
0131 455 6161

**Lincolnshire and Humberside University**
- Advertising and business
- Advertising and communications
- Advertising and computing (internet technologies)
- Advertising and computing (multimedia)
- Advertising and graphic design
- Advertising and media production
- Advertising and media technology
- Advertising and management
- Advertising and marketing
- Advertising and PR
- Advertising and psychology
- Advertising and TV and film design.

01522 886622/01482 463950

**Luton University**
- Advertising and marketing communications
- Advertising and social sciences.

01582 734111

**Thames Valley University**
- Advertising with design for interactive media
- Advertising with digital arts
- Advertising with film and television studies
- Advertising with languages
- Advertising with media studies
- Advertising with marketing
- Advertising with multimedia computing
- Advertising with new media journalism
- Advertising with photography
- Advertising with radio broadcasting
- Advertising with sound and music recording.

0800 036 8888

**SCOTVEC HND in Advertising, Perth College**

A full-time, two-year course (with a 60 per cent practical component) aimed at those interested in a media career.

Perth College
Faculty of Arts
Goodlyburn East
Crieff Road

Perthshire
Scotland
PH1 2NX
01738 621171

## School of Communication and Creative Industries, University of Westminster

Full-time and part-time courses:

- MA Film and Television Studies
- MA Audio Production
- MA Communication
- MA Art and Media Practice
- MA Hypermedia Studies
- MA Design for Interaction
- BA (Hons) Photography and Multimedia.

Admissions and Marketing Office
University of Westminster
Watford Road
Northwick Park
Harrow HA1 3TP
020 7911 5903
harrow-admissions@wmin.ac.uk

## MA Marketing, Certificate in Marketing and BA Marketing Communications

These are available from:

University of Westminster
Faculty of Marketing and Business Strategy
309 Regent Street
London W1R 8AL
020 7911 5000

University of Lancaster
Lancaster LA1 4YW
01524 65201

University of Central Lancashire
Preston PR1 2HE
01772 201201

University of Strathclyde

- MSc/PG Diploma in Marketing
- MSc in International Marketing.

Postgraduate Office
University of Strathclyde
Department of Marketing,
Stenhouse Building
173 Cathedral Street
Glasgow G4 0RQ
0141 548 4590
www.strath.ac.uk/Departments/Marketing/Index.html

## MSc/PG Diploma in International Marketing, South Bank University

The Business School
102 Borough Road
London
SE1 0AA
020 7 815 7720

## Short courses at The London Institute

- Desktop publishing
- Multimedia
- Introduction to the internet
- Guide to Apple Macintosh
- Digital typography
- Guide to website production
- Design
- Photography
- Marketing/sales promotion
- Advertising
- Copywriting
- Press and PR.

The London Institute
London College of Printing and School of Media
10 Back Hill
Clerkenwell
London EC1R 5EN
020 7514 6500/6562
www.lcp.linst.ac.uk
www.lcptraining.co.uk

## Graduate programs (USA)

This list is by no means exhaustive. Check out the IAA website for details of the advertising and marketing communications courses in your State.

University of Colorado, School of Journalism and Mass Communication.

Emerson College, Global Marketing Communication and Advertising Program, Boston.

Iowa State University, Greenlee School of Journalism and Communication.

Kansas State University, School of Journalism and Mass Communications:
• BA in Journalism and Mass Communications (Advertising Sequence).

Michigan State University, Department of Advertising.

Northwestern University, Integrated Marketing Communications Program (MA degree programme).

Pepperdine University, Communication Division (BA in Advertising).

Syracuse University, S. I. Newhouse School of Public Communications.

University of Alabama, Department of Advertising and Public Relations:
• BA in Communication (major in advertising or public relations)
• MA in Communication (major in advertising or public relations)
• PhD in Communication.

University of Florida, Department of Advertising, School of Journalism and Communications.

Florida International University, School of Journalism and Mass Communication.

University of Georgia, School of Journalism and Mass Communication.

University of Georgia, Advertising and Public Relations Department.

University of Illinois, Department of Advertising:
• PhD in Communications (major in advertising).

University of Missouri, Advertising Department.

University of Nebraska–Lincoln, Advertising Department.

University of North Carolina–Chapel Hill, School of Journalism and Mass Communication.
• BA in Journalism and Mass Communication
• MA in Journalism and Communication.

University of Texas Advertising Programs.
*Sources: University of Texas website and IAA Accredited Institutes*

**Useful websites for job-hunting in the USA**

The International Advertising Association:
www.iaaglobal.org

University of Texas advertising information:
www.utexas.edu/world

Internships, USA:
The Job Resource (thejobresource.com)
iInternsnet.com
internshipsinEurope.com

Career Builder Network (USA):
careerbuilder.com
thewashingtoncenterforinternships.com
job-hunt.org
www.workthing.com
www.prsa.org

Interbrand (for brand training programmes and information about financial
aid/scholarships in the USA):
www.interbrand.com

John Hartman Center for US Advertising and Marketing History:
http://scriptorium.lib.duke.edu/hartman

## Recommended routes

- Institute of Practitioners in Advertising (www.ipa.co.uk).
- The Advertising Association (www.adassoc.org.uk).
- The London College of Printing (www.lcptraining.co.uk/short_courses.htm):
  020 7514 6569.
- International Advertising Association (IAA) (www.iaaglobal.org).
- www.workthing.com
- University and College Admissions Service (UCAS) (www.ucas.ac.uk).
- Information about grants and courses (www.merlinfalcon.co.uk).
- Directory of Postgraduate Studies (www.postgrad.co.uk).
- *Prospects*: information about universities and postgraduate courses
  (www.prospects.csu.ac.uk).
- The Open University (www.open.ac.uk and www3.open.ac.uk/courses/).
- Milkround Online (www.milkround.co.uk).
- BTEC/EdExcel (www.demon.co.uk/btec).
- St Martins College of Art and Design (www.csm.linst.ac.uk): 020 7514 7022.
- *Times* Higher Education Supplement (www.timeshigher.newsint.co.uk).
- Guide to education and training in Scotland
  (www.ed.ac.uk/~riu/GETS/index.htm).
- Further education in England (www.wwt.co.uk/colleges/colleges.html).
- UK education web pages (Eduweb)
  (www.rmplc.co.uk/eduweb/eduweb.html).
- London Careers Net (www.londoncareers.net).

## Recommended reading

Hart, N. and Waite, N. (1994) *How to Get on in Marketing*. Kogan Page.

*Media Courses UK*. An annual guide to media and production courses.

BFI Publishing
21 Stephen Street
London W1P 2LN
020 7255 1444

*Prospects Postgraduate Funding Guide*

CSU Ltd
Prospects House
Booth Street East
Manchester M13 9EP
0161 277 5200

*The Journal of Brand Management*

Henry Stewart Publications
Russell House
28–30 Little Russell Street
London WC1A 2HN

Henry Stewart Publications
North American Business Office
810 E. 10th Street
PO Box 1897
Lawrence KS 66044
USA

The *Guardian* supplement on jobs and courses (Mondays and Saturdays)
The *Independent* (Thursdays)
*The Times* Media (Fridays)

See Directory (Chapter 17) for more information about publications, agencies and websites.

# 14 Ask the students

Students who have recently studied on advertising and marketing communications courses tell you what was good and bad about them.

## BA (Hons) Cultural and Media Studies, The University of the West of England (Bristol)

Amy Hellerman

### Course modules
Year 1

Compulsory:

- Introduction to media studies.
- Introduction to cultural studies (practical).

Options

- Literary studies: ways of reading.
- Psychology: individual experience and social learning.

Year 2

- Popular culture.
- Approaches to the mass media: the era of the blockbuster.
- Understanding culture.
- Making meanings with the media: critical practice (practical).

Year 3

- Documentary and realist film and TV.
- Gender and sexuality in film and TV.
- Continuing production (practical).
- Dissertation.

### Percentage of course work to examination

Examinations in the first and second year accounted for 50 per cent. No examinations in the third year. Two timed assignments worth 20 per cent and the dissertation.

- First year: examinations in literature, psychology and media.
- Second year: understanding culture examination.
- Third year: timed essays under examination conditions for gender and sexuality and documentary and realist film.

### Percentage of the course with a practical component

Twenty-five per cent.

### What made you choose this particular course?

I wanted a media course which had practical elements but also a lot of theoretical parts – essays etc. I also particularly liked the fact that you could choose basically what you wanted – not *having* to do practical work and not having lots of exams.

### What other media courses did you consider? How did they differ from the one you are on now?

On reflection, I did not look that hard, although there seems to be more interesting courses now with the chance of a year's work experience, which I would have really enjoyed. I liked the courses at Sussex and Birmingham – again combining practical and theoretical elements.

### What's good about your course?

It gives an interesting grounding – a good understanding of how 'the media' operates. Also, I enjoy the cultural studies side – it makes you think about the relationship between media forms and modern culture. It is also good that particularly in the third year you can concentrate on different aspects of the media and continue using and improving practical skills with broad project briefs.

### What's bad about your course?

I wish I had the chance to do more practical work now (although I did realize how it was going to be). Also, it is a shame that our course does not offer work experience opportunities or connections for finding jobs in the field of media (again, it did not claim to). Finally, there is a lack of equipment/library – resources could be better.

### How relevant do you think the course will be in helping you to get a job?

I think it has given me basic practical skills and I have enjoyed the theoretical aspects of the course. It is not really designed to help in finding a job, although I know what areas of the media interest me now.

**What advice would you give to someone who is considering taking a media course?**

Think seriously about whether it is a practical-based or theoretical-based course you want. Think about what you want from the course (i.e. contacts and a specific skill/job or just a more general grounding).

## BSc in Business Studies with Marketing, University of Salford

Adam Baginsky

### Course modules
Second year

- Organizational behaviour
- Statistics
- Economics and marketing
- Management science.

Final year

- Corporate strategy
- Consumer behaviour
- International marketing
- Marketing communications
- Market research
- Marketing management.

**What percentage of the course has a practical component?**

Only the placement year (which is optional).

**What made you choose this particular course? What attracted you to it in the first place?**

I didn't know what I wanted to do, but business interested me. Business studies meant that there was a wide choice when it came to final-year options.

**What other courses did you consider?**

I didn't really consider anything else. I felt it was too specialized to go into one stream (e.g. advertising) at the beginning. Business studies kept my options open.

**What's good about your course?**

The project (20 per cent) in marketing management – very useful. It involved analysing an internet site and making recommendations. Because of my placement year I could see how useful the project is for students. In the final year so far – consumer behaviour, marketing management and market research. Interesting modules and applied to the real world.

**What's bad about your course?**

The second year was very much theoretical and there was little application to the real world. There were no options in the second year and some modules were of little or no relevance, e.g. statistics. We also had a couple of bad lecturers who need lessons in presenting. There was a lack of help in getting a placement. This has now changed and they do give help.

**How did you go about finding your placement?**

I made a list of all the companies that I could think of and called them to see if they took students on placements. I then sent a letter and CV to those who did.

**What work did you do on your placement?**

I was assistant to the marketing manager. I did research in specific projects for the director of marketing and the managing director. I placed advertising for hotels, had budget control of new hotel openings for marketing materials and ordering, gave support to hotel managers in marketing activities and updated the internet and replied to emails sent to the site.

**Did your placement make you more interested in a marketing career?**

Yes, very much. I enjoyed all the work and projects. I was lucky that the job entailed a wide range of marketing elements, e.g. advertising, finance, research, promotions, etc.

**How relevant do you think the course will be in helping you to get a job?**

Relevant in the fact that it's a degree and that it gives exemptions from the first two papers of the Chartered Institute of Marketing exams. Really, it's a necessity for some jobs, so for me it's very relevant, but a bigger factor is the year I worked.

**What kind of jobs do people get at the end of the course?**

Advertising positions, marketing and research.

**Do most people from your course go into media?**

From those I saw from last year and this year I wouldn't say that most go into media.

**What do you plan to do when the course has finished?**

Travelling – three months in South East Asia and then three months in Australia and New Zealand. I hope to find work in Australia in marketing or a related type job for a year.

**What advice would you give to someone who is considering taking a media/marketing course?**

I would recommend it. However, for someone who definitely wants to get into advertising, business studies is too broad a course. Going on a placement is advantageous and well worthwhile. Consider doing two six-month placements – one in an advertising agency and another in a job where you have to deal/liaise with an advertising agency, to give you an inside and an outside view. It would develop your skills that much more.

## The Postgraduate Diploma in Advertising, Watford School of Business and Management, West Herts College

Liam Cronin

### Course modules
- Advertising strategy and management (including brand management and planning)
- Media communications (including media planning/buying and sales promotion)
- Consumer behaviour
- Marketing and market research
- Advertising presentation (including presentation skills, IT, CV writing and interview practice)
- Creative strategy and execution (including copywriting, art direction and workshops in video or radio)
- Campaign planning (the planning, preparation, execution and presentation of advertising campaigns to ad agencies).

### What percentage of your course has a practical component?
About 60 per cent.

### What made you choose this particular course? What attracted you to it in the first place?
It has a sound reputation with employers.

### What's good about your course?
It is extremely practical and gives a good solid overview of the industry.

### What other advertising course did you consider? How did it differ from the one you are on now?
The MSc in Advertising at the Dublin Institute of Technology. It is a much more theoretical course.

### Have you had any work experience in advertising? If so, where?
Everyone on my course has the option of a week or more of work experience.

**What did you do in a 'typical day/week' on work experience?**

Began work at 9.30 a.m. Reported to the 'boss' and was given something to do. Work was often related to pitches being done by the agency. Time was allocated to pursue people of interest in the agency with what were probably most annoying questions!

**Did your placement make you more interested in an advertising career?**

Yes, because it gave me the opportunity to experience the environment at a top London agency – BBH.

**How relevant do you think your course will be in helping you to get a job and why?**

The course is helpful because it gives me an extra bit of experience ahead of other applicants.

**What kind of jobs do people get at the end of your course?**

Mostly graduate trainee positions or junior executive positions. Six people have found jobs already, although the course still has a month to go.

**Do most people from your course go into advertising?**

Yes.

**What do you plan to do when the course has finished?**

I hope to apply for as many jobs as possible in media (planning/buying) and hopefully be successful within two months after the course ends.

**What advice would you give to someone who is considering taking an advertising, media or marketing course?**

I believe a practical course is the better option.

*Liam is now working as a planner/buyer at a media independent in London.*

# The Watford Postgraduate Diploma in Advertising, West Herts College

Charlotte Middleton

**What made you choose this particular course?**

I was looking for a postgraduate course in advertising and found out about Watford from the Oxford University Careers Service. I was very impressed by the course prospectus and the fact that the course has an excellent reputation within the advertising industry.

## What's good about the course?

The variety – the course isn't just about ads, but looks at people's reactions to campaigns and how relevant advertising is to everyone regardless of whether they take an active interest in ads. There are opportunities to investigate other ad-related areas such as marketing, consumer behaviour and media – these all present new career opportunities that might not have been considered before the course. The course is very 'hands-on'. I feel so much more confident about presenting now!

## What advice would you give to someone who is considering taking an advertising course?

It's a great experience and can confirm for you whether you really are contemplating the right career direction. Alternatively, the course presents many other options (and contacts) in other related careers that may, ultimately, suit you better.

*Charlotte is now working as an account manager for a London advertising agency.*

# HND in Advertising and Marketing Communications, Watford School of Business and Management, West Herts College

Dan Chambers and James Muggeridge

## Course content

Marketing, business strategy, management information systems, managing financial resources, organizations and behaviour, advertising, media, copywriting, art direction, production, direct response, public relations, sales promotion and the option to study a foreign language. Plus a four-week work placement in the second year.

## What percentage coursework to examination?

Sixty per cent coursework, 40 per cent examination.

## What made you choose this particular course? What attracted you to it in the first place?

*Dan*: It was close to my home town. I knew Watford had a good reputation for advertising. I applied for university degree courses but was not accepted.

*James*: While doing Media A level, advertising was my favourite part of the course. When I found out that there were advertising courses it seemed like the natural progression. Watford was chosen because of its reputation.

## What other courses did you consider? How did they differ from the one you are on now?

*Dan*: Pure advertising degrees at Bournemouth, Lancaster and other universities.

They just concentrated on one subject rather than a range.

*James*: I wanted to be near London, so I kind of put all my eggs in one basket. If I had been rejected I would have applied elsewhere.

### What percentage of the course has a practical component?
*Both*: 20 per cent.

### What was good about your course?
*Dan*: It was very varied in subjects and most were relevant to the career I wanted to pursue.

*James*: An excellent introduction to a business environment and solid foundation for further studies in business. The work placement was very beneficial. Course subjects were diverse in some ways and tightly connected in others.

### What was bad about the course?
*Dan*: It was not practical enough – a little too much business and theory. A lot of the business was similar to what I had previously covered in my BTEC National.

*James*: Assignments all coming at the same time and having to do examinations!

### Did the course include a work placement and how long was it?
*Both*: Yes – four weeks.

### Describe a 'typical' day/week on your work placement.
*Dan*: I went to Media Campaign Services (MCA), a media agency dealing with media planning and buying. A typical day involved lots of telephone work contacting major newspapers/magazines for a variety of reasons. Research was another aspect. The placement made me more interested in an advertising career because I experienced a modern, lively and young working environment. I discovered that working in a media agency was not for me and that I was more interested in the creative side.

*James*: I worked as a creative at Saga holidays in Folkestone, organizing brochure layouts and images. As we only had the one client it was rather limiting and I was put off for a while.

### How relevant was your course in helping you to get a job?
*Dan*: Some aspects will help but I want to be a creative and getting a job will be down to me at the end of the day. West Herts College definitely broadened my knowledge of the advertising industry.

*James*: I want to work as a creative but the background to business was invaluable to a career.

### What kind of jobs do people get at the end of the course?

*James*: Very diverse – from creative to finance. Basically anything in the business world.

### What do you plan to do when the course has finished?

*Both*: Do a 'top-up' degree.

### What advice would you give to someone who is considering taking a marketing communications course?

*Dan*: Look at all the colleges/universities offering courses and visit them on open days to see exactly what the content of the course is. If you want to be a creative, pick a course with a high level of practical work.

*James*: It is hard graft and a stepping stone which can help you decide which direction to take in your career path. Two years' thinking will help you and it is a solid foundation on which to build.

## BA (Hons) Advertising and Marketing Communications, West Herts College

Sabrina Jhumann

### Course content

- Preparatory course (the summer before you start the degree course)
- Business strategy (two modules): 50 per cent coursework, 50 per cent examination
- Dissertation (two modules): 100 per cent coursework
- Integrated marketing communications
- Consumer behaviour
- Advertising effectiveness
- Brand management

60 per cent examination, 40 per cent coursework

### Why did you choose this particular course?

I chose this course as I have a great desire to work in advertising. I thought that studying a degree in advertising would enhance my prospects of securing a position within the industry.

### What other courses did you consider?

I considered doing a similar course at Southampton but I had already spent two years doing an HND in advertising at Watford, which I thoroughly enjoyed. I was familiar with the college and the tutors' high standards, so it seemed natural to continue my education in an environment I liked.

I was also aware of Watford's good reputation within the industry, not just in the UK but internationally, and the strong links it holds with them. This, together with the fact that many past students have gone on to become extremely successful in advertising, was one of the reasons I chose to study at Watford.

## What do you like about your course?

I think this course is good as it gives me an opportunity to study some interesting areas of advertising and marketing in greater depth. I am responsible for my own motivation and can work at my own pace, to an extent. Though completed work is independent, we are encouraged to research and prepare presentations for seminars together, which creates a good balance between working independently and with others. The tutors at Watford give a lot of help and support, even those who no longer teach you are willing to give you their time. The college also uses its links for the students' benefit – members of the industry visit the college to talk to students.

## What don't you like about your course?

The only problem I can really identify is that there is *no* practical work, but you are fully aware of that from the start. We have, however, written a creative brief and prepared and presented presentations on a wide range of issues, though these are not assessed. I also would prefer more emphasis on an advertising module throughout the year rather than the present business-orientated module. This is only the second year that this course has run, so I imagine they are learning as they go along. Changes were made this year from feedback they received last year.

## Where do students find work at the end of the course?

Many students in the top-up BA AMC have successfully completed an HND or similar, either at Watford or elsewhere, in marketing or advertising. Last year, the students who completed their degree appeared to follow either of these previous paths when seeking employment. This is only the second year of this course, so we will have to see what happens to our year. I do know that one person is now working in the marketing department of British Gas, two went to D'Arcy – one through graduate recruitment and the other through perseverance. Another is working for a large Watford-based flooring company in marketing and is jet-setting around the world. A few have taken a year out, some are temping while they decide what to do or are looking for jobs in agencies.

## Do you think your course will help you find a job in advertising?

I initially thought that having a degree in advertising would put me at an advantage over other candidates and show potential employers that I was enthusiastic and serious about wanting a career in advertising – but now I am not so convinced this is true. On the one hand my degree and the fact that I studied at Watford may be a plus point, and on the other it may be a disadvantage as agencies don't want 'ready-made account executives'. I hope I will be judged purely on academic merit and how I perform at interview. I think that when I start out in the industry, this course, together with the HND, will have provided me with a good background by having introduced me to advertising and will have given me an excellent foundation on which to build my future career.

# BA (Hons) Advertising, Southampton Institute

Dan Chambers and James Muggeridge

## Course content

- Persuasion and communication
- Advertising strategy development
- Research skills
- Art direction
- Major project
- Consumer studies
- Ad process/media industries.

## Percentage of coursework to examination

One hundred per cent coursework (one examination in advertising strategy contributed about 30 per cent of one subject).

## What made you choose this particular course? What attracted you to it in the first place?

*Dan*: It was a top-up to my HND, giving me a degree in one extra year. I didn't have enough points to stay on at Watford. However, Southampton Institute offered a more practical approach to their course, which was going to help me towards becoming a creative.

*James*: Southampton had a practical-based course, which is my strength, particularly as I wanted to follow a creative career path.

## What other advertising courses did you consider? How did they differ from the one you are on now?

*Dan*: I didn't have enough points to stay on for the West Herts College top-up. Watford's course content was more business-related.

*James*: Watford was too business-oriented for my career path and had too many exams.

## What percentage of your course has a practical component?

*Both*: 50 per cent. Many subjects required you to produce campaigns.

## What's good about your course?

*Dan*: A small class of about nineteen students. Many tutors had previously worked in advertising. Interesting and practical subjects, all of which had some relevance to my future career as an art director.

*James*: Lots of regular briefs set and regular creative teams visit to give feedback on ideas. Very practical and very useful.

## What's bad about your course?

*Dan*: It was the first year that it had run and some problems did occur. Art direction was only covered in the first semester – it would have been nice to have carried it over into the second. Some changes will now have been made!

*James*: Ten thousand word dissertation, as exams and essays are not my strong point. There were some teething troubles as it was the first year – I assume that these have been ironed out.

## Does the course include a work placement?

*Both*: No.

*Dan*: The course has links with BBH and four students used their Easter holiday for a placement there.

## How relevant do you think the course will be in helping you to get a job?

*Dan*: I learned much more about ad agencies' specific departments, and through visits from creative teams I was given a lot of valuable advice. Just because you have a degree, it doesn't guarantee you any job. It's all about you as a person and the people you know and get to know – contacts.

*James*: Seventy per cent relevant as all the creatives would go for a drink with us afterwards and tell us how they got in.

## What kind of jobs do people get at the end of the course?

*Dan*: Temping – to start paying off the debts! A variety of media-related jobs.

*James*: Creative to account planner to media buyer. All kinds of media-based jobs.

## Do most people from your course go into advertising? If not, where?

*Dan*: No. Only a few of us have teamed up as creatives. Some have gone into account executive positions, others work in media departments of TV companies and other media positions.

*James*: No. Some have drifted into television production, while others have gone into marketing.

## What do you plan to do when the course has finished?

*Dan*: Have already finished. Teamed up with James and we're putting a book together. We've started making contacts and visiting agencies to get work placements and a possible job.

*James*: We're in the process of visiting agencies for crits.

## What advice would you give to someone who is considering taking a marketing communications course?

*Dan*: Try to work out what job you want in advertising and base your choice around a practical or theoretical course. If you are positive about a career in advertising, start contacting agencies as soon as possible to make contacts – and to get your name remembered. Pester people for placements. If you don't ask, you don't get.

*James*: Make sure the industry is for you. It's fast and pressurized. Advertising is a very competitive business. After studying for three years, I have just realized how competitive. If you want to succeed, be tenacious and confident. Above all, have patience and faith.

Since completing this questionnaire, we have been very busy. We have visited about eight agencies now and our book has improved so much we are becoming quietly confident that we may be getting somewhere. After a little more work on our book we will start getting back to see creative teams for the second time.

*(Dan Chambers and James Muggeridge, 1999)*

*James is now working as a copywriter. Dan returned to Watford, where he obtained a place on the copywriting/art direction course. He is now looking for work as an art director.*

# 15 The value of work experience

If people have had work experience, it helps.

*Corinne Fahn, Personnel Assistant, Saatchi & Saatchi*

Twenty per cent of the people at Saatchi & Saatchi started on a placement.

*Carol Wilkins, former Strategic Planner, Saatchi & Saatchi*

In a survey of graduates (HEFCE, 1996) students generally concluded that work experience had been a crucial factor in their finding employment, rather than their degrees.

## Puts you ahead in the selection process

Students who have had work experience are often much clearer about what they want from a job and also what they want to avoid. Experience in applying for and getting a work placement can also put you ahead in the selection process (Lock, 1998).

Employers say that students who have been on a work placement understand the world of work better – the combination of both academic study and agency experience makes you much more desirable to them as an employee.

## Work experience or placement?

The term 'work experience' has been used throughout this book to describe any time spent working within an ad agency. However, it's a good idea to think about your choice of words when approaching companies for work. As far as agencies are concerned, a *placement* tends to be for a longer period and now will often mean paid work, whereas *work experience* might just be for a day, a week or perhaps two weeks and will normally be unpaid, although you might be reimbursed for your expenses.

## One of the best ways of getting into advertising

Work experience is known to be one of the best ways of getting into advertising. You do, however, need to be determined to find a placement/internship. Use any contacts that you have, however remote. If someone you speak to can't help you, ask them to recommend someone who can.

You can phone up the agency, write or apply online. I would recommend phoning first, following up with a letter and then phoning again if you don't hear. If you have someone's email address, it's always worth emailing them, although there's a good chance that your email will be deleted rather than read. However, it's worth a try and I know of quite few students who have managed to find work in this way.

## How to phone an ad agency

- Know who to ask for (so do your homework beforehand) or speak to their PA (personal assistant/secretary).
- Don't expect to get through first time.
- Persevere.
- Always be polite.
- If you're asked to phone again, do so.
- Don't phone more than twice in succession – don't be a pest.
- Don't expect the agency to phone you back – you will have to keep trying.
- If you leave a message, don't expect a response.
- The best time to get hold of someone is either first thing in the morning or early evening.
- Plan in advance what you are going to say and if necessary rehearse it beforehand.
- If you get through, speak clearly and not too quickly. Give them your name, mention your contact (if any), explain that you haven't spoken before and that you would be grateful if they could spare the time to . . .
- Expect to fit into your contact's schedule and not vice versa.
- If you arrange a meeting, phone on the day to confirm.
- Keep a note of all arrangements, contacts, etc.
- Always thank people afterwards for their help.
- It's sometimes a good idea to follow up a telephone conversation with a letter of confirmation or an email, depending on the circumstances.

## The advantages of work experience, a placement or intern program

- Familiarization with ad agencies – get your foot in the door of as many agencies as possible. Find out which agency suits you best – the ones you like and the ones you don't.
- The opportunity to make contacts, meet people. It's known that networking is far more likely to land you a job than if you answered an ad.
- The chance to put any skills you have into practice and to learn on the job.
- Looks great on your CV/résumé, far more impressive than stocking shelves in your local supermarket.
- Most agencies prefer to employ people who have had work experience.
- It's a fun way of discovering what area of advertising you're most interested in.

- You get to see the realities of day-to-day life in an ad agency and to find out if it comes up to your expectations.
- You find out whether you can work under pressure and to deadlines.
- The opportunity to see how things work in practice.
- Possible involvement in 'pitches' (when an agency attempts to acquire new business by making a presentation to the company concerned).
- You get to see the progress of an idea from the first briefing to the finished campaign.
- Gives you the opportunity to work as part of a team or to observe teams at work.
- It will confirm (or not) your determination to follow an advertising career.

## The right career for you?

If you are lucky enough to get work experience, don't expect to be paid. You will be fortunate if you are reimbursed for your travel expenses. Don't expect to be meeting clients or making ads. You are more likely to be making tea, collating paper, delivering parcels and ordering sandwiches. Even if you only end up photocopying and making tea, you will still experience the buzz and excitement of working in an ad agency and the opportunity to find out if it's the right career for you.

## Think of it as an interview

The secret of a successful work placement is to treat it as a one-week interview. Do everything you are asked to do, however demeaning you think it is, with a smile. However, don't imagine that you have to agree with everybody. If you are asked for your opinion, don't be afraid to give it. Use the opportunity of your placement to talk to people – do as much networking as you can. Make yourself useful so that they will want you back. Or, better still, that they won't want to let you go.

### How to turn your work placement into a job

Carol Wilkins:

"Approximately 20 per cent of the people at Saatchi & Saatchi started on a placement. Here is how to turn a placement into a job offer:

Once you are in a placement decide that you will remain on placement until either the agency you are in, or some other agency, gives you the job you want. The great advantage of applying for jobs from within an agency is that you can put that agency's name at the top of your CV/résumé. You do not have to tell prospective employers that you are not being paid.

*Satisfy needs*
Get under the needs of the people you are working with and lift them up.

When you are on placement you will be assigned to a particular person. Figure out what they need and give it to them. Make their life so easy and make them look so good that they never want you to leave. Remember that the only way to make money is to satisfy people's needs. If you want a job in advertising you will have to become particularly adept at this.

### Total commitment

You will need to be totally committed. If you want to turn a placement into a job, mentally assume that you have the job anyway. This will mean that you will have to deliver work that is as good as, but preferably better than, those around you. Clearly they will have more experience and knowledge than you, so the only way you will be able to keep up to speed is to work harder than them. I worked 90 hour weeks for the four weeks of my placement. Obviously you can't keep this level of work up for ever. However, my advice is to focus your energy on your goal until it materializes. It generally pays off. **"**

*It did for Carol. After her work experience she was offered a job as a strategic planner at Saatchi & Saatchi. She is now Brand Consultant and co-director for Wonderworks, the ideas consultancy.*

## Placement schemes

Many ad agencies now run placement schemes. These are ideal for students as they're often held during the summer vacation.

> I recommend the D'Arcy summer placement scheme to anyone who doesn't have any luck with graduate training. I worked at the agency for two weeks and they offered me an extension on my time there too. They give you proper experience in all areas of the agency and it was paid.
>
> *Emmie Sergeant (2001), Media Planner, MPG*

## Surf yourself into a job

You can find out about agency placement schemes by surfing the web. One way to start would be by checking out the ad agency websites listed in the Directory at the end of this book. You'll see that not only do many of them offer the opportunity for work placements but you can also post your CV on their website.

## The Saatchi scholarship

Saatchi & Saatchi run a summer placement scheme for undergraduates and recent graduates. You are assessed for selection and there are places for fourteen students. If you are successful, your five weeks in the agency will be spent in account management, looked after by an account manager and gaining experience in and knowledge of the role of the account handler.

You will need to contact Corinne Fahn, the Saatchi & Saatchi personnel assistant, in the April of the year you intend to apply and send a covering letter saying how you think you will benefit from the programme.

This scholarship is quite separate from their graduate training scheme, although it could possibly lead to a job if you are an outstanding candidate.

No payment is offered but you do get your expenses covered – and the Saatchi name on your CV.

## Plan ahead

In addition to the summer placement scholarship, Saatchi & Saatchi, like most large ad agencies, offer work experience throughout the year. If you wish to arrange a week's work experience, you simply write with your CV to the agency of your choice. You need to do this well in advance. Saatchi & Saatchi, for example, are booked up six months to a year ahead.

## The IAA (International Advertising Association) internship program

The IAA is the global network of marketing communications professionals. There are more than 5000 members in 94 countries working in all areas of the business – ad agencies, advertisers, media organizations and other related services.

If you, your employer or your college is a member of the IAA, you can apply for the IAA intern program, which provides work experience at an international ad agency. Applications can be from undergraduates anywhere in the world. Most of the placements are in the New York metropolitan area and some are in Europe. Some internships are paid, others offer academic credit. You are expected to fund your own travel and accommodation, so it could be a costly – although valuable – experience.

The program is competitive. In 1998, there were 350 applicants for 50 internships. If you accept an internship, you're expected to write a report evaluating your experience and to attend weekly seminars and social events.

> This internship increased my awareness of communication and media, and helped me make important connections.
>
> *Intern student, BBDO, USA, IAA, 1998/9*

### How to apply

You need to send in your application by 1 February. If you qualify for the program you'll then receive a telephone or personal interview with a member of the internship team. If considered suitable, you'll then be placed on the IAA database. If your application matches an opening, it will be forwarded to the relevant agency. They then contact you directly if they're interested in giving you an interview.

International Advertising Association
IAA Internships
521 Fifth Avenue
Suite 1807
New York
NY 10175
USA
212 557 1133
www.iaaglobal.org
tina@iaaglobal.org

## Work experience at BDS Beechwood

Emma Payne, postgraduate student:

"While studying at Watford, we had the opportunity to contact BDS Beechwood, an advertising agency who were offering creative placements.

My creative partner and I sent in some examples of our work. We were then asked to spend two weeks in the creative department, where we worked on briefs for Pro-Plus and the Eating Disorder Association. We were given our own desk and were showered with pens and paper to use. The people in the agency were very friendly and tea-making was a wholly democratic process. We had a tour of all the departments, including the managing director's office and the table-tennis room (otherwise known as production), where we were asked to come up and play ping pong as soon as we were able.

Even though we were placement students, briefing was a serious matter and the account handlers took a lot of time and effort, speaking to us as they would to any of the permanent staff at BDS. This made us feel that we were being taken seriously. Our creative ideas were then critiqued by the senior art director, which is always an uncomfortable process, but allows you to see your work from a different point of view. He spent a lot of time talking to us, making us feel a valuable part of the agency.

On the second Friday we were invited by staff in the agency to a big party with free drinks and a band. The party was full of people in the advertising and media industries and we felt really privileged to be taken along.

My creative partner and I will be going back to BDS for more work experience in the near future, where we know we will learn more, while having a thoroughly great time."

*Emma is now working as a web designer.*

## Work experience at Triangle Communications

Anna Forsyth, postgraduate student:

"Everyone I worked with at Triangle was extremely kind and friendly. They really made me feel a part of the team and treated me more as a freelancer than a girl on work experience. I was included in most of the brainstorming sessions, and from day one was set up with my own email account and voice mail. The team that I was placed with could not have made me feel more at home and it was so nice to be part of a place where everyone was so happy and enjoying their work.

I was in charge of coordinating a sampling activity by Cadbury's Fuse. This was carried out by Cadbury's 'Fuseliers', handing out Fuse bars throughout the country in all of the major cities. Because of the problems in Kosovo, I had to organize new uniforms for the Fuselier sampling team, as for obvious reasons we had decided to drop the normal camouflage uniform.

While this sampling activity went on, I organized prizes from a local paintball centre, to do a joint venture with Fuse. By negotiating with a large regional paper, I was able to get free space for the siting of Cadbury and paintball centre logos and free exposure of the sampling activity in return for paintball prizes for the newspaper's readers.

I devised a press release for both the newspapers, and also the regional radio stations that I chose from *BRAD*. In order to get each radio station to read out the press release giving the details of where exactly the sampling activity was taking place in that area, I arranged for boxes of Cadbury's Fuse to be delivered by courier to each radio station along with the press release.

I feel that I got an awful lot out of the work experience. Not only did it do wonders for my telephone manner and confidence but it also reinforced my interest in working in that area because I was given so much responsibility. It also developed my negotiating skills through working so closely with the newspapers and made me become so much more organized. I learned to chill out a lot more as a result of the heavy workload. At the end of my three-week placement, the many messages on my voice mail that confronted me when I got in to work in the morning failed to faze me. As I became more confident, I became more laid back and was able to achieve so much more.

At the end of the placement I was very upset to leave and was surprised to receive a signed card and perfume as a thank-you for doing so much. I cannot fault my time at Triangle and would heartily recommend work experience to anyone. The practical experience that you receive cannot be gained through studies alone and focuses you on what you want to be doing when you finish studying. **"**

*Anna was employed by Triangle Communications. She is now working for 'Exposure'.*

## What can you earn?

An intern, typically, doesn't earn anything. Some companies, however, will pay a minimum wage, or just above, to summer interns. The point of an internship (in the USA) is to gain exposure and real-world knowledge, which is equated to education and you don't get paid to go to school (well, some of us do, but most don't).

After time an intern gets to be

an assistant account executive – a new college graduate with internships under his/her belt. After a year or so of work I would guess that an intern could earn around $20,000.

*Gini Arment, Rhea & Kaiser Marketing Communications, Illinois, USA*

### Minimum wage for placements

If you work at an agency for more than two weeks, you are now entitled to be paid a minimum working wage. Although this isn't a great deal, it's better than receiving nothing at all and will help to cover your expenses. However, because agencies now have to pay for placements you may find that they are not so willing to extend your time.

## Recommended routes

See the routes recommended at the end of Chapters 11, 12, 13 and the Directory. Also look at the advertising agency websites and at IAA and other internship programs.

# 16 Getting their foot in the door

This chapter features a selection of first-person accounts of how various people – myself included – found their first job in advertising.

## Recipe for a rare bird

I wrote to every ad agency under the sun asking for copywriting experience. I sent them all 'a recipe for a rare bird'. It began, 'Take one young girl sparkling with wit' and presented my CV in recipe form – a rather corny idea. 'Leave to simmer . . .' it read. 'Add a sprinkle of . . . and a dash of . . . Stir.' The postscript said, 'Hope you relish the sauce.' These were the pre-portfolio days, when it was possible to get a copy job by just demonstrating writing ability in a letter. I had some encouraging replies from creative directors – I have them still – but no real job offers: they all wanted someone with experience.

Then I was interviewed at an agency which now no longer exists. I got the job of junior copywriter. (This was before most agencies had creative teams – work was given to artists in a studio to complete.) There were three writers. A senior writer, the copy head. A technical writer. And me. Consequently I got most of the work, particularly anything that needed a 'youth' angle. Before long I was writing Hepworths Menswear radio scripts for Peter Murray, the disc jockey, to read over the air. I worked with him at the Radio Luxembourg studio in London – long before we had commercial radio. Radio Luxembourg – and pirate radio stations – were the stations young people listened to at the time.

I left the agency to travel, and then found myself out of work when I returned. I sold Avon cosmetics door-to-door, registered with creative recruitment consultants and hoped something would turn up. After a few months of signing on for the dole (benefit), I found myself a new job at Bates Dorland – although it was just plain old Dorland Advertising then. On my first day someone put a note on my desk which read, 'Welkum. We need someone in this room wot can write good English!' In my very first week I was thrilled to have my very first TV commercial accepted. My copywriting career had begun.

## Find a need and meet it

Salim Fadhley, Digital Project Specialist, OgilvyOne:

"I got my first job because of an unsolicited job application that I sent in. I sent an email to the chairman describing myself as a creative technical person. Previously I had identified a weakness in the company that they had nobody who could manage interactive production, so I set myself up to meet that need."

## The secretarial route

Cheryl Garber is an account assistant at BBH, one of the top advertising agencies. Here's how she got her first job in advertising:

"I left school with two A levels and an RSA in typewriting. I went to a secretarial employment agency called Changes and actually wanted to work for a magazine or something similar. However, I landed a job in BMP's media department as an office junior. I actually knew nothing about advertising and it was only a while later that I realized how lucky I had been landing my first job at BMP – and through very little effort! I was promoted to media secretary, then left to travel.

I later joined a small agency as team secretary and was promoted to account coordinator. I then left to travel again. I subsequently joined Leo Burnett's as secretary in charge/PA on the Kellogg's account and have recently joined BBH.

I would certainly recommend the secretarial route. It's a brilliant way to learn things about advertising and the company, as you have to do so much running around and organizing that you get to meet everyone!"

## Persistence pays off

An account handler tells her story:

"After I graduated in business and marketing with a 2:1 BA Hons, I applied to almost every agency in London. I only managed to get about five interviews and all of them rejected me. Reason? Mature student . . . and foreign. Or, at least, that's what I thought at the time. So I started to temp in order to survive and eventually got a job in the marketing department of a company specializing in information technology. During that year, I met, through my flatmate, a guy who used to work for an ad agency as a finance manager. He mentioned to me that there were some open positions and gave me some contact names. So I passed my CV on to him and waited.

A month went by and nothing happened, so I decided to phone the person I had addressed in my CV. He happened to be a very senior board director with very little time for anybody. Despite my messages he never responded, but I kept trying until, one day, I got him on the phone. He had never seen my CV (or he didn't remember it) but agreed to see me the following week. I went and got offered a job the week after. I started as an account coordinator for a big international client. Then got promoted to account executive and then to account supervisor. I now report to a board account director."

## Keep up contacts

Lara Richardson-Hill, PA in TV production, Publicis:

"While at Watford, we went to a TV production lecture at Publicis given by Caroline Black, their TV producer. Through this I obtained a work placement at Publicis with Judy Ross, head of TV, for the week after I had finished my course. During my placement I attended a shoot for Asda with Annex Films Production Company.

I kept in contact with Annex and then temped for two weeks for them as their receptionist. While there, I applied for a job in *Campaign* for a permanent receptionist at Harkness Sayers Film Productions. I worked there for a year and then got made redundant – as can happen, unfortunately, in this industry.

Throughout this time I had kept in contact with Publicis and I was invited back as a PA to Caroline Black, first as a freelance and then on a permanent basis. I have now been at Publicis for just over eighteen months. At the beginning of 1999 I was put on the IPA TV production knowledge course and I'm in the middle of it now. It's a great job but hard work."

*Lara is now a TV producer at Publicis.*

## A speculative approach

Ajay Shah, Account Executive, Smith Bundy Carlson (Direct Marketing):

"Following my completion of the Postgraduate Diploma in Advertising at West Herts College, I sent out speculative letters to a few above- and below-the-line agencies. I was called for a first interview at Carlson with the account director. The following week I was called back for an interview with the managing director. A day later they offered me the job!"

*Ajay is now an account director at Publicis.*

## Pure luck

Duncan Stokes, Creative Services Director, OgilvyOne:

"I got my first job in advertising by luck. I was trained as an apprentice compositor, moved into selling print and then sold money (hire purchase, corporate finance, etc.) mainly to companies. I was arranging car finance for an agency and started talking to the financial director about my previous production background. He suggested I send in my CV. Eight weeks later I had a job offer. I now run a creative services department of eighteen people."

## A baptism of fire

Nick Cumisky tells of his experiences at Bates Dorland. He had been unable to get on to a graduate training scheme so had accepted a temporary work placement in the agency's despatch (post) department (often a good starting place if you're not too proud to work in the post room).

"My time at Bates commenced the fortnight after the Watford course finished. Despatch was a true baptism of fire. I have never worked such long hours, constantly on my feet backwards and forwards for everyone in the building. From chauffeuring the chairman to a lunch in Oxford to copying documents of such proportions I still wake up in cold sweats at night screaming for more paper and toner cartridges.

Everything works around deadlines and the only deadline that exists is that everything has to be done by yesterday. 'If not, why not?' scenarios rule the fort, but I wouldn't really have it any other way. It makes the environment in which I work extremely efficient, as everyone is always on their toes and desperate to please.

At the end of week three we had the Royal Mail pitch (which, needless to say, we won!), where I was one of the pairs of 'hands' – basically one of a team of three responsible for helping pull all the strings together for the pitch team. One of our functions was to copy the pitch document twelve times for distribution to specific members of the prospective client post-pitch. It involved working through the night collating a 140–page full-colour document. I had worked a full day on the Thursday, put together the document on the Thursday night, and was then expected to work all day Friday.

Last thing Friday night before going downstairs to the wine bar, myself and one of the other 'hands' from despatch were called into the office of the agency director, thanked for helping out and offered permanent positions on an account as soon as they arose.

Since that day I have helped out temporarily on Lucky Strike for three weeks and currently on Compaq computers for the UK. I have been told that I will move on to the European side of Compaq to learn more about a pan-European account group and will ultimately end up working on Compaq UK after completion of the Bates Graduate Trainee scheme in February."

## I saw it on a notice board

Simon Prindiville, TV buyer, Universal McCanns:

"My first job as assistant TV buyer at Young & Rubicam was advertised on a board outside the West Herts College Careers Office. I had actually registered with some of the recruitment agencies – Lipton Fleming and The Stevens Company – but these were for sales jobs, whereas I wanted to work on the agency side."

## I wrote to all the TV companies

Andrew Canter, Broadcast Director, MPG:

"At the time I had to decide what career path to choose. I didn't have a clue what I wanted to do. I don't think I'd even heard about advertising (let alone media!) as a career.

So I thought I wanted to be a photographer. So that's what I became. A very low-paid photographer's assistant. That didn't last long. I then went into the jewellery trade for about a year.

It was around this time that my aunt told me about her previous career in TV airtime sales at Border TV. It sounded great. She suggested that I wrote to all the TV companies asking if they had any vacancies for TV airtime sales assistants. Eventually, after several interviews I managed to secure a job at Tyne Tees Television, based in London.

I spent the next eighteen months learning about TV airtime, advertising agencies and clients. This whetted my appetite for the 'heady world' of advertising and subsequently media."

## How I got started in sales promotion

Karl Perry, Managing Director, Promotional Campaigns Group, Manchester (PCG is a subsidiary company of the J. Walter Thompson Group):

"During the final two terms of studying for a psychology degree at Liverpool, I applied to all the big agencies for jobs, had an interview for Saatchi's – all with no success. During my studies I had become aware of Watford College (now West Herts College) and its standing within the industry. My first preference was to go straight into the world of work but Watford would be an acceptable safety net.

Getting into Watford proved more of a task than my naïve mind had considered. There were rumoured to be over 1000 applications for twenty positions on the postgraduate course. Somehow I got in. Had I not done so, I more than likely would have shelved my agency career there and then.

Throughout the course we were visited by numerous outside speakers, one of whom was the then general manager of Promotional Campaigns. I didn't have a particular drive for promotional marketing but their work and clients did seem quite interesting.

Late in May 1991 they advertised for account executives in *Marketing Week*. I applied with a hasty handwritten covering letter, explaining that I would like to be considered for a trainee position.

I was invited to a half-day recruitment session on 1 June. This comprised an interview, set brief, presentation, proofreading, creative writing and basic redemption calculations.

Convinced I hadn't got the job, I went back to Watford and sank two bottles of red wine, enjoying the summer sun in a friend's back garden.

The first of July was my first day at work. Four and a half years later I moved to Manchester to open PCG Manchester, where I have been since."

## Entered my first agency as an office boy

Michael Bartman, Sales Promotion Consultant:

"I wanted to make commercials and entered my first agency as an office boy, even though I had two good A levels. Eventually I progressed out of despatch to the media department and the position of junior executive. I left the large advertising agency and joined a well-known client company in the publicity department.

After six years I was promotions and advertising manager. I found myself frustrated at working with agencies whose creativity I thought I could match. Inevitably I left my client company to join one of the agencies I was working with."

## I just phoned creative directors

Gareth Dimelow, copywriter, Peter Kane Advertising:

"Ultimately, perseverance and resilience were pretty important for me. I found my current job a few weeks after losing my last one as the result of an unfortunate cost-cutting exercise. I gathered together the rudimentary makings of a portfolio and just phoned creative directors and asked them to see me. Some were shocked by my effrontery, others impressed by my tenacity and boldness.

There's no right or wrong in advertising, just a huge grey lump of 'maybes'. I was honest, ballsy and a little arrogant in my interview, and just stated my case. No cleverness or tricks of the light, just a straightforward, 'You need me because . . .'

After a week on the job and the imbibing of chronic amounts of alcohol, I was made a permanent member of the team. And that's how it is in advertising. This is a tough industry, and it really does help to know people. Don't worry, it won't be considered nepotism, because you're only as good as your work, and if your work is lousy . . ."

## Word of mouth

Paul Alexis, Creative Director at PCG Manchester (a subsidiary of J. Walter Thompson):

"I got my first job in advertising after four years at art college and a year out to work in print. One of my tutors told me that there was a junior position going at a new agency in Leeds. Although I had three months still to go on my HND vocational course in communication design, I went for it. I got an interview and got the job.

I got my current job via word of mouth. In fact, it's how I get all my jobs. 'PCG are looking for somebody and I mentioned your name,' they said. Two interviews later I was on my way to Quay Street, Manchester."

## An MSc in marketing

Wendy Milne, Account Executive, PCG Manchester:

"I began at the University of Aberdeen at the age of sixteen studying hospitality management. As a business degree, the three main subjects were personnel management, finance and marketing management. I found I preferred the third option, for I could always remember the layout of a marketing plan but could very rarely recall the layout of a profit and loss account! As the end of my degree drew near, my interest in marketing remained, so I decided I would like to specialize. I took the plunge and moved down to Paisley to study for an MSc in marketing.

I thoroughly enjoyed the course. I was the youngest in the class at the age of twenty and it was my first year of freedom. The course was very intense and led me on to my first job position in London as a research consultant for a hospitality training company. Although I enjoyed working in the research department, I craved a position in the marketing department, where, unfortunately, only two positions existed. As I was beginning to settle into London I was made redundant. I decided that Manchester would be my next challenge, so here I am, my first position in sales promotion."

## Cars were the key

Gareth Morgan, Marketing Manager, London Taxis International:

"I had been designing cars as a child. As I got older, I was attracted to car advertisements. Great BMW advertising from the newly formed WCRS stands out in my mind.

I left school to do an art and design foundation course at college. I wanted to create great advertising. After a year, I realized that I wanted to be a 'suit' (dreadful expression) because they got company cars (there we go again). I did my A levels and wrote to every ad agency listed in the West Midlands Yellow Pages. Loads of 'No thank yous' – it was the first recession of the 1980s. Amazingly I saw an advertisement in my local newspaper, the bizarrely named, *Kidderminster Shuttle*. It was for a trainee account executive. I applied and ordered a grey pinstripe suit from my mum's Grattan catalogue. I got the job, the only trainee account executive job I've ever seen to this day."

## I've not actually had to apply for any job

Louise Wall, Managing Director, EHS Brann:

"I got my first job via a boyfriend who was already in the business and then via a head-hunter who set up my interviews. I received three internal opportunities and was shortlisted with other graduates, although they had gone into the companies via the milk round. In other words, I was very lucky to get in via head-hunters already well known in the business.

I subsequently was poached to all my later jobs – that is, approached direct and then promoted internally. In other words, all my marketing positions have been referred to me via competitor agencies. I have not actually applied for any roles. However, if I had to I would select my recruitment agencies very carefully. **"**

## A fortunate student

Jan Newbold, art director:

**"**I entered the Creative Circle Student Award Scheme as a final-year student at Leicester Polytechnic (BA Hons Graphic Design) in 1979. The competition was to create an ad campaign to persuade people to use public transport. To my surprise, I was shortlisted, along with my creative partner.

We were invited to present our portfolios with other shortlisted students from various colleges at FCB. My partner and I were the only 'team' to be shortlisted. All the other finalists had worked on their own.

There were creative directors from approximately ten ad agencies at the presentations. Each one of us was called individually into the boardroom to present our work to this daunting panel of creative hotshots.

At the end of the day, we were assembled in the boardroom to be given certificates of achievement and, for some fortunate students, a placement. I was a fortunate student. I got a placement at Lansdowne Marketing, a subsiduary of JWT. This was for six months with a view to a permanent position.

I enjoyed my time at Lansdowne. I was involved with new business pitches and creating ideas for existing accounts such as Lyons Maid, Foster Grant sunglasses, Denim aftershave, Alpine double-glazing, Sketchley, Graff. I worked as part of a team and, individually, in the design department.

Lansdowne began as a below-the-line agency, supporting JWT's above-the-line campaigns. They became so successful creatively that they developed 'through-the-line'. For example, Lansdowne devised a press and TV campaign for Foster Grant sunglasses as well as the logo, design of the price tags, packaging, point-of-sale, promotions and trade.

My experience at Lansdowne, though I decided to leave after ten months, gave me a good all-round knowledge of advertising a brand. Every facet of advertising the brand was explored, from the creation of its name and the design of its label all the way through to a full-blown press and TV campaign. **"**

## I took a copy test

Tony Bodinetz, former Creative Group Head, DMB&B (now D'Arcy):

**"**After graduating with a law degree, I applied for a graduate trainee account executive position with the 'top' agencies – on the recommendation of two friends of mine who had worked in advertising, about which I knew absolutely nothing. One agency (London Press Exchange, now Leo Burnett) offered me a copywriting test – and a job as a writer.

One job led to another – writer at BBDO, senior writer at CDP, creative director at KMP and Kirkwood Co., and, just in time, to save me losing touch with my one craft skill, writer and group head at DMB&B. ''

## A resting actor

An account planner describes another route:

''While resting as an actor, I fell into qualitative research. Got fed up with the hours and lack of thanks so got into advertising – the best job so far. ''

## I met with anyone who would speak with me

Richard Eber (2001) Chief Creative Officer, MRM Partners Worldwide:

''It was 1976 and there was a real recession, much worse than now. I wrote to lots of people, finding their names in the awards annuals. I met with anyone who would speak with me. No one was hiring. Eventually, I was referred to Hank Seiden. He gave out assignments, and when he was satisfied with your work he would give you some names. One of those was a guy he worked with years earlier at Compton. It was a small place in New Jersey. I showed my work and was hired. It only lasted for about eight months, but I managed to put together a good portfolio. I spent the next few years at a lot of other small agencies (the economy took a while to recover). ''

# 17 Directory

Although by no means comprehensive, this directory gives you access to valuable industry information that is not normally easily available. Every effort has been made to ensure that it is up to date. However, the advertising world (especially the agencies) can change rapidly, so it's advisable to double-check names and addresses before using them. And do read the relevant chapters before approaching any advertising agencies.

## Journals/publications

**Admap (published monthly): journal for marketing, research and media**
NTC Marketing Department
01491 411000

**Advertising Age:** www.adage.com

**Campaign (published weekly)**
Haymarket Business Publications Ltd
174 Hammersmith Road
London W6 7JP
Subscriptions: 020 8841 3970
Back issues: 020 8503 0588
campaign@haynet.com
www.campaignlive.com

**Cosmopolitan magazine:**
www.cosmopolitan.com

**Digit (journal of new media)**
99 Gray's Inn Road
London WC1X 8UT
www.digitmag.co.uk

**Digital Broadcaster (digital technology in broadcast media)**
PS Publishing
The Old Ale House
129 Bengeo Street
Bengeo
Hertfordshire SG14 3EX
01992 410486

**The Economist**
2 St James's Street
London SW1A 1HG
020 7830 7000
www.economist.com
www.ads.economist.com

**IPC:** www.ipc.co.uk

**Marketing**
174 Hammersmith Road
London W6 7JP
020 7413 4150
www.marketing.haynet.com

**Marketing Direct**
Subscriptions
PO Box 43
Ruislip HA4 0YT

Credit card hotline: 020 8841 3970

**Marketing Week**
St Giles House
50 Poland Street
London W1V 4AX
020 7439 4222
www.marketing-week.co.uk

**MediaWeek**
Quantum House
19 Scarbrook Road
Croydon CR9 1LX
Subscriptions: 01858 438872
www.mediaweek.co.uk

**New Media Age**: www.nma.co.uk

**New Scientist**:
www.newscientist.com

**Radio Times**:
www.radiotimes.beeb.com

**Revolution** (published weekly):
journal of interactive media
Haymarket Business Publications
174 Hammersmith Road
London W6 7JP
Subscriptions: 020 8841 3970
www.uk.revolutionmagazine.com

**Time** magazine: www.timeinc.com

**Time Out**: www.timeout.co.uk

**Yellow Pages**: www.yell.com

## National newspapers

**Associated Newspapers Ltd**:
www.associatednewspapers.com

**The Daily Telegraph**:
www.telegraph.co.uk

**Evening Standard**:
www.standard.co.uk

**Express Newspapers Ltd**:
www.express.co.uk

**Financial Times**: www.ft.com

**The Guardian**: www.guardian.co.uk
www.guardianunlimited.co.uk

**The Independent**:
www.independent.co.uk

**The Mirror**: www.mirror.co.uk

**Scottish Media Newspapers**:
www.smg.plc.uk

**The Times/Sunday Times**:
www.the-times.co.uk

## Useful Addresses

**The Advertising Association**
Abford House
15 Wilton Road
London SW1V 1NJ
020 7828 2771
www.adassoc.org.uk
aa@adassoc.org.uk

**Advertising Standards Authority**
2–16 Torrington Place
London
WC1E 7HW
020 7580 5555
www.asa.org.uk

**Association of British Market
 Research Companies**
22–23 Old Burlington Street
London W1X 1RL
020 7434 0094

**Association of Media and
 Communication Specialists**
163 Rickmansworth High Street
Rickmansworth
Hertfordshire WD3 1AY
01923 711981

**British Interactive Multimedia
 Association**
6 Washingley Road
Folksworth
Peterborough PE7 3SY
www.bima.co.uk

**British Library Business
 Information Service: www.bl.uk**

**British Market Research Bureau**
Hadley House
79–81 Uxbridge Road
London W5 5SU
020 8566 5000

**British Printing Industries
 Federation**
11 Bedford Row
London WC1R 4DX
020 7915 8300
www.bpf.org.uk

**CAM Foundation**
Abford House
15 Wilton Road
London SW1V 1NJ
020 7828 7506

**Chartered Institute of Marketing**
Moor Hall
Cookham
Maidenhead
Berkshire SL6 9QH
01628 427500
Fax: 01628 427499
www.cim.co.uk

**Committee of Advertising Practice**
2–16 Torrington Place
London WC1E 7HW
020 7580 5555

**Direct Mail Information Service**
5 Carlisle Street
London W1V 6JX
020 7494 0483

**Direct Marketing Association Inc.
 (USA)**
1120 Avenue of the Americas
New York
NY 10036–6700
www.the-dma.org

**Direct Marketing Association (UK)**
Haymarket House
1 Oxendon Street
London SW1Y 4EE
020 7321 2525
www.dma.org.uk

**European Direct Marketing
 Association**
36 rue du governement provisoire
B-1000 Brussels
Belgium
00 32 2 217 63 09
www.direct-marketing.org/english/
 assoc/europe.htm

**Forrester Research Centre**
Charlotte House
9–14 Windmill Street
London W1P 1HF
020 7631 0202
www.forrester.co.uk

**The History of Advertising Trust**
HAT House
12 The Raveningham Centre
Raveningham
Norwich
Norfolk NR14 6NU
01508 548623

**Incorporated Society of British Advertisers**
44 Hertford Street
London W1Y 8AE
020 7499 7502
Fax: 020 7629 2728

**Independent Television Commission**
33 Foley Street
London W1P 7LB
020 7255 3000

**Institute of Advertising Practitioners in Ireland**
8 Upper Fitzwilliam Street
Dublin 2
Eire
00 353 1 676 5991
www.iapi.ie
info@iapi.com

**Institute of Direct Marketing (IDM)**
1 Park Road
Teddington
Middlesex TW11 0AR
020 8977 5705
Fax: 020 8943 2535

**Institute of Packaging**
Sysonby Lodge
Melton Mowbray
Leicestershire LE13 0NU
01664 500055

**Institute of Practitioners in Advertising**
44 Belgrave Square
London SW1X 8QS
020 7235 7020
www.ipa.co.uk

**Institute of Printing**
8a Lonsdale Gardens
Tunbridge Wells TN1 1NV
01892 538118

**Institute of Public Relations (IPR)**
15 Northburgh Street
London EC1V 0PR
020 7253 5151
Fax: 020 7490 0588
www.ipr.org.uk
training@ipr.org.uk

**Institute of Sales and Marketing Management**
Romeland House
Romeland Hill
St Albans
Bedfordshire AL3 4ET
01727 812500

**Institute of Sales Promotion (ISP)**
Arena House
66–68 Pentonville Road
London N1 9HS
020 7837 5340
Fax: 020 7837 5326
www.isp.org.uk

**International Advertising Association (IAA)**
UK Chapter Secretariat
12 Rickett Street
London SW6 1RU
020 7381 8777
www.iaaglobal.org

**The Marketing Institute**
South County Business Park
Leopardstown
Dublin 18
00 3531 2952355

**The Marketing Society**
St George's House
3–5 Pepys Road
London SW10 8NJ
020 8879 3464

**The Market Research Society**
15 Northburgh Street
London EC1V 0JR
020 7490 4911
Fax: 020 7490 0608
www.marketresearch.org.uk

**The Museum of Advertising and Packaging**
The Albert Warehouse
Gloucester Docks
Gloucester GL1 2EH
01452 302309

**NABS** (the charity for the marketing communications industry, offering help and support for those in and out of work)
32 Wigmore Street
London W1H 9DF
020 7299 2879
Fax: 020 7299 2887
www.nabs.org.uk

**National Museum of Film, Photography and TV**
Pictureville
Bradford BD1 1NQ
01274 727488

**National Readership Surveys Ltd (NRS)**
42 Drury Lane
Covent Garden
London WC2B 5RT
020 7632 2915

**Newspaper Publishers Association**
34 Southwark Bridge Road
London SE1 9EU
020 7207 2200

**The Radio Advertising Bureau**
77 Shaftesbury Avenue
London W1V 7AD
020 7306 2500
www.rab.co.uk

**The Radio Authority**
Holbrook House
14 Great Queen Street
London WC2B 5DG
020 7430 2724

## Advertising agencies offering graduate training

(For more detailed information see the IPA Factfile on the IPA website – www.ipa.co.uk)

**Abbott Mead Vickers BBDO Ltd**
151 Marylebone Road
London NW1 5QE
020 7616 3500
Fax: 020 7616 3600

**A. V. Browne Advertising**
46 Bedford Street
Belfast BT2 7GH
028 9032 0663

**Bartle Bogle Hegarty Ltd (BBH)**
60 Kingly Street
London W1B 5DS
020 7734 1677

**Bates UK Ltd**
121–141 Westbourne Terrace
London W2 6JR
020 7262 5077
Fax: 020 7258 3757

**BMP DDB Ltd**
12 Bishops Bridge Road
London W2 6AA
020 7258 3979
Fax: 020 7402 4871

**Carat**
Parker Tower
43–49 Parker Street
London WC2B 5PS
020 7430 6000

**D'Arcy**
Warwick Building
Kensington Village
Avonmore Road
London W14 8HQ
020 7751 1800
Fax: 020 7348 3855

**EURO RSCG Wnek Gosper Ltd**
11 Great Newport Street
Covent Garden
London WC2H 7JA
020 7240 4111
Fax: 020 7465 0552

**Grey Worldwide**
215–27 Great Portland Street
London W1W 5PN
020 7636 3399
Fax: 020 7637 7473

**Leagas Delaney London**
1 Alfred Place
London WC1E 7EB
020 7758 1758
Fax: 020 7758 1750

**The Leith Agency**
The Canon Mill
Canon Street
Edinburgh EH3 5HE
0131 557 5840
Fax: 0131 557 5837

**Leo Burnett Ltd**
60 Sloane Avenue
London SW3 3XB
020 7591 9111
Fax: 020 7591 9126

**Lowe**
Bowater House
68–114 Knightsbridge
London SW1X 7LT
020 7584 5033
Fax: 020 7584 9557

**M&C Saatchi**
36 Golden Square
London W1F 9EE
020 7543 4500
Fax: 020 7543 4501

**MBS Media Ltd**
84 Grosvenor Street
London W1X 0LD
020 7493 1616
Fax: 020 7409 0965

**Ogilvy & Mather Ltd**
10 Cabot Square
Canary Wharf
London E14 4QB
020 7345 3000
Fax: 020 7345 9000

**Partners BDDH**
Cupola House
15 Alfred Place
London WC1E 7EB
020 7467 9200

**Poulter Partners**
Rose Wharf
East Street
Leeds LS9 8EE
0113 285 6500
Fax: 0113 285 6501

**Publicis Ltd**
82 Baker Street
London W1M 2AE
020 7935 4426
Fax: 020 7487 5351

**Saatchi & Saatchi Ltd**
80 Charlotte Street
London W1A 1AQ
020 7636 5060
Fax: 020 7637 8489

**TBWA London**
76–80 Whitfield Street
London W1T 4EZ
020 7573 6666

**Walker Media Ltd**
Middlesex House
34–42 Cleveland Street
London W1P 5FB
020 7447 7500

**WCRS**
5 Golden Square
London W1R 4BS
020 7806 5000
Fax: 020 7806 5099

**Zenith Media Ltd**
Bridge House
63–65 North Wharf Road
London W2 1LA
020 7224 8500
Fax: 020 7706 2650

For a full and up-to-date list of agencies offering graduate training, consult the IPA Factfile the year *before* you wish to join an advertising agency.

## Ad agency websites

Abbott Mead Vickers BBDO: www.amvbbdo.co.uk

A. V. Browne Advertising: www.avb.co.uk

Bartle Bogle Hegarty (BBH): www.bbh.co.uk

Bates UK: www.bates.co.uk

BMP DDB: www.bmpddb.com

The Bozell Group: www.bozell.com

Carat: www.carat.co.uk

cdp travissully: www.travissully.com

Cogent: www.cogent.co.uk

D'Arcy: www.darcyww.com

Duckworth Finn Grubb Waters: www.dfgw.com

EURO RSCG Wnek Gosper: www.eurorscg.co.uk

Galley Slater Group: www.gsjobs.co.uk

Grey Worldwide: www.grey.com

HHCL & Partners: www.hhcl.com

J. Walter Thompson:
www.jwtworld.com

Leagas Delaney Partnership:
www.leagasdelaney.com

The Leith Agency: www.leith.co.uk

Leo Burnett Ltd:
www.leoburnett.com

Lowe: www.loweuk.com

McCann-Erickson Manchester:
www.mccannmcr.com

McCann-Erickson World Group:
www.mccann.com

M&C Saatchi: www.mcsaatchi.com

MBS Media Ltd: www.mbs.co.uk

Ogilvy & Mather: www.ogilvy.com
www.ogilvy.co.uk

OgilvyOne: www.ogilvyone.co.uk

Optimedia: www.optimedia.co.uk

Partners BDDH Ltd:
www.partnersbddh.co.uk

Publicis: www.publicis.co.uk

Publicis Networks: www.publicis-
networks.com

Rainey Kelly Campbell Roalfe/Y&R:
www.yr.com

St Lukes: www.stlukes.co.uk

Saatchi & Saatchi: www.saatchi-
saatchi.com

TBWA London: www.tbwa.co.uk

Walker Media Ltd:
www.walkermedia.com

WCRS Ltd: www.wcrs.co.uk

WPP Group: www.wpp.com

WWAV Rapp Collins Ltd:
www.wwavrc.co.uk

Zenith Media:
www.zenithmedia.com

## Websites for careers in advertising

Advertising Association:
www.adassoc.org

American Association of Advertising
Agencies:
www.AAAAdvertisingjobs.com

IPA: www.ipa.co.uk

Advertising jobs in India:
www.adjobz.com

IAA: www.iaaglobal.org

Advertising and media careers:

www.nationjob.com

www.brandera.com

www.brassring.com

careerbuilder.com

www.e-job.net (jobs in e-commerce)

www.guru.com

www.headhunter.net

www.knowthis.com

www.marketingjobs.com (USA and
Canada)

www.talentzoo.com

www.vault.com

## Other useful websites

AC Nielsen (Research):
www.acnielsen.com

*BRAD*: www.brad.co.uk

The Chartered Institute of Marketing
(CIM): www.cim.co.uk

D&AD: dandad.org

The Direct Marketing Association:
www.dma.org.uk

DoubleClick UK:
www.doubleclick.net

Emap Media Web: www.emap.com

European Direct Marketing Associations: www.direct-marketing.org

General media: www.ukmedia.com

The Institute of Direct Marketing: www.theidm.co.uk

Interbrand: www.interbrand.com

IPA and IPA Factfile: www.ipa.co.uk

Jobs: www.workthing.com

The John Hartman Center for US Advertising and Marketing History: http://scriptorium.lib.duke.edu/hartman

L'Express: www.lexpress-net.com

Mad: www.mad.co.uk

McCall's: www.mccalls.com

Media publications: Publications@zenithmedia.com

Mintel: www.mintel.com

Radio Advertising Bureau: www.rab.co.uk

Source of text books: www.abe.com

UK Media Directory: www.ukmedia.com

UK Media Internet Directory: www.whatson.com/ukmedia

University of Houston College of Business: www.cba.uh.edu/

University of Texas (Advertising): www.advertising.utexas.edu/world

US DMA: www.the-dma.org/

World Advertising Research Center: www.warc.com

YAHOO! home page: www.yahoo.co.uk and www.yahoo.com/business

Yellow Pages: www.yell.co.uk

## Broadcasters

BBC: www.beeb.com and www.bbc.co.uk/education

BSkyB: www.sky.co.uk

Carlton Online: www.carltonline.com

Capital Interactive: www.capitalFM.com

Capital Gold: www.capitalgold.com

Channel 4: www.channel4.com

Channel 5: www.channel5.co.uk

CNN: www.cnn.com

ITN: www.itn.co.uk

Virgin Radio: www.virginradio.co.uk

## Integrated marketing communication agencies

### 141 Communications
141 Westbourne Terrace
London W2 6JR
020 7706 2306
www.141worldwide.com

### Archibald Ingall Stretton
Berners House
47–48 Berners Street
London W1T 3NF
020 7467 6100

### Clarke Hooper Momentum Ltd
Oriel House
16 Connaught Place
London W2 2ES
020 7535 0500
Fax: 020 7535 0501

### Joshua
Wells Point
79 Wells Street
London W1P 3RE
020 7453 7900

**The Marketing Store Worldwide**
Brand Building
14 James Street
London WC2E 8BU
020 7745 2100

**Promotional Campaigns Group**
Astley House
Quay Street
Manchester M3 4AS
0161 832 8006

**Robson Brown**
Clavering House
Clavering Place
Newcastle-upon-Tyne
NE1 3NG
0191 232 2443

**Robson Brown**
No. 10 The Office Village
Exchange Quay
Salford Quays
Manchester
M5 3EQ
0161 877 2004

## New media agencies

**Agency.Com**
8 Crinan Street
Battle Bridge Basin
London N1 9SQ
020 7964 8200
www.agency.com

**Bates Interactive**
121–141 Westbourne Terrace
London W2 6JR
020 7724 7228

**circle.com**
100 Victoria Street
Bristol BS1 6HE
0117 914 6000
www.circle.com

**Grey Interactive (UK)**
65–66 Frith Street
London W1V 5TA
020 7439 2686

**i-level**
The Ballroom
26–30 Strutton Ground
London SW1P 2HR
020 7340 2700
jobs@i-level.com

**Interactive1**
132–140 Goswell Road
London EC1V 7DY
020 7490 5773
www.interactive1.com

**Mediawave Group Limited
(digital broadcasting)**
Hudson House
Hudson Way
Pride Park
Derby DE24 8HS
01332 866700
www.mediawave.co.uk

**Saatchi & Saatchi Vision**
80 Charlotte Street
London W1A 1AQ
020 7636 5060
www.saatchi-saatchi.com

## Direct marketing agencies

**Barraclough Hall Woolston Gray**
191 Old Marylebone Road
London NW1 5DW
020 7298 1000

**BBH Unlimited**
60 Kingly Street
London W1R 6DS
020 7439 4404

**Brann Cirencester**
Phoenix Way
Cirencester
Gloucestershire GL7 1RY
01285 644744
www.brann.com

**Brunnings Advertising Manchester**
Carterbench House
Clarence Road
Macclesfield
Cheshire SK10 5JZ
01625 572556

**EHS Brann**
6 Briset Street
London EC1M 5NR
020 7017 1000

**GGT Direct Advertising**
82 Dean Street
London W1V 6HA
020 7439 4282

**IMP Group Ltd**
Warwick Building
Kensington Village
Avonmore Road
London W14 8HQ
www.implondon.co.uk

**JWT Direct (Manchester)**
Astley House
Quay Street
Manchester M3 4AS
0161 832 9960

**Target Direct Marketing**
Royal House
Parabola Road
Cheltenham
Gloucestershire GL50 3AH
01242 258700

# Regional agencies

**1576 Advertising Ltd**
25 Rutland Square
Edinburgh EH1 2BW
0131 473 1576

**A. V. Browne Advertising Ltd**
46 Bedford Street
Belfast BT2 7GH
028 9032 0663

**Barkers Communications Scotland**
234 West George Street
Glasgow G2 4QY
0141 248 5030

**Barrington Johnson Lorains & Partners Ltd**
Sunlight House
Quay Street
Manchester M3 3JZ
0161 831 7141

**BDH TBWA**
St Paul's
Wilmslow Road
Didsbury Village
Manchester M20 2RW
0161 908 8600

**Cheetham Bell JWT**
Astley House
Quay Street
Manchester M3 4AS
0161 832 8884

**Cogent**
Heath Farm
Hampton Lane
Meriden
Coventry
West Midlands CV7 7LL
0121 627 5040

**Faulds Advertising**
Sutherland House
108 Dundas Street
Edinburgh EH3 5DQ
0131 557 6003

**Golley Slater Recruitment**
Wharton Place
Wharton Street
Cardiff CF10 19S
0292 066 3300

**The Leith Agency**
The Canon Mill
Canon Street
Edinburgh EH3 5HE
0131 557 5840

**McCann-Erickson Belfast Ltd**
31 Bruce Street
Great Victoria Street
Belfast BT2 7JD
028 9033 1044

**McCann-Erickson Bristol Ltd**
6 King Street
Bristol BS1 4EQ
0117 921 1764

**McCann-Erickson Central Ltd**
1266 Warwick Road
Knowle
Solihull
West Midlands B93 9LQ
01564 779321

**McCann-Erickson Manchester Ltd**
Bonis Hall
Bonis Hall Lane
Prestbury
Cheshire SK10 4EF
01625 822200

**Poulter Partners**
Rose Wharf
East Street
Leeds LS9 8EE
0113 285 6500
www.poulterpartners.com

**Robson Brown Advertising**
Clavering House
Clavering Place
Newcastle upon Tyne NE1 3NG
0191 232 2443

**Saatchi & Saatchi Advertising
(Dublin)**
4 Clonkskeagh Square
Clonkskeagh
Dublin 14
00 353 1269 8844

## Recruitment consultants

### Media planning/buying and sales

**The Davis Company**
4th Floor
Canberra House
315 Regent Street
London W1R 7YB
020 7580 4580
www.daviscompany.co.uk

### New media

**Major Players**
73–75 Endell Street
London WC2H 9AJ
020 7836 4041
*and*
3 Russell Street
Leamington Spa
Warwickshire CV32 5QA
www.majorplayers.co.uk
talk@majorplayers.co.uk

**Pricejamieson**
Paramount House
104–108 Oxford Street
London W1D 1LP
020 7393 1350
www.pricejam.com
newmedia@pricejam.com

**Secretarial**

**Christopher Keats**
020 7637 7555
www.christopherkeats.co.uk

**Pathfinders**
020 7434 3511
www.pathfindersrecruitment.com

**Regan and Dean + Adland**
23 Old Bond Street
London W1S 4PZ
020 7409 3244
www.regananddean.co.uk

**Marketing communications**

**EMR Marketing Search and
  Selection**
33 Sloane Street
Knightsbridge
London SW1X 9NR
020 7823 1300

**Direct Recruitment**
020 7287 1171
www.direct-recruitment.co.uk

**Michael Page Marketing**
www.michaelpage.co.uk

**SPCA graduate recruitment**
www.spca.org.uk

**Creative**

**Liz Harold Creative Recruitment**
61–63 Beak Street
London W1R 3LF
020 7437 7863
www.lizh.co.uk

**Kendall Tarrant UK**
56–60 Hallam Street
London W1W 6JL
020 7907 4444

**Kendall Tarrant New York**
41 East 11th Streeet
11th Floor
New York
NY 10003
001 212 645 8433
info@kt-ny.com

## Advertisers/brands

Adidas: www.adidas.com

Body Shop: www.bodyshop.co.uk

British Airways:
  www.britishairways.com

Cadbury's:
  www.cadburyschweppes.com

Campbell's Soup:
  www.campbellsoup.com

Capital Radio: www.capitalfm.com

Carling: www.fa-carling.com

Coca-Cola: www.cocacola.com

Colgate-Palmolive: www.colgate.com

Easyjet: www.easyjet.com

Ford: www.ford.co.uk

Gillette: www.gillette.com

Guinness: www.itl.net/guinness

Harrods: www.harrods.com

Heinz: www.heinz.co.uk

Irn-Bru: www.irn-bru.co.uk

Lever Brothers: www.persil.co.uk

Levi Strauss: www.levi.com

National Lottery:
  www.national-lottery.co.uk

Nestle: www.nestle.com

Pepsi: www.pepsi.co.uk

Perrier: www.perrier.com

Sainsbury: www.j-sainsbury.co.uk

Tango: www.tango.co.uk

Tesco: www.tesco.co.uk

Toyota: www.toyota.com

United Biscuits:
  www.unitedbiscuits.co.uk

Van den Bergh Foods:
  www.vdbfoods.co.uk

Virgin Atlantic: www.virgin.com

Virgin Records: www.vmg.co.uk

Volkswagen: www.volkswagen.co.uk

Waterstones: www.waterstones.co.uk

Wrigley: www.wrigley.com

# Notes and references

## Chapter 1

Institute of Practitioners in Advertising (1998) *Graduate Careers in Advertising Agencies.* IPA.

Institute of Practitioners in Advertising (2001) *UK: Business Gateway to Europe*, information pack. IPA.

## Chapter 2

Arment, G. (2001) Personal communication.

*'Just do it'*, Nike campaign slogan.

*Campaign Report* (2002) The top 300 agencies (ranked by billings/revenues – based on accounts handled on a creative-only, creative and planning or full-service basis). Data supplied by AC Nielsen MMS, Haymarket Business Publications Ltd, 22 February.

*Campaign Report* (2002) Regional agencies (ranked by billings/revenues). Data supplied by AC Nielsen MMS, Haymarket Business Publications Ltd, 22 February.

## Chapter 3

*Advertising Age* (2001) Top Ten agency brands worldwide.

*Campaign Healthcare Report* (2001) Top healthcare agencies (ranked by declared billings/revenues). Data supplied by MMS, Haymarket Press.

*Campaign Report* (2002) Business-to-business agencies (ranked according to declared income). Compiled by *Campaign* with the aid of the Association of Business-to-Business Agencies, Haymarket Press, 22 February.

Carter, M. (1999) How many doctors do you need? *Campaign*, 8 January, p. 17.

Cook, R. (1998) The joys of being a creative – and the woes. *Independent* Media Supplement, 6 April.

Newland, F. (1999) Agencies rethink role in world where anything is a medium. *Campaign*, Haymarket Press, 26 March.

Stuart, L. (1998) Why space is the new frontier. *Guardian*, 31 October.

## Chapter 4

Bolles, R. N. (1998) *What Color Is Your Parachute?* Ten Speed Press.

Burnett, L. (1995) *100 Leo's: Wit and Wisdom from Leo Burnett.* NTC Business Books.

Leagas, Shafron Davis (1996) Graduate application form.

Ogilvy, D. (1995) *Ogilvy on Advertising*. Prion Books.

## Chapter 5

Fraser, I. (1990) The boss. *Campaign*, Haymarket Press, 3 August.

## Chapter 6

Beattie, T. (1998) (cited by Meg Carter) How to get ahead in advertising. *The Times*, 25 September.

Burnett, L. (1995) *100 Leo's: Wit and Wisdom from Leo Burnett*. NTC Business Books.

Child, B. (1996) Want to create award-winning soaps, comedies and thrillers? Recruitment advertisement, McCann-Erickson, Manchester.

Coughlan, D. (1998) Write me off this page. Recruitment advertisement, Barkers.

Human Resources, *Guardian* Media supplement.

Eber, R. (2001) Starting out in a real recession. *Admap*, September, p. 12, World Advertising Research Center.

Fahn, C. Personnel Assistant, Saatchi & Saatchi, personal communication.

Fisher, A., cited by R. Cook (1998) The joys of being a creative – and the woes. *Independent* Media supplement, 6 April.

Gettins, Dominic (2000) *The Unwritten Rules of Copywriting*. Kogan Page.

*Guardian* (1995) Recruiting drive – what we're looking for. *Guardian* Careers supplement, 6 May.

Holker, N. Barker Human Resources, personal communication.

Hunt, T. (1999) Applauding the ideas that count. Direct Awards 1999.

*Campaign*, Haymarket Press, 12 April.

IPA Survey of Salaries (2001). Institute of Practitioners in Advertising, April.

Lord, R. (1999) Does this man need to get a life? Judge for yourself. *Adline*, April.

Rayfield, T. (1998) Hidden talent revealed in your jeans. *Guardian* Jobs supplement, 13 June.

Souter, P. (1999) Should agencies recruit creatives from diverse backgrounds? *Campaign* Forum, 19 March.

Sullivan, L. (1998) *'Hey Whipple Squeeze This'. A Guide to Creating Great Ads*, Chapter 10, p. 229, 'A good book or a crowbar'. John Wiley & Sons.

Welch, J. (1998) How to get the dream jobs that are never advertised: why waste time on second best when you deserve better? *Guardian*, 28 November.

## Chapter 7

AGCAS Graduate careers information booklet.

Burrows, R. (1999) Recruitment consultant, visiting speaker to the Watford Postgraduate Diploma in Advertising.

*Campaign Report* (2002) The top ten media specialists ranked according to billings/revenue – based on accounts handled on a media buying basis. Data supplied by AC Nielsen MMS. Haymarket Business Publications Ltd, 22 February.

Canter, A. (1998) MPG, lecture to Watford School of Business postgraduate students, 9 November.

Digital Broadcaster (1999) *Digital Television Is Changing All The Rules*. Chapter 7. PS Publishing.

Duff, G. (1998) Report on Zenith Media. *Campaign*, 27 November.

Girling, Mark (2001) *MediaWeek*, Quantum New Media, 28 September.

Jacobs, Kathryn (2001) (Commercial Director, Virgin Radio) In search of the tomorrow people. *MediaWeek*, 24 August.

*Market Monitor* (1998) MPG UK.

Media Planning Group (2001) website.

*MediaWeek* (2001) Average media salaries (Data supplied by The Davies Company). Quantum Business Media, 6 July.

*MediaWeek* (2001) BMRB: The media habits of internet users in the UK, 17 August.

*MediaWeek* (2001) August cinema audiences at their highest for 30 years. Quantum Business Media, 28 September.

*MediaWeek* (2001) Rajar data reveals long-term change in radio listening. Quantum Business Media, 28 September.

Optimedia (1999) Agency credentials.

Peerless, J. E. Advertising Manager, *Financial Times*, personal communication.

Sadie, S. (1998) Director of Innovation, MPG UK, Time for media planners to take more risks. *Time and Space*, Fourth Quarter.

## Chapter 8

*AdWeek* (2001) The top 100 interactive agencies. adweek.com, 3 September.

AQKA.com (2001) website.

Bonello, D. (2001) *Campaign*, February.

Digital Broadcaster (1999) *Digital Television Is Changing All the Rules*. Chapter 7. PS Publishing.

Foley, K. (2001) Second sight: floating bellies ride out storm. *Guardian* Online supplement, 4 October.

Freeman, M. and Young, J. (2001) *Technology and the World of International Marketing Communications*, IAA, May.

Gray, R. (1999) quoting Don Pepper in Do you still believe in one-to-one marketing? *Revolution*, May.

*Guardian* (2001) Endlessly expanding web of fun, New Media supplement, 13 August.

*MediaWeek* (2001a) *BMRB: the media habits of internet users in the UK*. Quantum Business Media, 17 August.

*MediaWeek* (2001b) Survey shows internet power. Quantum Business Media, 24 August.

Parente, D. (2000) *Advertising Campaign Strategy*. The Dryden Press (Harcourt College Publishers).

*Revolution* editorial (2001a) Online ads can put up a fight, 21 February.

*Revolution* (2001b) Which way now?, August.

Salzman, A. (2001) *It all started with the PC: Technology and the World of International Marketing Communications*. IAA, May.

## Chapter 9

Hobsbawn, J. (1998) If only Clinton had taken Viagra. Media Times, *The Times*, 25 September.

*Marketing Report* (2000) *Top 20 Direct Marketing and Sales*

*Promotion Agencies*, 30 November.

Pandya, N. (1998) Sales promotions: it's all about the image. *Guardian*, 20 June.

Pandya, N. (1999) Cool companies: No. 4: The Marketing Store Worldwide. Rise: next moves for graduate professionals, *Guardian*, 6 February.

Trickett, E. (98) The Direct Future. *Campaign*, Haymarket Press, 18 September.

Wall, Louise (1999) Managing Director, EHS Brann, Careers talk at West Herts College, 11 February.

Woolf, K. (1999) Institute of Direct Marketing, lecture to postgraduates at Watford School of Business and Management.

## Chapter 10

Budimir, O. (1998) Head of Production, Burkitt DDB, lecture to Watford postgraduate students.

Herron, B. (1999) WCRS production is riled by punter. *Campaign* letters, 12 February.

Rowe, J. (1998) Creative Services Director, Duckworth Finn Grubb Waters, Trade body aims to promote profession of creative services. *Campaign*, 25 June.

## Chapter 11

Budimir, Olga (1998) Head of Production, Burkitt DDB, lecture to Watford postgraduate students.

Wall, Louise (1999) Managing Director, EHS Brann, careers talk at West Herts College, 11 February.

## Chapter 12

Lowe Lintas (formerly APL) (1997) Graduate application form.

Burrows, R. (1999) Recruitment consultant, visiting speaker to the Watford Postgraduate Diploma in Advertising, February.

Fahn, C. Personnel assistant, Saatchi & Saatchi, personal communication, February.

Freeman, H. (1998) Suits that make you suitable. *Guardian* Money supplement, 28 November.

IPA (1996) *Best Practice in Graduate Recruitment: A Guide to Finding, Choosing and Keeping the Best Graduates*. Institute of Practitioners in Advertising.

Morgan, A. (1999) Recruitment Consultant, lecture to Watford postgraduate students, February.

## Chapter 13

Burchill, Julie (2001) *Guardian*, 16 August.

Canter, A. Head of Broadcasting, MPG, personal communication, 3 February.

Cope, Nick. (2001) (as cited by Midgley) Netting the best. *Guardian* Education supplement, 20 August.

Falmouth (1998) Admissions prospectus, Falmouth College of Arts.

Golding, P. and Kilgarriff, R. (1999) (cited by H. Marsh) Action plan for wannabees with stars in their eyes: switch off your television set and do something less boring instead. Rise: next moves for graduate professionals, *Guardian*, 16 January.

Humphrys, J. (1997) Advice to tomorrow's John Humphrys: My

Big Break. *Guardian* Media supplement, 17 February, p. 6.

Open University (2001) Advertisement for an MBA in the Management of Technology.

Pandya, N. (1999) Working week: student can compete for introduction to marketing. *Guardian*, 16 January.

Woolf, K. Institute of Direct Marketing, personal communication.

## Chapter 15

HEFCE (1996) *Review of Postgraduate Education, Evidence Volume, Section 9, Report of the Employers' Task Force, 13, 7.* HEFCE, CVCP, SCOP.

IAA (1998/9) Internship program information leaflet.

Lock, A. (1998) Makes you think doesn't it? *Guardian* Higher Education supplement, 8 December.

## Chapter 16

Canter, A. Broadcast Director, MPG, personal communication.

Eber, R. (2001) Starting out in a real recession. *Admap*, September. World Advertising Research Center.

Other contributors to this chapter have asked to remain anonymous.

# Index